Privatization: Tactics and Techniques

Privatization: Tactics and Techniques

Contributors
include:

Wendall Cox
Thomas Kierans
Oliver Letwin
Madsen Pirie

Edited by:
Michael A. Walker

THE FRASER
INSTITUTE

Canadian Cataloguing in Publication Data

Main entry under title:

Privatization : tactics and techniques

Proceedings of a symposium held July 22-24,
1987 in Vancouver, B.C.
ISBN 0-88975-118-8

1. Privatization - Congresses. 2.
Privatization - Canada - Congresses. I.
Walker, Michael, 1945-   II. Fraser
Institute (Vancouver, B.C.)
HD3842.P75 1988   338.7'4   C88-091028-3

Printed in Canada.

CONTENTS

PART TWO
INSTITUTIONAL AND POLITICAL ASPECTS
OF PRIVATIZATION

PREFACE

INTRODUCTION — THE BIRTH OF PRIVATIZATION

This is the second book on privatization that I have had the opportunity to compile and edit. The first, entitled *Privatization: Theory and Practice,* was published nearly a decade ago and dealt with the first major privatization of public assets which, up to that time, had been attempted. In the intervening period, and in part because of that earlier experience, privatization has become one of the most significant and important features of the public policy landscape.

The development of this surge in interest in privatization serves to illustrate a very important fact about how ideas are transmitted throughout the world and it is worth taking a brief detour away from our central journey to consider this.

In 1976, Milton Friedman gave a talk entitled "Curing the British Disease" at an Institute of Economic Affairs gathering in London, England. In the spring of 1977, the Fraser Institute republished this essay in Canada in a book entitled *Friedman on Galbraith and on Curing the British Disease.*

One of the issues discussed by Professor Friedman in his essay was how to go about unwinding the government of Great Britain. A particular subject was what to do about the nationalized industries. I think it is worthwhile repeating what Professor Friedman had to say:

> The obvious thing do so with the steel industry, the railroads and all those industries currently governmentally operated is to get rid of them by auctioning them off. Here there are various devices. At the moment it would be very hard to auction off the steel industry, because a Tory government did it once and then Labour re-nationalized it and anybody who buys it again would now be very uncertain that he would be able to retain ownership. One suggestion a number of people have made which I think makes a great deal of sense, would be, not to auction it off, but to give it away by giving every citizen in the country a share in it.

> After all, the supposed argument is that the people of Great Britain own the steel industry; it is the property of all the citizens. Well, then, why not give each citizen his piece? Now you may say this raises some questions of feasibility. You might say fifty-five million shares are a lot of shares—in order to have a market in them you would have to reintroduce

> the farthing to enable people to buy and sell them. That's true. But it
> seems to me you could go at it in a very different way. You have not only
> the steel industry, but electricity, the BBC, railroads, road transport, etc.
> Suppose you constructed a mutual fund to which you assign the shares in
> all these enterprises and then gave every one of the fifty-five million
> citizens of the United Kingdom a share in it. Now you are talking about
> magnitudes that are perfectly feasible.

The substance of these thoughts was subsequently picked up by those
who were advising British Columbia's Social Credit government which, in
microcosm in 1975 inherited the same sorts of problems about which
Friedman spoke in the United Kingdom. The problem was that the socialist
government which had preceded it, had nationalized a number of forest
products firms, and acquired other assets into the public sector which it
was felt ought properly to be in the private sector. One of the financial
advisers to the government at the time suggested that the government
should establish some sort of mutual fund into which the government's
assets could be placed, a suggestion which came directly from Milton
Friedman's essay.

The likely transmitter of the idea was Mr. Austin Taylor who, at the
present time is Chairman of McLeod Young Weir, Canada's largest
brokerage house and, for trivia collectors, also William F. Buckley's
brother-in-law. (This may be the first case of *de jure,* retro-genetic
transfer.)

Eventually, the British Columbia government did create a kind of
government-owned mutual fund company, The British Columbia
Resources Investment Corporation, which was given, in addition to the
various nationalized firms, some oil leases, shares in private sector
companies, and other assets which had been held in the public sector. It
also undertook a distribution programme of free shares in BCRIC as well
as selling a large tranche of shares to the general public. The privatization
of B.C.R.I.C. turned out to be a very large undertaking, indeed. It was the
third largest common stock sale in history exceeded only by the Ford
Motor Company and TWA sales, both of which had exceeded $500
million. In the end, the BCRIC issue raised $487.5 million in 1979 dollars
and was well over twice the previous record in Canada for a common stock
issue. Millions of individual shareholders had to be serviced for their free
shares. The organization and sales process was quite sophisticated.

The Fraser Institute followed this closely and in 1979 commissioned a
book to be written about the BCRIC experiment, including the difficulties
that had been encountered and the things that might be learned from having
gone through the privatization process. The book, *Privatization: Theory*

and Practice which appeared in the Spring of 1980 was the first book ever written on the subject of asset privatization and it enjoyed a very broad circulation in Canada and elsewhere. In particular, it attracted the considerable attention of the newly elected government of Prime Minister Margaret Thatcher. We soon received visitors from the department responsible for the privatization of the energy assets of the government of Great Britain who, we are told, learned a great deal about privatization from the BCRIC experiment.

Recent conversations with Sir John Moore, a senior Minister in the Thatcher government and the Minister responsible for the early privatizations, have revealed that one of the things the British government and he personally learned was that the extent of shareholder interest in purchasing such assets might be much higher than was commonly thought.

In the case of the British Columbia Resources Investment Corporation issue, whereas the best guess in advance of the sale had been that 60,000 investors at most might be interested, the number who actually participated was 170,000 within the Province of British Columbia—a very high fraction of the total potential market.

The most important thing that the government of Britain learned from the BCRIC experiment, however, was some of the areas to avoid, in particular, limitations on the shareholding, how to deal with problems of xenophobia and how to structure the continuing influence, if any, of the government over the corporation, once privatized. I don't wish to take away any of the credit which the Thatcher government deserves for having perfected the process of privatization in its second term. However, it is interesting to ponder whether they would have had such confidence had the BCRIC experiment in all of its multi-faceted splendour not occurred.

In any event, I like to ponder the delicious irony of the fact that the idea for privatization which was enunciated by Milton Friedman in London in 1976 should have found its way to Vancouver, British Columbia, and be implemented in a most marvelous way; the lessons of which were then applied back in Great Britain several years later.

A HUNDRED QUESTIONS ABOUT PRIVATIZING ASSETS AND SERVICES

The foregoing privatization story concerns largely the privatization of assets which one way or another had found their way into the public sector—either by nationalization or because they were created in the public sector in the first instance. In the Canadian case, the latter is more prevalent.

There is an entirely different aspect of privatization and that is the contracting-out of public services. This sort of privatization has been a standard part of public sector conduct for many years but has assumed greater proportions in recent years in part because of the work conducted by the Centre for Local Government at the Reason Foundation based in Santa Monica, California. A book *Cutting Back City Hall,* written by Robert W. Poole, Jr. was an important instigator of interest in privatization of public services in the United States, a trend which has recently been spreading to Canada.

The present book considers both asset privatization and the privatization of service production and attempts in each of those areas to consider the most recent experience and information available about how to privatize and about the operational aspects of the privatization process itself. It might well have been entitled *A Hundred Questions about Privatizing Assets and Services* because the discussion which is included at the end of each chapter provides a gold mine of information for those who have to engage in privatization or those who wish to understand it.

INTERNATIONAL LESSONS IN PRIVATIZATION

Part One collects a number of papers dealing with international lessons in privatization. The first, by Dr. Madsen Pirie, President of the Adam Smith Institute in London, is an insightful and highly readable account of the political motivations which might have produced the explosion in interest in privatization in the United Kingdom. He also provides an overview of the basic principles which must guide the privatization process if it is to be successful from a political and operational point of view.

From that relatively high level overview, John Williams of Kleinwort Benson and the person primarily responsible for the privatization of British Telecom, from the merchant banking point of view, sketches out a case study in privatization. His analysis of the various elements which were involved in the privatization of British Telecom, which at the time was the largest privatization project ever attempted, is both challenging and revealing.

One of the most insightful aspects of Williams' session is the distinction he draws between the benefits of privatization which accrue from severing the link to the public sector and those which accrue as a result of increased competition which the privatized firm faces. In effect, the implication of Williams' discussion paper is that while major benefits are, in fact, acquired because of the competition which is faced by privatized public firms, there is also an independent and additional benefit which accrues because of the severing of the umbilical cord that ties public firms to the political fortunes of their governmental masters. The very practical details about privatization, and in particular its relation to the stock market, which John Williams provides, should be a useful guide to any government considering a privatization effort or any private sector observer trying to ascertain the likely impact of such a manoeuver.

The scope of the international privatization movement is given some measure in Oliver Letwin's discussion of this topic. Letwin was the deputy head of the privatization unit at No. 10 Downing Street, and though a philosopher by training, he brings a piercing political and economic insight to the international developments in privatization. His expertise is also very evident in the wrap-up panel discussions. Those interested in the politics of privatization will find his contribution fascinating and insightful.

Perhaps the most difficult paper in the volume was prepared by Kenneth Stein, the head of Canada's federal privatization effort and a person who was placed in an unfortunate position by virtue of the fact that the federal government which employed him had, just before he presented his paper, cancelled a privatization effort in full flight. The tentative nature of Stein's presentation reflects the tentative posture in the federal government at the time the paper was delivered but also serves to point out an important difference between privatization in Canada and that in Great Britain. Most Canadian public or Crown corporations were created deliberately by governments to pursue particular policy objectives whereas most nationalized industries in the United Kingdom emerged as a result of the nationalization of previously private firms. This and other features of the Canadian political climate with regard to privatization are skillfully explored by Mr. Stein.

Part One of the book closes with two papers on the privatization of public services. The first by Robert W. Poole, Jr. entitled "The Limits of Privatization," reveals that there are no limits on the extent to which public services can be privatized as long as the privatization is appropriately structured. Poole documents the wide range of services which have been privatized in the United States and shows that even services like the operation of prisons and social services can effectively be privatized.

The second paper on the privatization of services in Part One, by Professor James McDavid, is an investigation of a particular kind of public service in Canada, namely solid waste removal, more popularly known as garbage collection. McDavid's path-breaking work on the cost of the provision of this service in Canada reveals that the savings to the taxpayer from the privatization of service production can be quite significant. His work also reveals that many of the standard prejudices about privatization do not stand up to careful scrutiny. For example, the major factor contributing to the reduction in the cost of garbage collection does not arise because the private firms are non-unionized, but emerges from the fact that they are differently organized and involve different incentive systems. Employees working for private firms are also considerably more productive than public sector employees and simply collect more tons of garbage per worker than those in the public sector.

INSTITUTIONAL AND POLITICAL ASPECTS OF PRIVATIZATION

Part Two of the book, entitled "Institutional and Political Aspects of Privatization," provides a consideration of Canadian experience with privatization as well as the issues and institutional peculiarities which must influence the implementation of a privatization programme in Canada. The first paper in the section, written by Thomas Kierans, provides an interesting guide to the particular differences that attend the existence of public enterprises in the Canadian context. Kierans notes that public corporations in Canada have tended to be a conscious outgrowth of social and economic policy rather than the by-product of the failure of a private sector firm.

From the point of view of the individual provincial governments which establish these public institutions, the existence of the Crown corporations is often an integral part of government policy and they, therefore, present special problems when they are to be dismantled. From the federal government's point of view, one of the central policy conflicts is to be found in its historic role of operating a national policy which is sensitive to the requirements of the individual regions. As Kierans notes, privatization in a unitary state such as Great Britain has very different ramifications than privatization in a federal state such as Canada which has ten quasi-autonomous political units within its borders.

Notwithstanding his reservations about privatization in the Canadian context, Kierans has played an active role, both in advising the federal government on the privatization of some of its most significant assets and in the actual privatization of Fisheries Products International which was recently privatized with great success.

Success in privatization has also been experienced in other parts of the country and Graham Walker of Pemberton Houston Willoughby Bell Gouinlock Inc., who has advised several governments in Western Canada on privatization ventures, describes some of that success in his paper.

All Crown corporations are not created equal in the sense that some are more intimately involved in the lives of citizens than others. A peculiarly

Canadian institution in this regard is that of publicly owned insurance corporations providing automobile insurance to citizens on a monopoly basis. Manitoba, Saskatchewan and British Columbia all have Crown-owned automobile insurance corporations and their privatization, because of the intense political activity which can attend their operations, requires special consideration. In his paper, Michael C. Burns provides a discussion of some of the difficulties that can emerge in the privatization of such an organization and suggests a novel alternative to standard privatization in the form of mutualization. Burns's paper is interesting, both because of its exploration of the political difficulties which can be involved in privatization initiative, and because of the demonstration that privatization policy must be flexible in adopting different techniques for different situations.

That is also illustrated in the paper by Pierre Matuszewski who discusses some of the success that has been enjoyed in the privatization programme in the province of Quebec. His particular case study of the privatization of the Soquem/Cambior mining venture is a hands-on, nuts- and bolts-type description of how a privatization can proceed in a particular circumstance.

The last two papers in the second section deal with public service provision and both draw on experience with privatization in the United States where this activity has progressed to a later stage than in Canada. The two papers together serve to illustrate some very interesting principles about the privatization of public services and some of the difficulties which can be encountered.

The paper by Wendell Cox "Privatization in the Public Services" discusses some of the facts and fallacies that attend the privatization of public transportation facilities. Because it is often felt that transportation is one of those areas wherein it is very difficult for the private sector to operate effectively, Cox's paper is very valuable in documenting the extent to which privatization can actually help more effectively to achieve the ambitions of the public ethic in urban transportation. His work also contains some fascinating reflections on the relative safety levels in public and private transport and demolishes the mythology which persists about the inferior safety record of private operators.

The paper by Davis R. Schwartz "Privatization of State and Local Government Services in the United States" is a description of a particular privatization effort undertaken by the State of Washington which currently requires, by law, that certain aspects of public services be privately provided. Schwartz's taxonomy of public service provision and the systematic approach taken to it by the privatization unit in his firm is an

intriguing illustration of the opportunities and the pitfalls which may attend
any privatization activity.

QUESTIONS AND ANSWERS ABOUT PRIVATIZATION

While the formal papers themselves provide a wealth of information for
anybody who wishes to learn about privatization, its ramifications and
prospects for its adoption, the book also contains the results of an intensive
discussion period between the various authors and the audience which attended the symposium upon which the book is based. This question and
answer interchange represents some of the most valuable information about
the privatization process that is currently available. Some of the world's
most informed experts about privatization effectively deal with many of
the social questions that must be addressed in considering and implementing a privatization programme. These sections are must readings for
politicians, public servants and others directly involved in the privatization
process.

Privatization is one of the most important policy issues of our time and
the Fraser Institute has been very pleased to support the work of the
authors contained in this book in the interests of raising the level of public
awareness about this issue. However, each of the authors has worked
independently and opinions expressed by them, therefore, are their own
and do not necessarily reflect the opinions of the members or the Trustees
of the Fraser Institute.

Michael A. Walker
Director
The Fraser Institute

PART ONE

HOW TO PRIVATIZE:
INTERNATIONAL LESSONS

MADSEN PIRIE

(Introduction by Michael A. Walker)

The first of our speakers, Madsen Pirie, is the president of the Adam Smith Institute in London—a man who has probably done more to spread the good news about privatization around the world than any other. Madsen has a Ph.D. in philosophy, and one of his best works in that area is called *The Book of the Fallacy*, which is probably what prepared him eminently well to become interested in the privatization issue. He has been a research associate with the Republican Study Committee on Capitol Hill in Washington, a distinguished visiting professor of philosophy at Hillsdale College, and in the late '70s formed the Adam Smith Institute to prompt his fellow citizens to be more interested in market-oriented issues and, in particular, in the issue of privatization. Madsen Pirie has travelled to every continent and probably to most of the countries of the world singing the praises of privatization. I'm sure you'll agree that he is an able spokesman for this process.

CHAPTER 1

PRINCIPLES OF PRIVATIZATION

Madsen Pirie

INTRODUCTION

Since I spoke last in Vancouver, Mrs. Thatcher has been re-elected for a third term, as I said she would be, with a majority of more than 100, as I predicted. She is, of course, the first British Prime Minister in modern times to achieve this feat. It was done before by Lord Liverpool who took office in 1812, but since that was before the vote was given to the working classes in 1867 or to the middle classes in 1832, it's rather less of an achievement than Mrs. Thatcher's. It is a staggering and unprecedented political success. The most significant policy of the Thatcher administration since 1979 has been privatization. Therefore, this third-term victory with a huge majority for her administration is, to some extent, a vindication of the success of that amongst other policies.

THE POLITICS OF BRITISH PRIVATIZATION

I want you to imagine how it must have been. Mrs. Thatcher coming into office in 1979, finding that she'd won the election, and then uttering those immortal five words all incoming leaders utter—What do we do now? The following conversation is imaginary, and I will not attempt to reproduce Mrs. Thatcher's accent—first, because I'm not a very good mimic, and secondly, that would kiss good-bye to any hopes I might have of a peerage. The conversation, as Mrs. Thatcher confronted her aids after the election, might have gone something like this.

"Who voted for us?"—"Prime Minister, principally the home owners." —"Right, I want more of them." She is a very direct woman. So, during the next eight years, policies are pursued which result in 2.5 million more families in Britain owning their own homes. That is one result of privatization. Of course, people in those 2.5 million families who now own their own homes are members of a group more inclined to vote for the Conservative Party.

"Right, who else?"—"Prime Minister, there is considerable evidence that people who own shares tend to vote Conservative."—"Right, we need more of them." Like I said, she is pretty direct. And the results of the policies since 1979 have been to ensure that we now have four times as many share owners as we did before, even more than that if you count the number of families owning shares.

We are reaching a landmark in Britain toward the end of this year when the number of persons in the country holding shares will exceed the number of persons who are members of labour unions. That is a significant and profound change taking place in Britain, and it has happened since 1979. In 1979 there were many times more people who were members of labour unions, now the one is just about to pass the other.

"All right, who else voted for us?"—"Prime Minister, there is considerable evidence that people who are self-employed voted for you." —"Well, I want more." So we now have three-quarters of a million more people who are self-employed.

"Who else?"—"Prime Minister, people who own shares in the company they work for tend to vote Conservative."—"Right, I want more of those." And indeed there are now hundreds more companies where the workers own shares in the firm that they work for. The average take-up rates of privatization issues when shares are offered to the labour force is in excess of 90 percent. The unions tell them to oppose privatization. The firm offers them a free share issue or a reduced option share issue, and the take-up rate of that is over 90 percent. So, another large group of Conservative voters.

"All right, who votes against us?"—"Prime Minister, of course, we tend to find the Labour Party dominated by members of the labour unions." —"Right, I want less of them." And indeed, there are now one-third fewer members of labour unions than there were.

"Who else votes against us?"—"The people who live in council houses as tenants of state-owned houses."—"Right, I want less." So we have one million fewer families living in state-owned homes, and the target is another million purchasing their own apartments in the next two years after the sale of the houses.

"Who else tends to vote against us?"—"Prime Minister, we do find that people who work for the state-owned firms in the public sector tend to vote against the Conservative Party."—"Right, I want less of them." So, there are now two-thirds of a million fewer of those.

"Who else?"—"Civil servants don't tend to vote Conservative." —"Right, I want those down as well." And, lo and behold, we have a 20 percent reduction in the number of civil servants.

"Who else votes against us?"—"People who own no capital assets, tend to vote against us." So we now have a situation in which 70 percent of all persons retiring have an additional income as well as their pension. Over two-thirds of those of retirement age now have capital assets in excess of 25,000 pounds.

You begin to see that there's a kind of remorseless system. Some people suspect this conversation did take place, but I assure you it is all imaginary.

A SOCIAL REVOLUTION

What we have in fact is a complete social revolution. That conversation I described did not take place, but you begin to see that it might as well have because every single group which supports the Conservative Party has found its numbers expanded. And every single group which tends to oppose the Conservative or capitalist policies has found its numbers diminished. The conversation never took place; it didn't need to because privatization has helped to do all of that, just as if it had been planned systematically. The results of those eight years have been exactly as I described. I don't think it was planned demographically in order to gerrymander future election results, but that certainly appears to have been a consequential effect. It is hardly surprising, therefore, that Mrs. Thatcher won her third term. The surprise, indeed, is that there was anyone left to vote against her.

Privatization, you can see from that very short example, has an important political dimension. When government engages in an activity such as privatization, it is speaking to several audiences. Among the audiences that government speaks to are the managers of Crown corporations, the workers who are employed in them, the members of the general public who are customers of Crown corporations, the general public who are taxpayers and who pay subsidies to support the losses of those corporations, potential investors who might buy shares in those corporations, the financial and business community which takes an interest in their performance, and the media commentators who observe this process and comment on the results and declare it to be a success or a failure. Every act of privatization speaks to all of those audiences, and every act should be tailor-made to maximize the support of each of those different groups.

PRINCIPLES OF PRIVATIZATION

Never Cancel A Benefit

The first task when contemplating an act of privatization is to list all of those groups and to identify their advantage. Start any particular operation by asking: "who are the groups involved, who benefits now, who could gain?" Then list their advantage. The golden rule about privatizing is always to give people greater advantage than they previously enjoyed. When you have listed all the groups involved and estimated the advantage they currently enjoy, devise the privatization policy in such a way that they will gain more advantage from it. In Britain, we say the rule is: never cancel a benefit.

If people are deriving a benefit from the state from a public activity of a Crown corporation, never cancel it however unjust it is. When people have a benefit from the public sector stretching over many years, they begin to think of it not as a benefit but as a right. After a time, it becomes a civil right. Shortly after that, it progresses into becoming a human right. The public does not take very kindly to governments which cancel their human rights. So, the rule is to never cancel a benefit, especially if you can buy it instead.

For example, take the pensions enjoyed at British Airways. When that was being prepared for privatization, one of the obstacles was that the work-force enjoyed index-linked pensions. Being employed in the public sector, they had pensions which were linked to the rate of inflation. There is no way you could put that into the private sector. It is an unlimited liability, so you could not put that kind of obligation into the private sector with any kind of reasonable price on it. Instead of cancelling those index-linked pensions and arousing the fury and opposition of the work-force of British Airways, through management the government offered cash funds to the workers to trade in those pensions for conventional ones. Of course, all of them traded in their index-linked pensions for a more conventional pension and took the cash sum. The benefit wasn't cancelled; it was bought. The workers who might otherwise have opposed the move, supported it instead and were quite grateful for the cash sum received.

Make Friends Out of Your Enemies

This brings us to the first principle of privatization: make friends out of your enemies. Find out who the people are who might lose on the privatization process and structure the policy to make sure they gain instead. In other words, determine who could become your enemies and make them your friends, whether it's the management, the work-force, customers or the general public. Whichever group it is, identify them and secure their advantage.

When we attempted to privatize the Gas Showrooms in 1981—a tragic mistake—the policy was to separate the high street stores from which gas appliances were sold and maintained, and sell those as a profitable separate entity. It was opposed by the management of British Gas. The workers staged a one-day strike to show that if privatization met with their opposition they were in a position to disrupt the industry and undermine its value. The head of British Gas, Dennis Brooks, set up a lobby in the House of Commons and conducted a campaign against the privatization of his Gas Showrooms. The general public bombarded their Members of Parliament with worried letters, thinking that they were going to lose their Gas Showrooms and that unqualified people would come in to connect dangerous appliances. The result was that after a few months the proposal was withdrawn—an example from which we learned. We had alienated almost every possible group in that particular case: the management, the work-force, and the general public.

By the time British Gas was privatized successfully last year, all of the lessons had been learned. All of the groups were given greater advantage. The same management and work-force which had opposed it the first time made it a success the second. So principle number one: make friends out of your enemies.

The National Freight Corporation, which was one of the very first groups to be privatized, was sold to a management/work- force buyer. A 1979 examination and analysis of the National Freight Corporation, a state-owned trucking company in Britain, had concluded that it would be impossible to privatize it because of the attitude of the work-force. But that survey assumed it was going to be sold to someone else. When it was actually sold two years later, it was that same work-force that bought it.

Management organized a syndicate. About two-thirds of the workers came into it. They mortgaged homes and pooled their savings, and they bought the company between them. So, National Freight was privatized successfully to its management and work-force, and as a result of its increased profitability—every time I tell this story it changes—the current value of each 1 pound invested then is now 41 pounds. The company is worth 41 times what it was worth when they bought it in 1981. That's simply because they're more productive and more profitable working for themselves than they were working for the state. Again, I emphasize the first principle: make friends out of your enemies.

Disarm the Opposition

The second task is to identify all possible objections to privatization. For example, when we were contemplating the privatization of Telecom, one possible source of objection was from people who use pay phones in remote areas—not terribly economic. Would a private company maintain those pay phones if they were not profitable? What would happen to the price if the company went private? Would they be able to jack-up prices, exploiting their dominant position in the market? Obviously, customers were a potential source of objection. What would happen if the Americans bought up our telephone network? What kind of strategic independence would that give us if our entire communications network was owned by a foreign power? What would happen to the special rates and privileges given to disabled people? One can go on through the list, examining everyone who benefits in some way and all the possible sources of objection to the privatization.

The next stage is to tailor-make the policy so that every single one of those objections is dealt with in advance. The act which privatized British Telecom requires them to maintain a certain number of rural pay phones. It is in the law that makes them a private entity. That same law imposes a condition upon them. We call that technique legislative preconditions; you write some of the conditions that the company must meet in the future into the act. Sometimes this is in perpetuity; more commonly it's for a number of years—how they must behave for the next 10 years and perhaps subject to parliamentary review after that time. They're required to maintain the rural pay phones.

The prices they can charge for their services are limited by a formula which says that any increases must be set below the increases in the cost of living. We call that formula RPI-X, in this case X is 3. Whatever the current cost of living index or rate of inflation, the telephone company is only allowed to increase its prices 3 percent below that. In other words, if inflation is running at 4 percent, they are allowed to increase their prices by a maximum of 1 percent. It's written into the act. That dealt with the objection over price.

The golden share retained by the British government gives them voting control in the event of ownership of Telecom passing into foreign hands. It is like a poison pill, activated to maintain the strategic interest of Britain over its communications network. We used it before in British Aerospace. The golden share is quite a common formula now. It indicates a determination to retain control of vital strategic industries. That, of course, defuses the patriot argument. You've dealt with it in advance.

And, of course, all the special privileges and facilities for the disabled were announced as being maintained and improved by Telecom. That defused another possible source of objection. We systematically went through every single possible group and dealt with the objections in advance. So, if principle number one is make friends with your enemies, principle number two is: disarm the opposition. Find out every single objection and deal with it in advance.

When we privatized the National Bus Company, for example, one possible objection was what would happen to the remote areas that don't pay very well. We knew that a privatized bus company would run innovative services with smaller vehicles and experiment and probably be able to make money anyway. Although we knew that, how could we convince people in advance that that is what it would be like? The answer is that we couldn't. That is hypothetical, and they're worried about losing their remote bus services. So we introduced the principle of competition for least subsidy. Where there are certain services we deem essential for social reasons, we will maintain these at a loss and invite private companies to bid against each other to see who can perform it for the least subsidy. In that way we get all the benefits of competition and innovative techniques, but at the same time we're spending as little of the state's money as possible to provide this essential service. The main thing is that the people who live in these remote areas see that their service is going to be maintained and therefore don't provide a focus of objection to the privatization that they might have otherwise.

We're going to privatize the electricity supply industry in Britain. It's in the manifesto for this Parliament and is probably coming next year. Do watch it in the light of what I've said. Observe how carefully written into that bill are ad hoc measures designed to deal with every single conceivable objection that could possibly be raised against it. I was taking a bet with someone that they would, if necessary, make the areas around power stations into bird sanctuaries if it took that to get the environmental lobby to support the privatization. Watch that one very carefully. If you see new bird sanctuaries being designated, you'll know it wasn't a joke.

So, we're now at the stage where, armed with principles number one and two—make friends with your enemies; disarm the opposition—you satisfy the management, the work-force, the customers, the investor, the financial institutions and, by means of adding on special clauses, you deal with the patriot lobby through such things as the golden share and you deal with people like the bird watchers. I'm sure when we privatize the railways, there will be a clause put in maintaining a certain number of steam trains in order to get the railway enthusiasts to support it and, if necessary, the whale lobby. Whatever it takes, no matter how ad hoc it seems, these are worth doing because privatization has a political as well as an economic dimension. It is very important to secure the support of the groups who might otherwise have fought it.

TECHNIQUES OF PRIVATIZATION

Fixed Price Shares

Let's give you some examples of the techniques that have evolved during this process. You watch the big public flotations in Britain and you see that several million new share owners are attracted. There is invariably a premium. The price goes up on the first day, and everyone says the government sold it too cheaply. Yes, of course, it did, because it's very important that the people who buy the shares should perceive an immediate gain. This makes them support privatization. It means they'll be along next time, and it means that if by the prospect of that gain we can spread share ownership very widely, it's going to be very difficult for subsequent parties to come along and threaten to reverse the process and concentrate those shares. So you will always see this little premium.

Tendering

Sometimes we sell the shares at a fixed price; sometimes we use the tender process. The process of entering bids by tender is thought to be too complicated for the unsophisticated small investor in Britain. Depending on whether we think the company is risky or not, we try to sell it to a particular market. In the case of the oil companies such as Brit Oil and Enterprise Oil, considerable use was made of the tender method of sales because we didn't want to get little old ladies bringing out their tin boxes from under the bed and putting their life savings into a potentially very risky business such as the oil industry. On the other hand, for something like Telecom or British Gas, which is a solid blue chip asset-backed thing, we do try to entice little old ladies with their tin boxes.

In the British Airports Authority sale currently going on in Britain, which is the privatization of seven of our leading airports, we used both techniques for the first time. One-quarter of the shares sold at fixed price, and three-quarters through the tender process. We are trying to attract both types of investor by a very widespread and diversified share ownership by the fixed price method and, at the same time, bring the special investors and institutions in for a large whack with the tender method. Interestingly enough, the applications for British Airports Authority, which closed at the end of last week, were ten times over-subscribed. The share allocation is such that if you applied for between 100 and 1,000 shares, you get 100. If you applied for more than 1,000 shares, you get none. So, everyone is automatically a member of the 100 club of British Airports Authority —they get 100 shares—and none of the personal investors get more than 100. In other words, the government has deliberately maximized the spread of share ownership and minimized the concentration. This is reckoned to be very good for social and political reasons. You can maximize the number of people with a stake in it.

Management/Work-Force Buy-Out

The Vicker's Shipyard was privatized last year and was indeed a landmark because it was sold to the second-highest bidder. The highest bid for the Vicker's Shipyard was received from a multinational conglomerate, Trafalgar House. The second highest bid was from a consortium of the management and the work-force and members of the communities in which the ships were built and the local banks. It was reckoned that that syndicate had a better chance of making privatization a success because it involved all the participants in the process. While we could have gotten a higher price simply by selling it to a company, there would have been, if you like, less satisfied customers. There would have been less support built in. By selling it to that consortium we have the work-force involved, the local community and the management. It's very much more likely that they'll do a National Freight and make a successful go of it because they have a stake in it. But interestingly enough, it went to the second highest bidder.

We're in the process now of privatizing National Bus. It's been broken up into 66 companies which are being sold off one at a time. There are about 38 gone so far, and all but three have gone to management and worker buy-out. In other countries you read about the big share issues such as Telecom and British Gas, but the unsung story of privatization is the leverage management/work-force buy-out. There have been many hundreds of these. If anything characterizes privatization in Britain—a typical example—it would be where the management and work-force have gotten together to form a syndicate to purchase it. It doesn't make international news; they tend to be smaller. But it certainly makes for success.

You probably read the enormous fuss we had over the potential sale of Leyland Bus and Leyland Truck about a year ago. Great was the outcry in Parliament about letting these vital British assets go to the Americans. The idea of General Motors or Ford buying this was reckoned to be a total disgrace to the British character and besmirched our flag and so on. A classic example of how not to have a political debate, incidentally. I wonder how many people know that in the months after that we sold Leyland Truck quietly. It's gone into partnership with a Dutch firm. Leyland Bus has been bought by a management buy-out. Both of them quietly privatized as if there were no fuss at all. The management/work-force buy-out is the hidden weapon of privatization. It's the one that accounts for most of the numbers.

Privatize the Process

There is one further principle I will give you. You must maximize your chances of success several ways. First of all, don't do the difficult and un-popular ones first. Do the easy ones first, and use the success and popularity of those to gain support for the other ones.

In Britain we learned very rapidly that there is no reason why the government should have to learn how to buy and sell companies and how to win public support and interest. There are companies which do this everyday on the stock market. We found very early on in Britain that by buying that expertise we could maximize the chances of success. The third principle is: privatize the process of privatization. Don't try to do it as a government. Hire in the expertise—the merchant banks, the brokerage houses, the public relations firms, the advertising agencies—the people who do this for a living. The people who have been buying and selling firms and promoting share issues for many years on the private market are the people to do it for the government. They know how to do it. They have a reputation in the financial community, and they have the contacts. The idea that a government should try to learn what these people have spent a lifetime learning when you can simply buy it is simply nonsense. We learned very quickly that if we hire expertise, we stand a much better chance of success.

Also, it gives us a hands-off approach. Because you hire a commercial firm like a merchant bank, the government can step some distance away from the process. Can you imagine what privatization would be like if each bill had to go through Parliament and have 650 Members of Parliament try to amend it in the interests of their own districts, their own electors and constituents. You can begin to imagine what a torturous process it would be if everyone sought to affect it politically. Firms would be required to keep open a little factory in Puddlethorpe Lesser because of the 850 jobs it guaranteed. Whereas, if you hand it to experts—hand it to a merchant bank and say, I want to privatize this—in a sense you are distancing yourself from it.

When you use expertise from the financial community, they will advise on the method of sale, the timing of it, the advertising of it, and how to promote public awareness. Again, there are innumerable case histories in Britain. I thought the advertising campaign for the Trustees Savings Bank privatization was brilliant. They used the symbol of the British financial community, which is the bowler hat. The series of ads they ran showed ordinary people doing ordinary things but wearing bowler hats. The message was hammered home, now is your chance to become the owner of a bank. Then you saw a window cleaner wearing his bowler hat, and everyone was geared up to apply for the shares. As the time grew near to the dates of the stock being kicked off, everyone in Britain knew what the Trustees Savings Bank was and that it was being privatized and the date on which share applications had to be in. The result is that they were swamped with applications.

If anyone was in Britain while the British Gas campaign was running, you saw a character they called Sid. The message read, "tell Sid that British Gas is going to be sold on November 13th." The mysterious Sid started appearing in cartoons and became a national character. He represented the ordinary man with an interest in British Gas.

GO FORTH AND PRIVATIZE

By the time you have dealt with every group involved, by the time you've dealt with all possible sources of opposition, and by the time you've minimized the risk of failure, you know why privatization is easy. It is because it's about politics as well as economics. If you start at the very beginning and recognize that, you're more likely to be successful.

It is significant that some people in Canada say that if only the Prime Minister had done some privatization early while there was still time he might have achieved very different results to what is currently shown in the opinion polls. Privatization isn't something unpleasant that you need to do quickly in order to have a few years to get over it. It's not like that. We were privatizing right up to our general election and through it. The privatization of Rolls Royce and British Airports Authority were taking place even while the general election campaign was going through in Britain.

It's not something unpopular that you need to do in a hurry so you can live it down afterwards. It is not only going to be very successful but extremely popular. As I say, the interesting thing in Britain is that the government was doing it right down to the wire almost to polling day. It is definitely an electoral asset. After this, one can understand why Mrs. Thatcher managed to win three elections in a row. All of those groups which support capitalism in general—the Conservative Party philosophy of choice and opportunity—have been maximized and increased by the privatization process. The groups that favour state dependence have been diminished similarly. So it makes what would otherwise appear to be inexplicable electoral success understandable in demographic terms.

My advice to you today as we start this conference is: go forth and privatize. You'll find that it enables you to bring opportunities to ordinary people. It gives your citizens a chance to take part in the wealth-creating process. It speeds up economic growth. It cuts the costs of government. It turns losses into tax revenues. In Britain it's ending the old politics of division—the old politics of "us who don't have it and them that do." As I said, it is getting so there are more people who own shares than who belong to labour unions. It is letting ordinary people in Britain own property and capital. It has spread on a world dimension to more than 100 countries so far, providing choice and opportunity. It is without doubt the most significant economic fact of our age, and I would predict we are at the beginning of probably a fifty-year cycle of retreat by the state in the public sector and promotion of opportunities for private enterprise and participation by ordinary people.

DISCUSSION

Edited by Michael A. Walker

Question: What are the negative aspects of privatization?

Answer: That's easy. There aren't any at all. If privatization is done right, there is no downside whatsoever. A way to rephrase this question would be, "what mistakes did we make along the way that we haven't made again?" The answer to that is that we've learned several things—it's very much a learning process. For example, we were criticized early on for getting the price wrong, allowing people to make a quick killing by having the price very much below that which it settled at in the market.

It's extraordinarily difficult to actually price a Crown corporation. In many cases, they've had nothing remotely resembling accounts for decades. Indeed, if any private company had turned in accounts like those of our Crown corporations, they'd go to jail. Given that, it's quite difficult to put a price on it, and sometimes you get it wrong.

We've learned one really good trick with Telecom—sell only part of it. If you sell just over 50 percent, you put it into the private sector. There's a very big premium on the Telecom price, but that's fine. The government is sitting on 49.8 percent of the shares, which it can quietly unload on the market as we did with British Petroleum. Wherever we've done that, we've gotten far more for the second sale and the third than we did for the first. So, there's no downside at all if you do it right, but you do learn tricks like that as you go along. It's a learning process, and every country is different.

Question: Was privatization an act of leadership or a reflection of shifts in public opinion?

Answer: I tend to think it was an accident. The word itself didn't appear in the 1979 manifesto. There was late talk of "returning" Aerospace to the private sector. This was the old game of de-nationalization that was played immediately after the war when the Labour Party would nationalize British Steel and the Conservatives would de-nationalize it, then Labour would re-nationalize it—taking it from its former owners and giving it back to its former owners.

That's not what privatization is. Privatization is creating new forms of ownership. Some of the things we've privatized had never been in the private sector at all.

How was it done? The first one was British Petroleum. The government made a small sale in 1979 which took its holding below 50 percent. That made it technically a private company. Under our Treasury rules, any capital it raised was therefore treated as purely private—not part of the public sector borrowing requirement limits. Once it was a private company, British Petroleum started making commercial decisions and it became very profitable. I'm sure someone in government said, "hey, we can do this again." Very modestly at first—British Aerospace, Cable and Wireless, Amisha International—the trickle became a flood, the flood became a torrent.

Question: With all respect, the question was, was there an act of leadership involved?

Answer: No intellectual battle was won. We didn't win the argument first. We privatized first and used the success of privatization to win the argument. We didn't have to win it in theory in advance. We didn't get public opinion to support it until after it was done. So, in that sense, it was an act of leadership. But then, fortunately, for the last eight years we've had a Prime Minister who believes in acts of leadership.

Question: Has privatization had a broader economic impact, and what about the structural unemployment one hears about?

Answer: First of all, the broader economic impact of privatization has been wholly good. Firms that were marginal or loss-makers before have been turned into profitable private corporations. More than that, the fact of becoming commercial and responsive to commercial and sometimes competitive pressures has meant that they've offered better service to the rest of British industry, which finds, for example, that all of its input costs—telecommunications, freight, transport—are very much less and better service is provided than previously was the case. So, it has had several beneficial effects on the economy at large.

It has not contributed substantially to unemployment. The decline of our mass manufacturing industries has done that. It's been going on for many decades. The policy of previous governments was to try to prevent it from happening by supporting declining industries through subsidies instead of allowing the normal recycling process and redeployment of resources into growing industries. The result was that we spent an increasing amount of money every year keeping old and declining industries going through subsidies. We didn't have the investment there to promote new and growing industries. That was part of the so-called "British problem". That's why we were in such a bad way in the late 1970s. That process of adjustment has now been done very rapidly. It did, of course, create record levels of unemployment. The only good news is that unemployment has been going down every month now for eleven months and is below 3 million and falling, so it seems as if we're over the worst of it.

Question: A very practical question. On a municipal council of nine, two of us favour privatization, how do we convince the other seven members of council to become believers?

Answer: You have an advantage that we didn't have. I said we didn't win an argument in theory—we did it and it worked—but people doing it now can cite foreign experience. You can show an overwhelming weight of evidence that privatization—particularly at the municipal level—does provide better services and saves money and is more responsive. Take Dr. Robert Poole over and have him talk non-stop for an hour and a half. If you haven't won at least four of those seven over by then, I'll be very surprised. Simply cite the record of what's happened elsewhere in the world—you'd have to be almost a narrow-minded bigot not to want to give it a try.

The answer is, first of all, show them the evidence from elsewhere, and then suggest one or two services be privatized as an experiment.

Question: Are there examples of failures? Have some of the new companies gone broke?

Answer: Yes, there are examples of failures. They're very small, and they're almost all of the same type. They're where the state closed down an operation such as a shipyard, for example, and the workers applied to buy it out and keep it going after it was already deemed to be commercially unsound. We've had a couple of failures like that, where even with the workers taking it over they weren't able to make a go of it.

The lesson we learned is that when a thing has been closed down, it's a bit late to start privatizing it. And secondly, to have it as a worker co-operative isn't as good as the leveraged buy-out that is led by management with strong work-force participation. If you want to make a go of it, it will be the management that leads the consortium and involves the work-force, rather than the workers coming together as a group of individuals and buying a factory that's already been closed because it was uneconomic. So, we've had a couple of small failures like that along the way, and those are the lessons to be learned.

Question: In Britain what structure is in place to carry out the privatization process? For instance, is there a "minister" in charge, such as there is in Canada? Could you explain the process?

Answer: No, it's very informal in Britain. It developed as it went along. It got to the stage where a Treasury minister now has a special responsibility for privatization. So, one of the two new ministries in the economics department, which we call the Treasury in Britain, is given special responsibility for privatization.

Most of the initiative comes from the department concerned. If it's transport, it will be the Department of Transport; if it's privatization of local government, it will be the Department of the Environment which takes the initiative. The ministry with responsibility generally takes the initiative. Gas was privatized by the Department of Energy. Of course, we've had ministers virtually competing with each other to show that they can do more privatization than the other guy.

Question: What is going to happen to your budget when you run out of things to sell?

Answer: That's a very good question. The current rate of privatization is just in excess of 5 billion pounds per year. Incidentally, in 1982 there was an inquiry by the government which estimated that privatization would never be able to reach 1 billion pounds a year because the stock market wouldn't be able to absorb those kinds of claims made upon its finances. It's now running in excess of 5 billion per year just a few years later, and still increasing.

It's making a contribution toward our national budget equivalent to four-tenths of income tax. For the first year ever, the proceeds from privatization are currently exceeding our borrowing. We're borrowing 4 billion, at least that's the announced figure, and we're selling 5 billion. But, in fact, privatization is going to be more than 5 billion and borrowing is going to be very much less than 4 billion, so it's an even bigger split. It's quite conceivable we could end up with no borrowing at all, closing the gap with privatization sales.

We're not going to run out for a long time. Currently, we've put the privatization of water before Parliament; the Water Authorities in Britain is valued at 10 billion. Electricity is coming next year, probably something approaching the same. Then we have the remainder of the auto industry, the rest of Leyland and the steel industry. Looking down the road we have the railways, the post office and the coal mines. When we start selling publicly-owned land, the Adam Smith Institute estimates we can go on at the current rate for more than 40 years before we begin to run out. So, the answer to what will happen when we do run out is, I'll be dead and it will be someone else's problem.

John Chown: (Intervention from the floor) I've come all the way from London to take part in this. I feel a little bit like a skulker in the weeds because I entirely agree with Dr. Pirie about the virtues of privatization. However, as a mere financial technician I want to criticize the details, and I am terrified to do so in my own country in case I give too much succour to our enemies.

Four issues I looked at were underpriced, 11.5 billion gross to the government, 11 billion after expenses—worth in the market, 14 billion. Where did that money go?—1.2 billion went to the state. The great British public who applied enthusiastically got cut down to a couple of hundred shares and made a few hundred pounds profit a head for our 3 million people. The advantage was in winning votes for Margaret Thatcher, if nothing else. However, 1.4 billion of that didn't go to the state. It went to what I might call rabbit's friends and relations, if you remember the expression. That is, the underwriters were offered 55 percent in the case of British Telecom, 25 percent in the case of British Airports Authority. So, the profits to the underwriters were not one percent—which people say could have been three-quarters of a percent and perhaps the government should have bargained it down. The average profit to the underwriters' financial institutions was 11 percent with a maximum of 33 percent to the overseer underwriters of British Telecom.

This is quite an unjustified method of operation which shows there's a conflict of interest between the city of London's financial community as the government's advisers and the government, which has been resolved in the way one would expect. It is ultimately a device to encourage underpricing. Look at BA, the institutions are saying we've got it up to 200; we're going to take more than 200, possibly 220 or 245. What do they do? They all put in their tenders at 283. The stock is limited and they instinctively start talking it up. The answer for Canadians is that you do need your investment bankers—only they can sell the issue—but for heaven's sake, get some independent advice on structuring the issue and pricing.

Answer: First of all, distinguish between the fees which these people are paid for their services, which are in general quite low compared with what is charged in the private sector, such as 2.5 percent whereas 4 percent would be normal. The commission on fees charged has been less than is normal for the private sector. You could argue that since these are pretty solid, secure, automatic success blue chip sales, they ought to be getting even less. What you're talking about is the risk element which goes to the underwriters, and they turn out to make a whacking profit on it. They didn't in the case of Enterprise Oil and Brit Oil. The underwriters got caught there and had to take shares that opened at a discount instead of a premium. So, to some extent there is a risk element.

But, granting everything you say, I still think it's worth doing. The most important thing about each privatization is not that it must be priced absolutely correctly but that it must be successful. It's very important that the thing be a success and be perceived to be a success. One of the audiences that I said you speak to is the financial community. It's very important that the general perception of the financial community is that the privatization is a success.

There is a mansion somewhere in South America where retired Nazi generals argue with British financiers, and the Nazi generals show that in hindsight they, in fact, won World War II seven times over. And the British financiers show that with hindsight they could have gotten a very much better price for Telecom or British Gas or whatever. The answer is that it's all very easy after the fact to know that the price was wrong because the premium was too high. I'd rather have it that way than the other. My general view is that the nation has gained as a result of those privatizations.

Question: When privatization occurs, has management changed; i.e., have civil servants remained or has new management come in? If former civil servants remained, did retraining occur over a short or a long period?

Answer: The basic answer is, no. When we privatize, management stays right through, normally. That said, we often change the management in order to prepare for privatization. It's very important that you put someone at the top who believes in it. If you have management that has long been tied to the traditions of state ownership and control and locked into bureaucratic ways, then it's a good idea to change to someone who's given the brief, "go in and privatize, you've got four years." It concentrates the mind wonderfully, and you'd be quite amazed at the amount of restructuring and reorganization that can be packed into a couple of years. So, you might want to change management if the thing needs to be prepared for privatization.

When the thing actually hits the private market, no, we don't need to. We gave a lot of thought to whether someone working for the public sector would be any good at running a private corporation. The answer we discovered is that you don't need to worry, that happens automatically. Anyone of the desk-bound bureaucratic type gets quietly promoted upstairs into an honorary position within a year or two, and some smart youngsters who are very much more adept at the competitive and commercial climate they're now in get promoted. You don't need to make unpleasant decisions which may have unpleasant political consequences, because the private market does it for you automatically. It brings the talent to the top.

Question: What is the process of adjusting labour force work habits and expectations in privatized industries, especially those that have never been in the private sector?

Answer: If the work-force has to be trimmed down to make this thing economic in the private sector, one of the rules we try to follow wherever possible is, do it without firing people. We got British Airways down from 59,000 to 39,000 without firing anybody. We did it by generous terms of voluntary early retirement. In many cases it does involve renegotiating labour contracts. That's part of the reason you do it.

In general, there are more opportunities and incentives under privatization and less security.

Question: Has Britain privatized any Crowns which existed primarily to serve government, like the BC Buildings Corporation?

Answer: Yes, we've privatized the maintenance of military bases. We've privatized a lot of the servicing of public buildings—security, cleaning, that kind of thing. We privatized a branch of the armed forces in that the RAF Marine Auxiliary is now handed out to a private contractor.

Question: Do you not think that political leaders must take the leadership in setting the stage for acceptance by the general public?

Answer: No, I think that's up to independent think-tanks, academics and media commentators. The most important thing political leaders can do is to do it—get a couple of examples of privatization off and running so you can point to the success and encourage them to do more.

JOHN WILLIAMS

(Introduction by Michael A. Walker)

John Williams is a member of the Corporate Finance Department of Kleinwort Benson. He was graduated from the London School of Economics with a Masters degree in Economics. He joined the U.K. Treasury in 1978. Following a series of assignments, he spent two years working on the U.K. government's privatization programme. His principal involvement there was with the British Telecom privatization, although he also worked on the preparations for British Airways and British Airports Authority privatizations. He joined Kleinwort Benson in August 1986 and has since been involved in a number of takeovers, defences, and international privatizations, including advising the French government on the Saint-Gobain privatization and the New Zealand Electricity Division on its proposed corporatization.

CHAPTER 2

A CASE STUDY IN PRIVATIZING A MAJOR PUBLIC CORPORATION

John Williams

INTRODUCTION

This presentation examines the privatization of British Telecom in November 1984 as a case study in privatizing a major public sector organization. The presentation first looks at the background to this privatization and the nature and performance of the nationalized industries in the U.K. It goes on to consider in a more detailed way the approach to the B.T. privatization. This privatization has been chosen as a case study not simply because Kleinwort Benson was the government's principal adviser but because the structure devised for the B.T. flotation and the many innovations it contained have become standard features of subsequent privatizations in the U.K. and elsewhere. The presentation goes on to draw some comparisons between U.K. privatizations and Kleinwort Benson's experience in advising on the French privatization programme.

NATURE AND PERFORMANCE OF U.K. NATIONALIZED INDUSTRIES

The nationalized industries, before the present Conservative government was first elected in 1979, accounted for about 10 percent of the U.K.'s output and employed almost 5 percent of the working population. The nationalized industries dominated the transport, energy, communications, steel and shipbuilding sectors of the economy.

The key characteristic of the nationalized industries at that time was their diversity. Some, such as the electricity and gas supply industries, were near monopolies while others, such as British Airways and the British Steel Corporation, operated in highly competitive international markets. The reasons for their nationalization were also diverse. Some industries, such as coal and steel, were nationalized for ideological reasons. Others, such as shipbuilding, were nationalized for strategic reasons. Others, such as Rolls Royce, were nationalized in order to be rescued from bankruptcy. Some, such as railways and steel, had once operated in the private sector. Others, such as the Royal Mint and the Bank of England, had effectively been in public ownership for over a century.

The feature which all the nationalized industries shared was a history of frequent and widespread criticism. The nationalized industries were regarded as inefficient operations which paid little attention to customer demands or to the quality of the services which they provided. The reasons for the poor performance of the nationalized industries are complex but an important cause was the control framework and the relationship it defined between the government and each of the nationalized industries. The nature of this relationship is a key factor in a proper appreciation of the government's privatization policies.

The basis of the control framework was that the government should set each industry broad strategic objectives and the industry should be allowed to manage itself in a commercial way within those objectives. This relationship was set out in each of the acts of Parliament which established the nationalized industries. These acts typically gave the government the power to approve each industry's corporate plan, capital expenditure plans and borrowing, and gave the industry directions on matters which affected the national interest. Outside this legislation, successive governments developed a structure of financial and economic obligations for the nationalized industries. Government began to set financial and performance targets and limits on the industries' external financing requirements.

Increasingly, it became clear that the fundamental distinction between policy and management, which formed the basis of the relationship between the government and the nationalized industries, was not workable. The nationalized industries were economically, socially and politically too significant for the government simply to abdicate all control over their management. Governments were not prepared to allow the nationalized industries alone to determine commercial issues such as their prices or rates of pay because of the widespread implications of such decisions on the economy and the electorate.

Governments inevitably became closely involved in the detailed management of the industries in order to pursue a mix of social and macro economic objectives. Furthermore, governments often operated on the nationalized industries using informal pressure and guidance rather than by giving overt and clear directions. This detailed and unpredictable involvement by government and the absence of a coherent set of objectives for the industries caused the management of the industries to lose their motivation and enthusiasm. Performance suffered and recruitment became difficult.

At the same time, the imposition of non-commercial criteria on the nationalized industries caused their borrowings to increase and to become a more significant component of total public sector borrowing. Increasingly, the nationalized industries' financing requirements became subordinated to the government's public expenditure objectives and an instrument of macro economic policy. The finance and investment of the nationalized industries had become heavily constrained by the political process.

In sum, the nationalized industries, before the privatization programme, were operating in a confused environment. Their relationship with government was uncertain and unpredictable. Their performance as a result was inefficient and lacked energy. It was into this environment that Mrs. Thatcher launched her privatization policies in 1979.

These privatization policies were presented as an important element of the Conservative government's economic policy. The objective of privatization was to open up the nationalized industries to competition and so to improve their performance and the quality of their services. This government's view was that government control over the nationalized industries was unnecessary and inefficient and should be replaced by market forces combined with regulation where necessary.

The government argued that privatization benefited customers because of the greater efficiency achieved which fed through into lower prices, wider choice and better service. Employees of privatized companies benefit because they work in a company with clear objectives and the means to achieve them and are able to participate through share ownership. The economy benefits through the higher returns on the capital employed in the privatized industries which can no longer pre-empt resources from elsewhere in the economy but must compete for funds in the open capital markets.

THE PRIVATIZATION OF BRITISH TELECOM

The first stage in the privatization of British Telecom was the British Telecommunications Act 1981. The main features of this legislation were:

- the split of the General Post Office into the Post Office and B.T., with B.T. having all responsibility for telecommunications;
- the liberalization of the equipment market which brought to an end the monopoly which B.T. had previously enjoyed in the provision of equipment such as telephones;
- the framework to permit the setting up of an alternative telecommunications network, Mercury. This aspect to the legislation has proved to have been very significant in promoting competition in telecommunications.

Mercury has a licence to carry out telecommunications services within the United Kingdom and has been able to build up a trunk network linking the major industrial and commercial centres of importance. Its licence also permits it to interconnect with the B.T. network and provide direct international access. It now competes very aggressively with B.T., particularly for commercial traffic in the trunk lines and international traffic sector.

The primary purpose of the 1981 act was liberalization. The aim of the second Telecommunications Act in 1984 was privatization. This act permitted the government to implement a policy, which it first announced in July 1982, of selling just over 50 percent of the share capital of B.T.

There were five aspects to the preparatory stage of the B.T. flotation.

Regulation

It was clear that, despite the element of competition introduced by the 1981 act, B.T.'s share of the U.K. telecommunications market would remain dominant. The regulatory system which was devised to control this dominant position and to prevent any abuse of B.T.'s monopoly powers had a number of features. The first was the creation of the Office of Telecommunications (OFTEL) with a Director-General appointed by the government but whose approach was to be independent of the government. This office was modelled on the U.K.'s Office of Fair Trading. The first Director-General is Bryan Carsberg, a Professor of Accounting on leave of absence from the London School of Economics, who was appointed for a three-year term from 1 July 1984. The appointment of an accountant reflected the government's view that one of the main tasks of the Director-General would be to detect any cross-subsidization from an area where

B.T. had an effective monopoly to an area where B.T. was facing competition.

The second stage in devising a regulatory regime was to issue B.T. with a licence whose main terms and conditions were designed to ensure:

- effective competition through the prevention of cross-subsidization;
- the provision of a universal service in every part of the United Kingdom;
- the provision of certain special services such as the emergency service and services for the disabled; and
- the maintenance of public call box facilities.

The third and critical part of the regulatory framework was the inclusion within the licence issued to B.T. of a control over prices charged. There was considerable debate in the early stages of the privatization about the form such control should take. The initial view was that the control should be in the form of a ceiling on the rate of return on capital, typical of that employed for telecommunications companies in the United States and Hong Kong. However, following an influential report by Professor Stephen Littlechild, the government instead opted for control based not on profits but on tariffs. Under this scheme, B.T. is permitted to increase a basket of its charges by an amount relative to the U.K. Retail Price Index. This index monitors movements in the prices of a general basket of consumer goods and services. This approach to price regulation became known as the RPI-X formula because it allows the licensee to increase prices up to "X" percent less than the general level of inflation. The advantages of such a scheme are:

- it avoids the inherent complication in a return on capital scheme, where definition of profit and calculations of the asset base are difficult to make;
- from the government's point of view, it controls tariffs which are generally considered to be more politically sensitive than profits; and
- from the investor's point of view, it ensures that efficiency gains flow to investors and that there is no check on the incentive to increase profit which characterizes a rate of return control scheme.

In deciding upon the RPI-X formula, two further points were considered. Firstly, the basket of services to which the formula should apply, and secondly, the level of "X." These two points were related since the economics of local telephone calls are quite different from the economics of trunk and international calls. The level of "X" which it was reasonable to place upon B.T. consequently depended in part on the precise balance of services which were included in the basket. The government elected to include local calls and trunk calls (which together accounted for some 55 percent of B.T.'s turnover) but to exclude international calls and other services such as apparatus supply and private circuits; "X" was fixed at 3 percent for a five-year period. The RPI-X approach has also been applied to other privatized utilities. In the cases of British Gas and British Airports, the formula has been modified to reflect the significance to these undertakings of costs in a particular sector rather than the RPI generally. The formula applied is in an RPI-X+Y form. The "Y" factor allows changes in the specific sector to be reflected in the price ceiling.

Capital Structure

The next element of the preparatory stage was to determine the appropriate capital structure for B.T. The objective was to capitalize B.T. in a way which gave it the necessary financial strength to remain a major force within its own market and to compete successfully overseas. There was not a complete coincidence of views within government or between the government and B.T. about the appropriate balance of debt and equity.

The outcome was to give B.T. a level of debt and preference shares which amounted to some 75 percent of its equity capital and an interest cover of around four times. This structure allowed B.T. to be perceived by many within the international financial community as a company of substantial financial strength.

The Relationship between Government and British Telecom

There was one further significant factor in this preparatory stage. The relationship between the government and B.T. after the flotation was critical if investors were to be confident that the government would not use its residual B.T. shareholding as an instrument of social policy. It was agreed ahead of the flotation that the government should distance itself from the commercial operations of the company. That undertaking was set out in the prospectus in the following words.

> HM Government does not intend to use its rights as an ordinary shareholder to intervene in the commercial decisions of British Telecom. It does not expect to vote its shareholdings on resolutions moved at General Meetings although it retains the power to do so.

It was also agreed that, while the government would have the right to appoint two directors to the board of B.T., the responsibility of those directors would be to the company and not to the government.

A further aspect of the relationship between the government and the company relates to B.T.'s independence and freedom from takeover. Under the company's Articles of Association, no person can own more than 15 percent of the company's share capital and, in order to prevent this article being amended, the company issued to the government a special share. Any proposed amendment triggers special voting rights which the holder of the special share may exercise.

The Flotation

The principal feature of the flotation was its sheer size. The value of half the company was about 4 billion pounds, some seven times bigger than that of any previous U.K. issue and also many times bigger than anything attempted in the United States. It represented approximately the amount which the big U.K. investing institutions had put into the equity market over a two-year period.

It was clear that for an issue of such unprecedented size to be successful at an acceptable price, it would be necessary to achieve the widest appeal involving an intensive selling campaign in different markets. The four markets which were addressed were:

- the U.K. institutional market;
- the U.K. general public;
- B.T. employees; and
- overseas.

The Institutional Market

Discussions began in January and February of 1984 with a small number of major U.K. institutions, and over the course of the year the group grew to several hundred. There were three elements to this institutional campaign. The first was a series of discussions with the institutions led by Kleinwort Benson's team of stockbrokers. These discussions covered the size and the manner in which the offer was to be made. Secondly, a major programme of stockbrokers' research work about B.T. was instigated, not just by the sponsoring brokers. B.T. set aside a considerable amount of time to talk to brokers, and their research reports played an important part in building confidence in the company. Thirdly, a number of meetings were held for the institutions to get to know the company, including meetings with board members and company visits.

These lengthy discussions with institutions were essential in order to obtain their support, without which the whole exercise would have been impossible. While initially the attitude of many fund managers was that such a large issue represented a major burden (indeed a number of fund managers early in 1984 privately expressed the view that the size of the proposed transaction made it impossible), as the issue approached views shifted and enthusiasm grew.

The Retail Market

The main objective of the campaign to the general public was to aim the issue at a very wide audience and in particular at the 10 million or so residential subscribers to B.T.'s network. While widespread share owner-ship was a major policy objective of the government in the B.T. issue, the logic of the retail campaign was not solely political. From a merchant banking standpoint, it always seemed sound financial sense to aim an offer of this size at a wide audience. For B.T.'s part, although it recognized the administrative costs of a large shareholder register, it saw the advantage in having many of its customers as shareholders where they would have a wider understanding of what B.T. does and why it does it. The retail marketing campaign broke new ground in many areas and a number of its features are worth mentioning:

- a brief leaflet describing B.T. and the issue was sent to all 16 million residential subscribers in the summer of 1984;
- a major advertising campaign, using press and television, started in August with the general slogan "You can share in British Telecom's future." The purpose of this campaign was to make people aware that the issue was aimed at the small investor as much as at the big city in-stitutions. It also aimed at providing basic information to people about the risks and rewards of share ownership;
- those who responded to the advertising campaign (and by the time of the issue this list had grown to 1.3 million) were sent a booklet produced in conjunction with the London Stock Exchange which was a basic introduction to buying and selling shares. At the time of the issue itself, those on the mailing list were sent a prospectus; and
- during the summer, a team drawn from B.T., Kleinwort Benson and the stockbrokers travelled around the country talking to financial inter-mediaries about the coming issue and encouraging them to talk to their clients. In all, some 55 seminars were held at this time and this schedule, in a somewhat reduced form, was repeated at the time of the issue itself.

Employees

The government was anxious—and in this it was supported by the board of B.T.—to get the maximum support from B.T. employees for the privatization exercise. The official union's position during the run-up was one of hostility to privatization, but few employees heeded the official view of their union. The government effectively offered employees three incentives. Under the first, each employee would be given 70 pounds worth of shares free. Under the second, employees would receive two shares for every one they bought themselves, subject to a maximum of 300 pounds. Thirdly, employees were offered a 10 percent discount on the final instalment of shares they bought up to a maximum of 1600 shares. There was a substantial take-up by the employees, and B.T. now has some 95 percent or around 220,000 people of its work-force as shareholders.

Overseas Markets

The sale of B.T. was always considered as essentially a U.K. offer, and the marketing plans were designed to achieve a major success in the United Kingdom. There was, however, substantial interest from overseas markets and the decision to sell some shares overseas was based on two considerations. The first was the view taken much earlier in the year that, if an issue of this unprecedented size was to be successful at an acceptable price, it needed to generate interest from competing sources of demand. The second was that, if B.T. was to play an important role overseas, it needed to have some support among international investors as well as among the U.K. financial community. For these reasons, a proportion of the shares was sold in the United States, Canada, Switzerland and Japan.

The period of the issue itself, and its outcome, is well documented and can be briefly summarized. A pathfinder prospectus, containing full details about the company (including a forecast of profits through to March 1985) was released on 26 October 1984. Three weeks later, on 16 November 1984, the issue was priced and underwritten and the final prospectus was issued. The issue was then held open for twelve days, during which time it was widely advertised in the press, on television and radio. The overall response, both in the United Kingdom and overseas, was substantial. Over 2 million applications from the U.K. public were received and an allotment policy, heavily weighted in favour of the small investor, with those applying for over 100,000 shares getting nothing, was adopted. The final allocation between the four markets which were addressed was as follows:

U.K. institutions	47 percent
U.K. public	34 percent
B.T. employees and B.T. pensioners	5 percent
overseas	14 percent
	100 percent

This general structure—incorporating institutional, retail and overseas markets—has formed the basis for subsequent major privatizations. An important feature of the structure is the competition for shares it can generate between the separate targeted markets. A sense of scarcity develops which can enable the vendor to achieve a higher price than if the vendor was facing a monopoly buyer.

PREPARATIONS FOR PRIVATIZATION: CONTRASTS

This section considers some of the differences and similarities based on Kleinwort Benson's experience of U.K. privatizations and privatizations in France where we have advised on the privatization of Saint-Gobain and Credit Commercial de France.

Timing

The privatization programme in the U.K. has in practice been powerfully influenced by practicalities and short-term public expenditure objectives rather than by economic and political philosophy. The government first privatized companies which were already profit making, were reasonably capitalized, which had at some stage already been in the private sector and which did not require special regulatory regimes. British Aerospace, Jaguar and Cable and Wireless were among the first privatizations. This same approach has been adopted by the French government in that the initial privatizations were of companies which had been in private hands prior to the nationalization programme of the early 1980s. This approach allows privatizations to be completed relatively quickly.

The U.K. programme has now moved on to tackle public corporations which require considerably more preparation and whose privatization raises major issues of relation and competition. The privatization of British Telecom was the first of these "difficult" privatizations. The government has gone on to privatize British Gas and the British Airports Authority which also required the development of increasingly sophisticated regulatory regimes and sale structures. The government's declared intention to privatize the electricity supply industry in England and Wales will raise regulatory and structural issues which potentially are substantially more complex and intricate than in any previous privatization.

The problems encountered in these privatizations and the time taken to resolve them contrast with the preparations for the Saint-Gobain and Paribas privatizations. Both these companies had recently been in the private sector, had reasonable debt/equity ratios and had proven managements in place. The French programme is young and is addressing those kinds of companies which the British government dealt with first. The U.K. programme has matured and the easy targets have all been sold.

Parliament and Legislation

A second contrast between the two privatization programmes lies in the legislation which enables the privatization. Enabling legislation in the U.K. tends only to establish a broad framework in which each privatization is to be conducted. During the passage of the legislation, the government always tries to ensure that its discretion under the act is maximized. Normally, the government is left with complete flexibility on how to value the company to be privatized, how to structure the offer, whether and how to offer special concessions to the retail sector and when the privatization should occur.

The French government is typically faced with a number of legislative requirements and procedures which would be unusual in the U.K. One example of such a legislative requirement concerns valuation. In the U.K. the value of the corporation to be privatized is determined by the government and its advisers without any specific legal, judicial or parliamentary veto or input. In the U.K. the government is answerable to Parliament only after the valuation of the company has been determined and announced. These arrangements contrast with the role of the Privatization Commission in France. This commission is independent of the government and effectively and formally determines, before the privatization, a minimum valuation for the issue.

The French legislation also contains several further provisions governing detailed aspects of the privatization which are unprecedented in U.K. legislation. One example is the provision that all individuals who apply for up to ten shares must receive their application in full and that only up to 20 percent of an issue can be sold overseas. The U.K. government has wider discretion on allocation.

The Role of Government

A third set of contrasts concerns the respective roles of the government. In the U.K. the government and its advisers dominate the privatization. Although the company to be privatized will be closely involved in the lead up to the privatization and will normally share the costs of the privatization with the government, the government and its advisers are clearly in control of the operation. They typically chair the organizing committees and will take the key decisions about the structure and timing of the offer and its pricing.

In contrast, our experience in French privatizations is that responsibilities are more fully shared with the company. Indeed, the balance of responsibilities in the Saint-Gobain privatization fell mainly on Saint-Gobain and its advisers. Saint-Gobain was responsible for the retail marketing campaign, the arrangements for the overseas tranches and the documentation, all of which would have been controlled and organized by the government in the U.K.

This contrast may in practice be more apparent than real. Co-operation between the government and the industrial sector in France is historically much deeper than in the U.K. Interchange between the civil service and industry in France is also considerably more extensive. For these reasons the sharp dichotomy of objectives and perspectives between the government and the company which is often prevalent during a privatization in the U.K. seemed much less distinct in the Saint-Gobain privatization. In any event, the result was very successful and the working relations between the company and the government and their respective advisers was excellent.

Administrative Machinery

A fourth comparison is between the different administrative machines within the respective governments. In the U.K. privatizations are the prime responsibility of the sponsor department and the sponsor Secretary of State. The Department of Trade and Industry, for example, had sponsored British Telecom as a public corporation and so sponsored its privatization. The Department of Energy sponsored the British Gas privatization, and the Department of Transport sponsored the British Airways and British Airports privatizations.

The contact point with the government for both the government's advisers and the company to be privatized will almost exclusively be the sponsor department. The Treasury will have a very influential role, but as far as the company and the government's advisers are concerned, this role will rarely be visible or explicit. In contrast, our contacts with the government in French privatizations were conducted almost exclusively with the Treasury. The Treasury in France has a much greater presence in privatizations than the U.K. Treasury assumes in primary U.K. privatizations.

Another contrast is in the role of ministers. We, as advisers to the government, had considerably more contact with government ministers in preparing for U.K. privatizations than in the Saint-Gobain privatization. For example, in the British Telecom privatization we had a regular meeting once a week with the Department of Trade and Industry minister responsible for privatization and, as the privatization approached, we saw Department of Trade and Industry ministers very frequently. There was also a greater tendency in the U.K. for civil servants to refer decisions up to ministers. There was a committee of ministers which considered the major decisions, and the Prime Minister and her office were kept fully in touch with the progress of the privatization. The Prime Minister was on several occasions required to resolve disputes between the Treasury and the Department of Trade and Industry.

In the Saint-Gobain privatization, our experience was that civil servants themselves or ministers' "cabinets" were more prepared or able to take executive decisions. There appeared to be considerably less reference to ministers or interdepartmental differences of opinion.

Size of Issues

Both the U.K. and French governments have been faced with the prospect of privatizing companies which would have required an issue much larger than the new issue market had so far experienced. The U.K. government used two techniques. First, sometimes only a portion of the capital was sold. Provided more than 50 percent of the capital was held by the private sector, the company was not considered to be part of government and the company's financial operations did not impact on the government's borrowing requirement. Another technique used was partly paid shares, whereby the full price was paid over two or three instalments. Both these techniques are designed in part to alleviate potential market capacity constraints. The French government has so far sold all its interest in companies and has not yet utilized the concept of partly paid shares.

PREPARATION FOR PRIVATIZATION: SIMILARITIES

There are also similarities between the U.K. and the French privatization programmes. These similarities are as striking and as interesting as the contrasts.

There appears to be a broad coincidence between the objectives of both privatization programmes. Both governments aim to secure privatization in a way which maximizes proceeds while encouraging the spread of share ownership both among employees of the company and the retail sector generally. This coincidence of objectives results in several similarities.

Marketing

The marketing of issues on the scale employed by the U.K. government in the privatization programme was unprecedented in the London market. Marketing has become an essential part of the U.K. privatization programme and is now being adopted by private companies going public.

The type of marketing campaign used in the Saint-Gobain privatization and subsequently has a number of features which have become established components of the marketing strategy for the U.K. privatizations.

These features include the sophisticated use of the principal advertising media. The marketing campaign is normally divided into phases which aim first to alert the target market to the company itself and then to the timing and details of its privatization. As part of this strategy, a register of potential investors is built up during the campaign, often by inviting the target market to call a well-publicized telephone number or to return coupons from newspapers and journals. Domestic and international road shows are also used to heighten awareness of the company and to enhance investors perceptions of it. These features are common to both the major U.K. and French privatizations.

Retail Incentives

Special incentives to retail investors and to employees are another common feature of both privatization programmes. Loyalty bonus schemes, which provide small investors with the opportunity of a free issue of shares after a specified period, are now an integral feature of U.K. privatizations and aim to encourage the retail investor not to speculate but to continue to hold shares. Similarly, employees are encouraged to participate with the offer of free shares and discounts. In the case of the public utility companies in the U.K., such as British Telecom and British Gas, the government also offered credit vouchers for shareholders who held shares for a period of time to be used against telephone and gas bills.

Method of Sale

There are also close similarities in the method and structure of the privatization in both countries. Privatizations in the U.K. are typically on a fixed price basis, which is easier for the retail investor to understand, with an offer period long enough to allow the retail investor to consider the investment opportunity and to respond to it. Interestingly, the recent BAA privatization incorporated a partial tender mechanism to try to ensure that any excessive conservatism in pricing is recouped into proceeds rather than translated to a substantial premium in the aftermarket. U.K. privatizations, in the same way as French privatizations, also make use of overseas markets in order to encourage competing sources of demand for the offer and so to maximize proceeds.

Similar clawback arrangements are also employed. French privatizations typically contain provisions which enable a proportion of the overseas tranches to be clawed back to satisfy domestic demand in the event of a substantial oversubscription. Similar procedures apply to the underwriting of U.K. privatizations, and these procedures are becoming increasingly refined. In the recent privatization of British Airways, 60 percent of the domestic offer was initially allocated to U.K. institutions. This proportion was later reduced by 20 percent and made available to retail applicants because the domestic offer was more than three times oversubscribed. The tranches allocated overseas were also reduced by the same proportion.

Another recent innovation in the U.K. is that the government now invites underwriters to tender for a proportion of the offer. The rates of underwriting commission in such tenders have tended to be very significantly below conventional rates.

Flowback

Another concern shared by both the U.K. and French governments is flowback. Substantial flowback can expose the government to the accusation that it denied shares to the domestic market and allowed them to be used for speculative purposes overseas. The U.K. government has considered a number of formal mechanisms to try to minimize flowback, but each of these mechanisms tends to undermine fundamentally the marketability and attractiveness of the shares in overseas markets. Both the French and U.K. governments have concluded that the most effective method for minimizing flowback is to ensure that overseas tranches are placed with national syndicates led by institutions prepared to generate and sustain a liquid market in the shares.

Special Golden Shares

Both governments are concerned to ensure that the activities of companies with a strategic significance are not able, after privatization, to conflict with the national interest. While the requirements of the Treaty of Rome have to be borne in mind, both governments utilize various forms of "actions specifique" or special shares which effectively allow the government a veto on certain defined, key matters.

Administration

Finally, both U.K. and French privatizations are characterized by a similar structure of committees. Both sets of privatizations featured a regular marketing committee, a prospectus committee and a general organizing committee.

DISCUSSION

Edited by Michael A. Walker

Question: At what stage and in what manner did the politicians interact with the outside principal advisers to establish the political dimensions of the process so that all potential objections could be identified and addressed?

Answer: The government advisers are always very closely involved with the government during a privatization. It's very much a team effort. The government's principal advisers work alongside civil servants who work alongside ministers. The thing moves along in a very co-ordinated way. Government ministers tend to bring the political dimension to bear on things. There are a number of pressures—political, financial and so on—which all come together in making a privatization. Ministers have the final say and what they say goes. The role of the government's advisers is to tell the government: this is how we think it should be done; this is what you must do; what do you think? If they say they want to do it this way, for various reasons which are more political in character than financial, then we say, all right, we will do that but you should know that if you want to do it that way one effect of that will be this. So, a continuous discussion goes on all the time—a very close discussion.

Question: On the questions raised by Mr. Chown, has the fee and profit of the underwriters been an issue in the U.K.?

Answer: Yes, it has. It's an area evolving quite a lot. It was criticized very much in BP because the government played it quite safe in terms of the structure of the issue. It had the whole issue underwritten, and then it under priced it. That was an expensive process. There were some very good reasons why the government did what it did. As I said, this was, by quantum leap, the largest issue ever made anywhere in the world. It was essential to the government politically and for other reasons that the thing be successful initially. The government decided it wanted to underwrite the issue from day one. It knew at 10 o'clock on impact day, when the thing was underwritten, that it had success on its hands. It was out of the public sector and it was away.

The government looked at various options, such as not underwriting it—they considered a whole range of different structures—and decided to go this way after very careful thought. But the fees and tendered commissions made by underwriters and the advisory fees made by the government's principal advisers were an issue. Parliament looked at it and wanted to define some issues and problems. They looked very closely at the cost of the sale. One of the biggest components of the cost of the sale was the underwriting commissions. It was a big issue. I think there are reasons the underwriting commissions were the size they were, but it certainly was an issue. Subsequently, the government has reduced commissions dramatically.

Now, issues are not underwritten in the classical way on a fixed-price basis where you invite underwriters to underwrite the issue at whatever percentage. The government now says, we are going to privatize British Airports Authority. If you want to underwrite this, you're very welcome to. Let us know how much you'd like to underwrite, and also at what commission rate you'd like to underwrite it. So, the government has introduced a tender arrangement in underwriting, and commissions have fallen. It's competitive. Commissions have fallen from nearly 3 percent down to .003—it's fallen away completely.

This is a very shrewd move by the government because underwriters do take a risk. This is not money they get for nothing. They are taking a risk. A few may not perceive that risk because privatization tends to succeed. Nonetheless, there is a genuine risk there. At the rate underwriters now quote, they are not being paid to take that risk. You'd get more money by leaving your money in the bank overnight than you do by underwriting an issue. So, the government has a good deal. It has a risk taken off its hands for a very low price, and that's very good.

Certainly, it's an issue. Fees are always an issue in privatizations. The government has learned by this and has become more sophisticated about the way it appoints advisers and the way it underwrites issues.

Question: Could you distinguish the ways in which the underwriter's profits were made—fees, options, secondary trading?

Answer: Only with difficulty. Underwriters earn commissions for taking a risk. They don't typically end up with any shares because issues are successful and shares tend not to come back to the underwriters. But some underwriters, priority applicants as they are now called, earn commissions. The government hasn't yet broken classical underwriting commissions. It's broken secondary underwriting, it hasn't yet broken the underwriting commissions or managed to introduce tender arrangements there. People make money on the commissions they earn for sub-underwriting. They also receive a proportion of shares they sub-underwrite; that was mentioned earlier on. If the issue moves to a premium in the after market, the value of the shares they have retained increases, and they will make a gain on those too. It is hard to split that out. It depends very much on movement in the after market in the price. But, yes, the value normally will increase.

Question: Could you give us any advice about the structuring of this aspect of privatization flotations?

Answer: I could talk about that for an hour. The U.K. government has gone through the evolution of the words "structured privatizations". It's fascinating, and there's been a tremendous evolution as well. The government started with some rather crude ways of structuring privatizations and some very crude tender mechanisms. It did use a fixed-price offer. It was very simple. There was no effort to bring in the retail sector. The thing was more like a "bought deal", as people call them these days. The other objective was to take a more prominent share ownership. So, the structure has moved on until you see today in the BAA structure an extremely complicated and sophisticated arrangement which builds a tender element into a fixed-price offer which combines competitive underwriting with maximizing the retained input. They're very sophisticated.

It depends very much on what you're privatizing and where you are in your privatization programme and on the political objectives you're trying to secure. There isn't an easy answer to that. There are a whole ranges of options, and each option has its relevance to particular circumstances. The U.K. experience provides a very interesting history in the different structures that can be used and in how those structures have been refined. That's a highly evasive answer, but it is an enormous subject.

Question: There is an old expression which I've often found helpful; namely, "don't confuse brilliance with a bull market." What role did the bull market play in British Telecom's success.

John Williams: We weren't convinced there was going to be a bull market. There was a miners' strike on and the re-election of the president. There were a whole range of uncertainties around ahead of pricing that issue. It turned out that everything went right. All the big world events that would have wobbled the market tremendously came up in ways the market found acceptable, and that helped. There was a period of uncertainty ahead of pricing that issue. The uncertainty went away during the issue and just afterwards. The market stabilized, and the thing took off. It helped a lot. If the miners' strike had gotten worse rather than better, if the U.S. president hadn't come back—anything like that—then we would have been in major trouble.

Yes, the market helped, but we weren't sure how that was going to go. As it turned out, we were very lucky in the way it went. The bull market has subsequently helped in other privatization issues. Perhaps you could do without some of the insurance the government puts into the way it structures issues if you could be confident that the market is a bull market. It's a pity you can't know that, the thing could turn.

Michael Walker: I can't help but provide a footnote. Given the problems you have had to overcome in the British case and given the relative ease, it would seem, that we in Canada would face, it's almost an embarrassment that we haven't done anything yet.

Madsen Pirie: I just had a comment on the bull market. Some of the things that have been privatized were not in a bull market for that particular industry. Some of the shipyards, for example, were privatized successfully during a world decline in the value of shipbuilding companies. And the privatized issues have spectacularly and overwhelmingly outperformed the bull market by a very large margin. So, while the bull market is obviously significant, it's by no means all down to that. Privatization is a success in its own right.

Question: How important do you think it is to orchestrate a campaign of informed opinion—the financial press, the media commentators—when a privatization is in process to get some feedback of the ideas that the commentators are putting out and incorporate them into the process? In other words, to make it slightly a learning process as you go through.

Answer: I think that's very important. It is something that happens in every privatization. A characteristic of the big privatizations is the very intensive marketing campaign that goes on ahead of them, both to institutional investors and to the retail sector. It's very important to get the marketing right and get these people hungry for shares. It is crucial that the effects of the marketing campaign be monitored continuously to make sure the messages you think you're putting across are being received on the other end. If they're not, then you must tailor your marketing to make sure these messages get across. We always advise the government to appoint opinion pollsters to find out what is being received—what messages are getting across. Monitoring is very important indeed.

Question: Here are three questions related to the RPI-X formula. First, setting only the price of services delivered by BT, how did the government ensure that service standards would be maintained given that there is an opportunity, obviously, for the firm to increase its return by reducing the quality of service?

Secondly, does the formula apply to the average service delivered, or does it apply individually to the services delivered?

Finally, realizing that the political leaders are in a position of not wanting to have BT fail, how is British Telecom behaving with regard to executive salaries, wages and this kind of thing? Since BT cannot be permitted to fail, is there evidence that they could put pressure on the government for subsidies or whatever?

Answer: In terms of quality, one background remark to that is that the government doesn't want to necessarily do that. One of the objectives of privatization is to get these state-owned companies out into the private sector and for government to walk away and say, that is now going to be efficient because market forces are operating on it. To the extent that they are not working, we have a system of regulation that makes up for them. So, the whole idea is to cut loose from the government in a very visible, clear way.

Having said that, the question about the quality of BT service post-privatization is very timely because there have been a number of press reports recently suggesting that the quality, rather than being improved, has actually deteriorated since privatization in terms of number of wrong numbers and waiting time to get things put right. The government, strictly speaking, has no role now. It's a shareholder in BT, but it has neutralized its shareholding. So, according to the theory, it shouldn't care.

The people who do care about the quality of service are OFTEL, the regulatory body. They are shaking BT up very vigorously to make sure the quality of service is improved and maintained, and it has, under the terms of the licence, powers to make sure the quality is maintained and improved. So, OFTEL looks after quality to some extent.

An interesting point about OFTEL is that it is very small—very few people. A lot of the way OFTEL actually operates is very noisy, and I think a real pain to BT is the quality of the person heading it, Bryan Carsberg—he's very aggressive. They are doing a lot. The other thing is Mercury—the little telecommunications operator that operates mainly in the city but has a network around England now and competes on the trunk and international services. BT is losing a lot of its prime traffic to Mercury. That's its rightful competition, but it has to get its quality right if it's going to hold onto its real revenue-generating sources. So, there are two things operating on it.

RPI-X and what that applies to, it applies to a basket of goods and services. If the outgo increases by 5 percent in a year, take off the 3 percent—the X-factor, the efficiency factor—that means BT can raise the prices on the average of a basket of services, not all its services, but a specified basket, by 2 percent in the year. It applies globally to a basket of services; that's the way it operates. The benefit, apart from those I mentioned, is that it's very simple and not very difficult to understand. Investors think, "we can understand that; that's not a problem." What they will be worried about is the regulatory regime, which is complicated and which seems to allow lots of areas to be interpreted subsequently. It's not absolutely clear where the regulation is biting or how it's going to bite. RPI-X may be crude, but at least it's simple, and it seems to have been effective.

Question: What was the attitude toward privatization of those with whom you worked in the civil service? And, with privatization marketed as an exciting entrepreneurial opportunity, how do you deal with staff who remain in the sponsoring department, particularly if they see their colleagues leave to privatization and they remain in a reduced empire?

Answer: Yes, I'm one of them. I'll talk as an ex-civil servant now rather than anything else. The role of the civil service, and it does this, is provide the best professional advice it can to its ministers. It will do that, whatever the policy objectives of ministers. My experience with the civil service is that there is no particular view that the civil service wants to get across, other than to administer the country in the most professional way. So, if a government comes in and says, we want to sell off British Telecommunications and British Gas, the civil service—whatever their private views may be which they express outside of work—will say, my job now is to look at that policy objective and work out ways in which to achieve it in the best possible way. It's like a doctor. If a patient comes in and the doctor says, "I don't really like his face, I won't treat him"—that is not professional. The civil servant's thought is very similar. Here comes a policy and irrespective of what the policy is, you're there to advise your ministers on it in the best way you can and to implement it. Privatization comes along, and people work very hard to achieve it.

I mentioned that you sometimes find resistance on the part of the sponsoring departments for certain privatizations. You get that a bit because they will have become very close to their public sector organization. The whole problem with the relationship was that they got too close and they were almost running it. They thought they were doing a good job, and the suggestion that it be privatized is almost criticizing them. So, you do get a bit of opposition to privatization sometimes, but not seriously.

What do you do with the people who become redundant or lose their sponsorship function?—various things. The size of the civil service is shrinking very fast anyway, so that is a problem that otherwise wouldn't be. Most people seem to join merchant banks and investment banks after working on a privatization. It hasn't been a big problem.

Question: Why has no French privatization been marketed in the United States?

Answer: There are various technical reasons for that. One of them is that the size of the issues don't always necessitate tapping every overseas market that is available. Combining that with the French government's desire for swift and speedy privatization often means that the requirements of the SEC are such that it's not possible to complete them in the timetable for the privatization. Very crudely, I think the French government doesn't always need to tap that extra source of demand to get the best price. Indeed, to tap it is a fairly lengthy process which they are prepared to forgo in order to achieve a good privatization. It's mainly that type of reason— expediency combined with the different and strict SEC requirements that would be necessary.

Question: Did the government modify its personal income tax legislation to encourage people who were not investors in a traditional sense to purchase shares in privatized organizations, i.e., BT in England or Saint Gobain and Paribas in France?

Answer: I don't think either government has introduced tax legislation which would give a particular tax advantage or tax break for a privatization issue. In the U.K. one innovation is that you can now have your own personal equity plan packet, and there are certain tax dodges to that. That will allow you to nominate an investment banker or financial institution to build up and run a portfolio of equity holdings for you. The dividends you receive on that portfolio are subject to preferential tax treatment. It's linked to wider share ownership; it's not specifically linked to privatization.

Question: "If it ain't broke, don't fix it." If the public perception is that a Crown corporation is doing a good job, is it possible to sell the public on the idea that the Crown corporation should be privatized?

John Williams: Yes, typically the big ones in the U.K. government have all been very profitable, and they are ostensibly doing reasonably well, as you'd expect, because they're mainly monopolistic. I think the government's view is that they're doing okay, but they could do even better if they were unleashed and market forces were allowed to operate on them and they had to compete for their money and their customers. So, yes, I think you can persuade people of that.

Madsen Pirie: To which I would add, if it's in the public sector, it's broken.

Question: What position did the union leadership publicly take when a proposal was made to privatize "their" company? Did they buy shares themselves?

Answer: Their public position was opposition to the whole philosophy of privatization. Their members chose not to follow their leaders' advice and they bought in. In most privatizations you get one or two percent of the employees not buying in, perhaps they're the union leaders, I don't know. It depends how strongly they stand by their principles. But, overwhelmingly, employees come in, and why not?—the government's giving you money.

OLIVER LETWIN

(Introduction by Michael A. Walker)

John Redwood has been elected to the British Parliament in the last election and is required by his party to be in Parliament for voting purposes. He cannot therefore be with us today. We have been very fortunate to attract to the conference John Redwood's co-author of a forthcoming book on international privatization and his constant colleague at Number 10 Downing Street on the Prime Minister's Policy Unit on Privatization, where our guest speaker spent three years. Oliver Letwin was educated at Cambridge University, receiving his Ph.D. there. He has also been a fellow at Princeton University, at Darwin College, Cambridge, and at the London Business School. He has an incredibly large number of publications in academic and public policy environments in spite of his relative youth. Oliver Letwin is Assistant Director at N.M. Rothschild in London, where he is currently head of the International Privatization Unit.

He has been responsible for the privatization of the National Commercial Bank and the Caribbean Cement Company in Jamaica. He has done privatization studies for pulp and paper in Turkey, advised the New Zealand Treasury on the corporatization of New Zealand Telecom, and along with the French Rothschild House, advised the French government on the privatization of Paribas as well as various other privatization projects in the United Kingdom and abroad. He is currently working on a feasibility study for the privatization of the Public Utilities Board in Singapore for the government of Singapore and the privatization of Malaysian Railways for the government of Malaysia.

CHAPTER 3

INTERNATIONAL EXPERIENCE IN THE POLITICS OF PRIVATIZATION

Oliver Letwin

Number 10 Downing Street

I want to say two or three words about experiences inside Number 10—what it looked like from there—which is rather different from the perspective you had from both Madsen Pirie on the outside and John Williams from the Treasury. But mainly, I want to talk about what's happened around the world.

The Number 10 policy unit was a very small group of devotees and aficionados, selected by the Prime Minister because on the whole we agreed with her and believed in what she was trying to do. Our task was to try to help her steer policies—which were not easy to steer through the bureaucracy—through the bureaucracy.

My vision of the English bureaucracy is rather different from John Williams', not least because he was in the Treasury. The Treasury has the cleverest of officials in it and on the whole the most co-operative, people who I think more or less conform to the pattern he was describing. This is not so in very many other ministries. In fact from 1979 to 1983, during the later part of which I was working in the government, we encountered very considerable opposition from Whitehall, not dissimilar I think from things which you're facing now in Canada and various of the provinces.

People were, above all, frightened. I don't subscribe to the theory that civil servants are on the whole evil geniuses. On the contrary, I think they are trying to protect themselves. They are afraid—naturally, we all are—of a new policy which could go terribly wrong and land them fundamentally and forever in the soup. They were also, on the whole—I agree with John Williams that in France it was slightly different—rather ignorant about financial markets and financial opportunities and conservative by nature.

The result of those tendencies was roughly that every time we tried to suggest you could privatize anything they found 159 reasons why it was impossible. So, the first task was actually to persuade people that it was possible. I think that is where Canada now stands. On the whole your privatization programme is words, not actions, and the actions that have been taken, particularly with respect to de Havilland, were not politically well-judged. So I expect there is a good deal of fear here as there is in many other countries that I visit. That is certainly what we encountered in England.

The Evolution of a Policy

The second point is that from the inside we had no coherent policy. I repeat, no coherent policy. It was not the case that we knew privatization would bring in millions of new shareholders. It was not the case that we knew that all those shareholders would benefit from premiums. It was not the case that we knew companies would do better in the private sector. Almost nothing that has happened since was known in advance. It came upon us gradually and by accident and by a leap of faith. We had a fundamental distrust in the state running things—that we knew. We couldn't test it by a series of scientific analyses because you can never have the same company in both state and private control at the same time to test which is better. It was an act of faith. We didn't have any way of telling whether five or six years after the policy really got going it would look like a success or a monumental failure. The bets were on failure.

Because the Prime Minister had the will to go ahead with it, it was possible. It was done in the face of opposition from the industries themselves, from the financial markets, and from the civil service. As it slowly turned into a success story, the inertia which had acted against us started rolling in our favour. When the employees came in, when the number of shareholders went up, the whole thing began to look like a coherent policy that was destined to work from the very beginning. It's an illusion. You ought to be aware of that, because I am sure standing where you are now it looks very much like it looked to us then, not like it looks to us now.

Let me also say one further thing about what it looked like from the inside. We knew that there were tremendous technical problems, and it was no help to us to be told that the technical problems could be solved. We actually had to get down to brass tacks and go through one or two major privatizations before we discovered how the technical problems could be solved. We made a large number of mistakes on the way, and so will you.

If Canada engages in a serious privatization programme, it is not going to be a path of roses from one end to the other. There will be mistakes, there will be problems, there will be political attacks. They will vary from time to time and from case to case. As well as the initial leap of faith, it requires flexibility. You have to be prepared month by month to take on new political attacks and new financial problems. You have to find solutions which are suitable at the time. There is no recipe, there is no cookbook, there are no magic solutions. Anyone who peddles those things to you is a fool.

The fact is that it has worked, and it hasn't worked just in England. Let me try to give you a picture of just how far it really has worked. We try to keep a list of places in the world where privatization is under discussion, and it is always being updated. Being under discussion is very different from it actually happening, but we have tried to estimate what might happen in the next five years. It's a very rough guess, but it's not a lunatic's guess. It will probably prove to be too conservative. Even so we get to 100 billion pounds or 200 billion Canadian dollars. That, by any standards, is a large-scale international movement. I believe, in fact, that given the short period over which it will have occurred, it's the most remarkable change in the structure of capital markets that's ever occurred in the history of the world.

Reasons for Privatization

Why do governments do it? The answer is that we don't know. They have 101 different reasons. Governments aren't homogeneous entities to begin with. There are different people within them who have different reasons for any given policy, and there are many other players in and around government who also have different reasons. I'll try to list some of the reasons here. There is a general feeling that economic efficiency can't be maximized by having the civil service run companies. There is a general feeling that somehow or other privatization ought to be—alas too often hasn't been—a road to competition and choice. There is a general feeling that management and employees can get involved in a company in a way they never can when it's under state ownership. There is a desperate urge on the part of many governments to solve budget deficits, about which I'll have more to say in a moment. There is, on the part of some managements, a wish to get out from under, a feeling that they could do better, a feeling that if they were shareholders and could also run themselves they could become rich. Don't underestimate that desire as a factor. And finally, there is some kind of idea about widening share ownership.

If you think governments across the world have those as an orderly sequence of ideas with a set of priorities and that when there's conflict between one and the next they know exactly how to solve it in a kind of picture book way, you're quite mistaken. We've encountered these various ideas, half articulated, across the world. I'll come to the role of the financial adviser later, but one role is to help governments to articulate more clearly what it is they are really trying to achieve in a particular case and what their order of priorities really is. That takes a long hard slog of collective decision making.

Methods of Privatization

What methods are they using? Lots. At one stage Madsen Pirie produced an excellent list of the various types of privatizations there have been. You can combine companies for sale, as British Columbia knows very well. You can give it away to employees. You can contract out services. You can sell bits of property. You can have dozens of different varieties of privatization, but the three major ones that have been used around the world are: public offerings, the most high profile and the most politically significant form of privatization; selling to a corporate buyer, which is the easiest in many cases and often the most politically damaging; and the management/employee buy-out, which has been tremendously important in England and may be in a few other countries but which is often incapable of taking on the biggest slices. You couldn't have sold British Telecom or British Gas to its employees because there just weren't enough of them.

The point I want to make is that there is no perfect method of privatization. Just as there is no single truth about the way to do it, so there is no single perfect method for a given privatization. They all have their failings, and they can be mixed in numbers of ways. You have to look at it case by case. You have to try to get an image of what a government is trying to do in a particular case and an image of what the financial community will bear in a given case. Again, there is no recipe.

Let me just mention one interesting variant which is too often neglected and which is being practised widely in New Zealand. New Zealand has a socialist government. As a strong Tory, I would be voting for this socialist government if I were in New Zealand. The finance minister there, Mr. Roger Douglass, is one of the most admirable and clear-minded advocates of reducing state control and one of the most coherent thinkers about what privatization is really trying to achieve yet to have arisen on the world stage. But he's a socialist and didn't find it easy, to begin with, to persuade his colleagues that they ought to be engaging in a privatization programme, so he went half-way. What they've done in New Zealand is called corporatization. It is making companies which were previously departments of state into genuine stand-alone companies, issuing non-voting shares, so-called equity bonds, to the public and producing some kind of serious quasi-private entity which raises money on the normal financial markets through debt and doesn't rely on government.

That's an enormously powerful tool, but it's not the only one. There are other methods of partial privatization. You can take something which is already in existence and raise new money from outside, gradually turning a state corporation more and more into a private corporation. You can deregulate and allow former state monopolies to become competitive as the private sector acquires a gradually larger share. You can take a major construction project, like a bridge or an airport, and raise finance for it through private project financing without having to make any song and dance about its being privatized. But the result in the end is a private sector operation which would have been public sector. This is just as effective in many ways as building it first and selling it after.

The Role of the Financial Adviser

As financial advisers, what are we there to do? I should say, just like John Williams, I'm an example of privatization myself. I fled to the private sector when I was sacked from the civil service for taking up a political candidacy. We've been thinking ever since about what it is we are really trying to do for governments. What we're most commonly called upon to do is advise them on the following things: the legal framework; the question of competition; deregulation of monopolies; what kind of sale should be involved; and how to structure the balance sheet. That is at the stage when advice is going on.

There is another point I want to make very strongly. It's very easy to think that privatization is just political or just financial. There will be financial advisers who think it's just financial and lots of politicians who think it's just political. And they are as wrong as one another. The truth is that finance and politics are inextricably linked with one another in privatization in the most surprising ways. You will find minute changes in financial structure having huge effects politically through the kind of change in management attitudes that, for instance, a different debt equity structure can cause. A privatization can come to a grinding halt—has in one country, which I shan't mention—precisely because the debt/equity structure which looked like a pure financial issue turned into such a hot potato that the management of the company eventually blew their gasket and refused to have anything to do with the privatization. That put the whole political plot back.

When you're going into this business, it's very important to involve financial advisers from the start. I'd prefer you to employ Rothschild's rather than Kleinwort, but the fact is that there are several really experienced finance houses around the world who have some understanding of the intrinsic connection between the politics of the process and the finance of the process. It isn't enough to design a whole package and bring them in at the end to sell the item. You may be lucky, but in seven or eight cases out of ten you'll find that the politics go sour because the politicians have forgotten something which the finance men could have told you would have a political effect.

Marketing Privatization Issues

In addition to giving advice on the structure, we're also involved consistently in trying to market these issues. Privatization can sound too complicated. The truth is that it's just like selling coke cans. If coke is worth 45 cents and you sell it for 43 cents, an awful lot of people will buy it. But they won't buy it if they don't know it exists and that means marketing. Essentially, a privatization is a combination of structuring the issue right and marketing it like mad.

Marketing involves the technical financial marketing to serious investors who read a prospectus through the drafting. It involves a different kind of marketing to employees and consumers, often requiring long and patient negotiations and speeches and getting hold of somebody in the company and in the government who has sufficient charisma to persuade people that they're not trying to buy some kind of defunct coke can but that the thing actually fizzes. It means having advertising agents.

In Canada I think you have some of the best advertisers in the world. They need to be made use of. The experience in England has been that advertising can do an enormous amount. It can also do too much. There has been too much adverse comment in England in the end on the cost and scale of advertising. The only thing that has gone wrong is that some of the advertising has in the end looked too much like a marketing exercise. It's a subtle balance. You need to market very heavily, but you need the advertising to be sober enough so that the serious public commentators don't feel that the thing is a con job.

You also need serious distribution arrangements. Marketing doesn't just consist of advertising; it consists of getting the product to the customer. In a moment I'll talk about how that happened in a country at the very opposite end of the spectrum from the U.K.

Finally, pricing—impossible. You cannot price an issue accurately. What you can do is make the best possible guess and pray for rain. You can make wrong guesses if you don't do any serious analysis. But if you do all the analysis—multiple-discounted cash flows in addition to P/E ratios in addition to book value assessments in addition to market surveys—you still only come up with a range and a guess, not least because there is an exposure time. A major privatization is going to be out there, in effect, for days and even weeks. During that time the market will alter.

I would give the strongest possible reply to the gentleman who asked about bull markets. In the end, it will depend more on the market than on the price. If your market is a bear market, a price which would have looked good in a bull market the day before will look bad. There is nothing that a financial adviser or government can do about that. You ought to expect, if you're going to be serious about privatization in Canada, that there will be times when the price is too high and times when the price is too low. Goodness knows, it's happened in England.

You have to try to be conservative so there aren't a series of hopeless flops. But you can't expect—and it's very important to educate the public not to expect—that the thing will be sold within .002 percent of its aftermarket price. The larger the issue, the more divergence there is likely to be between the original price and the aftermarket performance. You cannot accurately assess it. But there is no reason to be frightened of it, because there are plenty of techniques for holding back a portion of the shares in government hands and selling them later if the thing has gone up. There are plenty of techniques for underwriting and insuring yourselves and the government against the risk of the price being too high. You needn't expect perfection, and you mustn't expect perfection.

What the Critics Say

No matter how hard one tries, the fact is that there will be powerful critics of privatization. Everywhere in the world there have been and there will go on being. There is a criticism which I imagine many people in this room are familiar with which was levelled by a former prime minister—a Conservative—Harold MacMillan, who said we were selling the family silver. He ought to know, he collected a lot of it in his time. But that was a serious comment, because he's not a fool. He looked at what was happening and had seen that on the one side you have a stock of debt and on the other side you have a flow of budget deficits. Privatization receipts, which are in some sense a capital asset, were being used to finance the flow of budget deficits and not to reduce the stock of debt. The French, observing that, put into place a system which is now being copied in some other countries, which uses privatization proceeds to reduce the stock of national debt or to increase the asset base of the companies themselves. That's one way around the problem.

Another way is to remind oneself, as is true in England, that the government, unlike the normal investor, is not a piggy bank. It's not just an account out of which cash flows and into which cash comes. It's a manager of the economy. The taxation authority has a direct interest financially, in the piggy bank sense, in the performance of that economy, but as the government it has a much larger indirect interest. If its privatization is used to reduce fiscal deficits, and if the effect of reducing fiscal deficits is to reduce taxation, and if the effect of reduced taxation is to increase growth, that growth will come to bear not only on the country as a whole in its performance but also on taxation receipts, and by golly it has in England. Nobody knows exactly how to do the assessment, but the latest analyses suggest that the effect of privatization on the exchequer may well have been massively positive. These are arguments and techniques you can use against the criticism, but don't imagine that the criticism won't come.

The truth is that there are a lot of people who will go on believing for many years, even in a country with a most successful privatization programme, that privatization is a dangerous thing and is giving away a precious national asset. That's a feeling rather than an intellectual assertion, and it needs to be addressed at the level of feeling. The only way of addressing it in the end is to prove that that asset is going back to the nation in the form of a wide shareholding and improved economic performance.

The next criticism: privatization reduces revenue to the state. That only applies to a profitable company, of course, but it's often true that you start with profitable companies because they're the easier cases. How do you explain the reduction in net present value to the exchequer that often attends the sale when the expected revenues are often very great far into the future? The answer is, you don't. Again, you have to point firmly to the opportunities for increased efficiencies and growth on the part of the company that's being privatized and hence the increased tax receipts. That's exactly what is happening in cases like British Telecom and British Gas. The tax receipts for major privatized industries in the U.K. have grown enormously. In fact, I should say they have grown spectacularly. The earnings of companies, post-privatization, in France look as if they're about to be vastly more impressive than we found in England, hence—again—increased taxes.

A far greater criticism and the one I think is justified in many countries is that it doesn't increase competition. In itself, privatizing a monopoly is a dangerous pastime. All you are doing is transferring a money-making machine into the hands of people who have a direct interest in maximizing profit. You can only counter that criticism by wide shareholding, by tough regulations and, wherever possible, by introducing competition. Often that competition has to be protected to begin with, as was the case with Mercury. When you don't introduce competition, you will find your own right wing coming back at you, just as it is in England now. British Gas is, in many respects, unpopular with the very people in England who have been promoting privatization, because it left the provision of an important national resource in the hands of a single monopoly. We have yet to see whether the government, in the case of electricity, will do more to increase competition. It's a very interesting point, however, that this time round they intend to have a study first of all of how to introduce competition.

Building Capital Markets

One last point about privatizing in other countries, which applies to England but applies much more in many other parts of the world and particularly the third world, is that it can be used to build a capital market on a scale previously unprecedented. Third world debt and debt in many other countries is a problem everybody knows about. What most people ignore is that debt ratios in the end depend upon the absence of equity. In most third world countries, 70 or 80 percent of large companies cannot raise significant amounts of equity on the market, either because there literally is no capital market or because that capital market doesn't function in anything like the necessary way. The result of that high gearing is massive—leading to volatility and a huge dive into bankruptcy as soon as the raw commodities which a third world nation often depends on shave a cent or two off their price.

Privatization can be used to build a market because government is in a unique position. It owns the shares. It can structure the offer. It can think not just about maximizing its receipts but about how the offer needs to be structured in order to build the capital market. The scale can be immense. In a few moments I'll come to the example in Jamaica, which is an interesting one at the farther end. But just to give you some clue in the middle, places like Malaysia and Singapore—not tiny countries but with capital markets which are in many respects similar to those of Canada—need desperately to increase the scope of their capital markets. They have an opportunity here, perhaps the last opportunity for many years to come. Governments in places like that have a chance to use a decent economic position now to raise equity and put equity into the hands of people who will later go on investing equity for the private sector—making privatization into a means of enabling the private sector to live on its own thereafter.

To do that you may well need to alter the entire nature of your stock market. We were lucky in Britain, and even the French to some extent have been lucky, in already having an active stock market. I think the Canadian market, if you'll forgive me the rudeness, is bound up with bureaucracy. There are all sorts of changes which may be required here and certainly in many other countries where the markets perform far less efficiently than in Canada. Dramatic changes may be needed. Local markets in Canada's provinces are also vastly underweight for some of the purposes which the private sector would like to use them for. Here's an opportunity to increase the volume of business, an opportunity which may require lengthened hours of trading, new stock exchange practices, and if used rightly, an opportunity which leads to a vast increase in the number of people who regard the market as something for them. In England, the stock market has to some degree become what bingo used to be—something which an ordinary person believes he has a part to play in. The danger, of course, is when we turn too much into bingo. That's not such a great danger as one might imagine, because the truth is that in almost every underdeveloped capital market and even in the U.K., the institutions provide a huge bulwark of pretty conservative money sitting there. The danger of volatility in the stock market is much smaller than the danger of an underdeveloped capital market for companies which have excessive debt.

The Problems Are Universal

Rothschild's is active in the U.K., the U.S.A., Mexico, Chile, Jamaica, Turkey, New Zealand, Malaysia, Singapore, and France. It's an interesting life wandering around these various places. It's fascinating to see that bureaucracies everywhere are almost identical. It's fascinating to see that although the problems of each place are different and differ across time, the range of problems is roughly the same. They occur in slightly different patterns, but there are patterns. I find that you can just about predict what the next problem over the horizon is going to be. Each success brings another problem with it. First you are told that the thing is impossible. Then when it proves to be possible, you are told that anything else more ambitious is too big and is impossible. When that goes successfully, you're told you've given away the family silver and sold it too cheaply. So you sell something too high, and you're told that the problem is that nobody can judge the scale of the market and so on.

Problems come and problems go, but around the world the experience is much the same. In Canada you can draw on that experience now. Five years ago, there was no one who could speak with any kind of authority about what privatization would look like in a country they hadn't dealt with for many years. Now there are such people because there are bases for comparison.

Some Recent Privatizations

We are involved in the BP offer for sale. It's going to be the biggest sale in history so far. It will be on offer, I've no doubt, in many countries including Canada. Let me give you an idea of the length of time it takes to conduct a major offer in the U.K., and I will bring up a comparison in a moment. British Gas started in May 1985, with a decision to do something. On 8 December 1986, eighteen months later, the sale took place. Bear in mind that is eighteen months of study, negotiation, legislation, and preparation.

Now let me take you to the other end of the world and the National Commercial Bank of Jamaica. Jamaica has a stock exchange which is not very active. It occurs on the mornings of Tuesday and Thursday. There are six people in the room. They have a blackboard. There are bids and asks. Traditionally, the volume of selling is, roughly speaking, equal to that of the sweet shop around the corner. The government, which is headed by an enthusiast, has in its bureaucratic bowels a man of vision who said to himself that he was willing to take the risks of developing that capital market by privatizing the single largest commercial company in the place, which had been taken over by the previous Cubanizing government. Impossible was what he was told because the size of the offer would have been more than four or five times the total volume of the stock market in a trading month. Impossible, because the total capitalization of the offer would be something like 5 to 10 percent. Nobody has every quite worked out what the total capitalization of the stock market is, but somewhere around 7 percent is my guess. Compare that with NGT, British Gas and BT, each of which made a call at any given moment of under 1 percent of the total capitalization of the British or Japanese markets. Impossible, because there's no postal system in Jamaica that works efficiently, and you can't expect people to return prospectuses and application forms on time by post. Impossible, because accounting isn't as well developed as it ought to be and for a hundred and one other reasons.

What happened? The total number of shareholders in Jamaica increased fivefold in one fell swoop. A new distribution system was created. We found the only way to do it was to use the commercial banks. At each bank branch counter people handed in their application forms. New standards for issuing procedures, for documentation, and for prospectuses were set up—a set of standards with which Jamaicans themselves are now familiar. How long did it take? From late September to the 23rd of December—under three months in a country where people said it was impossible.

Since then, the Caribbean Cement Company—vastly more difficult because it's still in the process of a major expansion programme and highly dubious because of cement restrictions around the world and new anti-dumping practices and so forth—has also been privatized. There is a chance that the Jamaican capital market will now become a serious entity that private sector investors and private companies in Jamaica will take advantage of to reduce their gearing ratios. It can be done in the most unpromising circumstances, but it's difficult.

Privatization Is Worth Doing

I want to leave you with one message. If it seems scary now, that's for good reason. It is scary. But there are people around who know how to do it. It can be done. When it's done, it doesn't always go right but slowly the lessons are learned. There comes a point when it all seems so obvious that one wonders why it ever seemed so difficult. Moving from the present theory in Canada to a substantial programme of action is not going to be easy. But if it happens, you'll look back on today and think I was crazy to say that it was all so difficult.

DISCUSSION

Edited by Michael A. Walker

Question: If New Zealand and Turkey and Malaysia and Jamaica can do it, why not Canada? What suggestions do you have for Canadians to enhance the possibility that we can pursue privatization?

Answer: My first advice is to stop looking for perfection. At this stage in a privatization programme, or perhaps I should say unprogramme, there is a tendency—in a large part of the world, not by any means just in Canada; other countries are in the same position—to think that if you go on studying long enough, you'll find some perfect case or some perfect method. You won't; you have to take a plunge. It's an act of faith—as much an act of faith as what we choose to start with or whether you're going to do it at all. So the first thing is to take the plunge.

Secondly, I think it's particularly difficult, in a sophisticated market with sophisticated people, to overcome the prejudice that there are too many difficulties. One of the advantages in Jamaica was that most of the people who were involved in the issue, apart from a general sinking feeling that it was impossible, really couldn't put their fingers on any of the particular problems that were likely to arise because they were not very experienced. In Canada you have a large number of experienced professionals, and that's a very dangerous thing. Experienced professionals know very well all the things that can go wrong.

So, my first advice is to take the plunge. My second advice is, don't listen too much to too many experienced professionals. Choose advisers who will take the plunge with you and get on with it. You will find, as I say, that it's not perfect, but it does work.

Question: In Canada foreign ownership is a fear played upon by the opposition parties. In the absence of building a larger domestic capital market, how can this criticism be countered on a level understandable by the general populace?

Answer: First, there's no reason to be afraid of foreign ownership. One retains strategic control over the industry and makes sure that no single foreign owner—particularly, I guess, in the case of Canada, no single American owner—is in a position to overwhelm the domestic investors and take control of the company. There are plenty of techniques for doing that. The golden share is one. Changes to the company charter and articles of incorporation is another. Legislation is a third. Those techniques can be used to avoid the most dangerous phenomena, but they will never do the whole trick.

When I was being coached for examinations at university, I remember being taught never to accept the implications of a question, and I don't want to accept the implications of this one. The question suggests that there are things you need to do apart from developing a capital market. There's no reason to think of it that way. The real way to overcome the problem of foreign ownership is to bring huge numbers of domestic small investors into privatization. When they hold the shares, they're not so worried about the fact that some overseas investors hold large portions too, because those overseas investors are actually giving them assurance that they're in the right place at the right time. If you don't have domestic investors, all the techniques in the world to protect the company against foreign ownership will never persuade the general populace that the thing is not really going abroad.

So, my answer is, do use this method of developing the capital market. Do market the shares widely. Don't, at any rate in the first instances, be put off by people who say it's difficult to get a wide share ownership in Canada. It is difficult, but it's not impossible. You just need to choose the right target.

Question: What is the official difference between partial privatization and full privatization?

Answer: In the kind of partial privatization I was talking about in the case of New Zealand, the government protects one hundred percent of the voting rights. You could not have more security that the government is not being ripped off than that.

The advantage, of course, is that the real discipline of the market in raising funds is still present. The company raises all its new capital either from non-voting shares or from debt instruments in the normal private sector financial market. So, the difference is where control lies through voting which is, in practice, a much less important difference than that between being controlled by government officials and the requirements of the exchequer on the one side or having the financial disciplines of the marketplace on the other.

It's more obvious, I think, what the differences are between full privatization and project financing, where you're not selling anything at all; you're just setting up a project in the private sector.

Question: Are unions always opposed to privatization, and what techniques of marketing have you found to deal with their opposition?

Answer: Unions are not always opposed to privatization. I can think of three countries where we've operated where the unions have been extremely co-operative.

The main technique for dealing with unions is not to deal with them. If you engage in lengthy negotiations with union leaders, you're giving them power in the privatization process which they don't need or deserve. In the end, they are going to be responsive to the views of their members. You can undercut them and put them at a disadvantage by going over their heads directly to the members with incentive schemes that have been described earlier. Once you have the members enthusiastic you can talk to the union leaders, and you will find that their mood is very different from what one might have supposed.

My experience in several countries has been that the union leaders directly involved in a particular company have themselves become major employee shareholders. The biggest benefit of privatization in some cases is actually the transformation of the relationship between union and management.

I think it's one of the great ironies of nationalization, as a matter of fact, that something which began with the highest aspirations and hopes for the relationship between management and union has all too often ended with either union capture or grotesquely bad industrial relations. The creation of a large body of employee shareholders including, if possible, the union leaders themselves is a major factor in changing that.

Question: Has privatization reduced the government deficit in the U.K., France, Jamaica and elsewhere, and if so, at what rate or amount?

Answer: The answer is that all over the world privatizations have reduced government deficits. I think some of the most spectacular reductions are yet to be seen. The U.K. deficit is now approaching infinitesimal. We may actually get to zero in due course. Whether that's a sound policy or not is an interesting question, but the scale of the deficit in the U.K., which used to be very worrying, is no longer a problem. Indeed, the Chancellor recently made the much quoted remark that "we no longer have to worry about public sector debt, we need to worry about private sector debt."

In France it has not had an immediate effect on the scale of the yearly budget deficit for the reason I pointed out, namely, that privatization proceeds are not being devoted to that. They have been devoted to reducing the stock of national debt or to increasing the asset base of companies. However, over the years reducing stock means reducing flow, and I've no doubt at all that with the absolutely massive privatization programme now planned, four or five years from now French deficits will be greatly less than they would otherwise have been.

In that connection, and it's particularly relevant to countries like Jamaica and Malaysia, which have terrible deficit problems, there is a snare and a delusion. It is possible to use privatization as a way of masking increased public spending. In the end it is a mask that falls off. Madsen Pirie is quite right that in England we have massive public utilities still available for privatization and that on any net present value calculation what happens 40 years from now is not of too much consequence. But there are countries, and perhaps some of the Canadian provinces, where the total amount available for privatization is not so great and you could quite quickly run out. If, in the meanwhile, those responsible for the budget allow public spending controls to go crazy, that will come home to roost. In the years when privatization is going on, it will look all right. The deficit won't be too bad, and a disaster point will come when Reaganomics hits. As financial advisers, it's not our responsibility to try to reconstruct people's budgets. But as a politician, I give you the advice that if you're responsible for any aspect of Canadian privatization, make very certain that those responsible for public spending don't regard it as an excuse for going wild.

Question: It appears that broad ownership, regulation and competition are the three factors which ensure quality. The first two are relatively easy to put in place, competition is more difficult to ensure. Can quality be assured without the benefits of competition?

Answer: My answer is that it's very difficult. John Williams was quite right when he said that Professor Carsberg, who is a highly intelligent and active individual, is trying masterfully to struggle against very poor standards of performance on the part of British Telecom. My guess is that he alone may well not succeed and certainly wouldn't succeed if he didn't have the aid of Mercury. The disadvantage of Mercury as a competitor is that it's very restricted. It doesn't compete, to speak of, on the domestic market. It's domestic services above all on which the political impact is felt.

The reason competition is difficult to install is not technical in most cases, it's political—I mean political with a small "p". When the senior management of large Public Utilities can't seriously be made enthusiastic about privatization by offering incentives, a chance to get free and a chance to make a large amount of money as private shareholders in a big utility, it is much more difficult to persuade them that they ought to give up a part of the empire. In most cases, because many of these things are actually natural monopolies, it's necessary that they should give up part of their empire rather than establish a free-for-all system because no one else will enter the market.

There are various techniques for dealing with that. I'll mention two or three in just a second. What I ought to say first is that the techniques are the easy bit; the difficult bit is finding a chairman or chief executive who will follow them.

The techniques are, one, establish a protected competitor with a duopoly or a series of such people for a period, as in the Mercury case. Two, split up an activity into various subactivities and create some degree of competition in those bits which are most easily competitive. For example, in the electricity supply industry, it would be quite possible to have a large degree of competition in generation, even though it's very difficult to imagine competition in the grids that transmit the power. Three, find some means of emulating the effects of competition. For example, it's perfectly possible to give price increases to the utility through a price formula—such as is being discussed for the water industry in the U.K. and for a few other privatizations abroad—which involves the average rise in costs for utilities of that kind. For instance, if you have competing water utilities in different geographical areas, there's no real possibility that the water utility for the south of England is going to start supplying large numbers of customers in the north of England. But, if they are only allowed to raise their prices by a factor which allows for the average rise in costs between them and the north of England, then each has incentives to reduce their cost base, because they clean off the difference between the average and whatever their cost is as profit. That's just one example; you can create emulative systems which mirror competition. There are a number of other techniques which I could describe some other time.

The techniques are not the problem. The problem, as I say, is breaking down resistance from those who are responsible for the cozy job of running a monopoly and turning them into people who are responsible for the much less cozy job of competing in an environment where they may lose out.

Question: Under what circumstances is the direct sale of a Crown corporation to an institution or firm, for example, ConRail or de Havilland, preferred to a public share offering, i.e, BT, BA, et cetera?

Answer: In my view, it's the last option. There are many companies which are simply too shaky or whose future is too uncertain to be sold to anyone except another trade investor who will understand enough about the business and be capable of sophisticated assessment to take on something which is said to be a loss-maker or which has hardly any great potential in its present form and try to transform it. Those are the difficult cases, and in many such cases you have to find a trade investor.

But I think it's the least satisfactory form of privatization because it brings none of the political benefits which the other forms bring. It may, indeed, cause concentration in markets and be adverse from the point of view of competition. In addition, the likelihood is that whoever buys, because he is in a very strong position vis-a-vis the seller, will extort conditions from the government which may be extremely unpleasant such as, for example, financial restructuring involving the writing off of debt, restructuring of the employees needed by sacking them before privatization and so on.

So, a government is in a bad position if it has to sell large numbers of its Crown corporations to individual investors. It can be gotten away with for the dogs, if the good cases are being privatized with a high profile through management-employee buy-outs or public offers. On its own, as a single method, I think it would prove a political disaster.

Question: There has been some suggestion that Mrs. Thatcher did not start privatization until her second term. If that is so, why? If it's so good, why wait? If it's not true, what would you say to Ottawa?

Answer: It is roughly true. There was some effort to privatization before 1983, which was the beginning of the second term, but the big ones all occurred after 1983. The reasons for waiting were not anybody's choice but because, as I said, nobody had a coherent policy, nobody knew how to overcome the tremendous inertia and obstacles inside the bureaucracy and in the companies themselves. No one quite believed it would work. No one knew how you actually went about the sales or what the market would absorb. In short, there was a great universal dither. That began to be overcome slowly through 1981 and 1982. It's a pure coincidence that BT occurred in 1984, in the sense that the preparation for BT was going on well before the election itself. The answer is that it takes a long time to overcome the dithers, and it would have been better if we had started early.

Question: It would appear that the recently announced acquisition of British Caledonia by British Airways goes against the view that competition is crucial. Please comment on this. What is the U.K. government likely to do?

Answer: These things are highly organized in the U.K., with a reference by the Office of Fair Trading and subsequently the Monopolies and Mergers Commission. The U.K. government comes in at the very end in many respects. What those various bodies will do is anybody's guess.

This is a purely personal view, but I don't think that the takeover of one airline by another is very adverse to competition in the sense that there are still plenty of foreign carriers. The serious competitive issues surrounding the air transport industry from the point of view of England have to do with deregulation of international traffic. Almost all our air travel is abroad, not within England. But there are some serious issues here.

Much more important, the takeover of a company with a weak balance sheet by a company with a strong balance sheet is a real danger in privatization. It could be much worse than it is in the case of airways. There are many other industries where internal competition and domestic competition are crucial. The only way you can protect against that is by making sure that the legislative constraints on them and the way in which their charter and articles are built up, are such that they have neither the incentive nor the ability to take over a market share which is excessive. You also have to pay attention to the balance sheet conditions of the company when it is privatized.

That's a very delicate balance. There are always people telling you that you've got to give the company a one hundred percent equity to debt ratio in order to sell it at all. And there are always people on the other side telling you that it's got to have one hundred percent debt because that's the only way the government will maximize its proceeds. You have to create a balance sheet which is strong enough for the company to sell but not strong enough for it to dominate a market it shouldn't be dominating.

KENNETH STEIN

(Introduction by Michael A. Walker)

Kenneth Stein came to the Privatization Branch in January 1987 in an indirect fashion from the private sector where he worked with IBM for a number of years, his own computer services company, and from there to the Department of Communications as a senior advisor. In 1974, he became Director of the Policy Secretariat, and in 1976, Director General in the Communications Department. Appointed to the Privy Council Office in 1977 as second in command for the Prime Minister's planning office, he had responsibility for analysis and advice on key issues and problems of direct relevance to the government's priorities.

In 1980, Mr. Stein was appointed Deputy Secretary of Finance at the Ministry of State for Social Development, with a mandate to develop the government's overall approach to social policy including medicare, post-secondary education and employment. In 1984, he was appointed Associate Deputy Minister for Fisheries and Oceans, with the specific task of establishing an economically viable direction for the fisheries sector and strengthening the policy and programme management of the department.

Mr. Stein is currently head of the Privatization Branch in the Office of Privatization and Regulatory Affairs. I, for one, am very much looking forward to his comments today on the privatization programme for Canada.

CHAPTER 4

PRIVATIZATION—
A CANADIAN PERSPECTIVE

Kenneth Stein

INTRODUCTORY REMARKS

In recent years, privatization has become a universal term. But it has also come to mean different things to different countries and regions of the world, each one tailoring this initiative to suit particular needs and objectives.

In the United Kingdom, privatization has taken the form of a massive programme keyed to improving the performance of the economy and stimulating market competition. In France, it has developed into an equally ambitious programme designed to reverse the tide of nationalization carried out under the former government. In the developing world, it has been promoted primarily as a means for nations to come to grips with a massive public debt and stagnating economy.

Canada, too, has its own perspective on privatization. The approach and process it has set out in implementing privatization, while inspired from international experience, are distinctly Canadian.

What I would like to do today is set Canada's programme of privatization in context by discussing how it fits into the history of the role of Crown corporations in the Canadian economy, how it is addressed as a policy issue, and how it is managed as a process by the federal government. You will appreciate that as a public servant my role will not be to advocate privatization but rather to explain the programme and put it into proper focus.

THE CREATION AND ROLE OF CROWN CORPORATIONS IN CANADA

A first reality which is central to understanding Canada's privatization programme is that Canada's Crown corporations, unlike state enterprises in many other countries, were not created under a broad nationalization effort. Nor was there ever, in this country, a strong ideological bent in favour of state ownership. Rather, Crown corporations were created one by one, to address real or perceived policy needs when it was felt the private sector could not or would not do the job.

The Canadian Broadcasting Corporation was created in 1932 by a Conservative Prime Minister, R.B. Bennett, to provide radio-broadcasting to all Canadians. The concern at the time was that the private sector would focus only on major markets and not support a national service.

Air Canada was created five years later. Its objective was to develop coast-to-coast airline service because it was felt that purely economic forces would favour a north-south rather than an east-west axis of development.

The Canada Mortgage and Housing Corporation was formed in 1946 in response to perceived gaps in long-term mortgage financing. The initiative was undertaken so that returning veterans could find adequate and affordable housing. The Crown corporation supported not public but private ownership of homes, consistent with the traditional North American view that ordinary citizens have a right to own their own homes.

The federal government also used ownership to restructure or revitalize key industries: the Canadian National Railway in 1919; the Cape Breton Development Corporation in 1967; de Havilland in 1974; Canadair in 1976; and Fishery Products International and National Sea Products in the early 1980s. These were carried out to salvage activity and jobs in sectors which were considered of primary importance for national or regional economies.

In this way, over time the federal government developed a fairly extensive corporate portfolio. There are currently 54 parent Crown corporations accounting for $60 billion in assets and about 190,000 employees.

At the provincial level, the approach to public ownership over the years was generally the same pragmatic one. The first major initiative was the formation of Ontario Hydro by the provincial Conservative government in 1906. The creation of this corporation, now Canada's largest in terms of assets, was essentially a policy response to the problem of managing a natural monopoly. The same initiative carried over to other provinces. Most of them also acquired their electrical utilities. Some, including the three Prairie provinces, took over their telecommunications networks.

The example of Pacific Western Airlines is also instructive. This corporation was acquired by the government of Alberta in 1974 in order to assist in developing the economic potential of the north, including oil and gas. But by 1983, the government realized that the corporation's strength lay in its ability to compete across Canada, so the corporation was returned to private ownership.

There were some exceptions to this general, case-by-case approach to government enterprise. The CCF government of T.C. Douglas in Saskatchewan in the 1940s clearly emphasized public ownership. Also, the Quebec government of Jean Lesage in the 1960s used public ownership extensively to ensure that the people of Quebec would exercise more control over their economic future. A landmark decision in this period was the amalgamation under Hydro-Quebec of all electrical energy facilities in the province. This initiative provided the institutional basis for the development, some years later, of the massive James Bay hydro project.

But overall, Canada's tradition is not one of resorting systematically to public ownership. Many of the country's key industries were developed from the start by emphasizing market forces. Where appropriate, the government used regulation rather than ownership to ensure that the national interest was served. Oil and gas, transportation, telecommunications, and insurance and banking are sectors where the regulation of private sector activity played a major role in achieving public policy objectives.

As a result, the extent of government ownership in the Canadian economy, while greater than in the United States, has been considerably less than in most European countries. Meaningful statistics on this are hard to come by but the following are illustrative. In the period 1975 to 1979, prior to the current world-wide privatization thrust, about 4.5 percent of Canada's work-force was employed in state-owned enterprises. During that same period, that percentage was 8.2 in the United Kingdom and 7.8 in West Germany. At the federal level, it is estimated that the contribution of Canada's Crown corporations to GDP is currently about 3 percent. In the U.K. that number in 1979 was about 10.5 percent.

Another distinctive feature of government enterprise in Canada has to do with public accounting. In the U.K. publicly owned enterprises have no value on the government's books, and so all privatization proceeds are applied against the deficit. In Canada, by contrast, Crown corporations are generally carried on the public accounts at the cost of investment. The impact of privatization on the deficit is therefore the difference between the realized proceeds of sale and the recorded value. That number may be positive, neutral or negative depending on the situation.

Under the circumstances, it is reasonable that Canada has developed an approach to privatization distinct from that in the United Kingdom or France, where state-owned companies have been put on the auction block at an extraordinary pace.

THE CANADIAN APPROACH TO PRIVATIZATION

The approach the Canadian government has adopted in implementing its privatization programme is consistent with the history of public ownership in Canada. The approach is case by case. It starts from the view that ownership is an instrument of public policy, which may or may not be appropriate to achieve certain objectives in particular circumstances.

Government has at its disposal a number of instruments to implement public policy. It can spend, it can tax, it can legislate and regulate, and it can own. All of these instruments have their relative strengths and weaknesses. All have to be carefully assessed and reassessed in terms of their contribution to national objectives.

In this context, privatization is not an unprecedented initiative for the Canadian government. Indeed, a very similar effort was launched at the end of World War II. During the war, the support of the Canadian military effort required a centralization of economic decision making in the hands of the federal government. The government used these powers to acquire or create 28 new Crown corporations, including eleven which were involved in the production of goods and services. But when the war came to an end, the government indicated that the wartime private/public sector mix was inappropriate to meet the challenge of post-war industrialization. The following quote from then Minister of Reconstruction, C.D. Howe, is remarkable for its time:

> If a private industry is not well managed—and plenty are not—it will go broke in a short time, be reorganized, and put under more efficient managementUnder public operation that usually does not happen. It goes steadily down grade. It is allowed to go down grade, unless it becomes

enough of a scandal, when the government is very apt to get rid of it and pass it to private hands.

It followed that most of the wartime Crown corporations were wound up or returned to the private sector.

The current privatization exercise of the government fits into this tradition of trying to strike the right balance between the private and public sectors—and act before things start to downgrade. The government aims to determine whether Crown corporations still have a public policy objective; and, if so, whether government ownership of the corporation is the best policy instrument for pursuing that objective.

The exercise is not a deficit reduction effort nor an ideological crusade. It is an attempt to realign government initiatives to fit current priorities.

Consider Air Canada. The decision to privatize or not to privatize is tied in with the transportation policy of the government. This policy was set out in the government's paper "Freedom to Move" and the consequent legislation recently passed by the House of Commons. The legislation establishes a new regulatory framework which emphasizes market forces and competition. It also puts in place a mechanism whereby carriers can receive compensation from the government to operate uneconomical routes, where necessary.

It is in this context that the privatization of Air Canada must be approached. The issue is not whether the management of the company wants it or whether the competition wants it. The issue is whether a privatized Air Canada will be in an improved position to provide all Canadians with better transportation services.

I realize that a number of commentators and editorialists believe the government is dragging its feet on this issue. But the issue is not a trivial one. In this regard, I appreciated Peter Cook's commentary in a recent *Globe and Mail* article, titled "Canadian Privatization Turtle Holds a Lesson for British Hare:"

> In Canada, privatization is...much more something to be justified on the grounds that it will improve efficiency or, as with the sale of de Havilland to Boeing, provide a guarantee of marketing skills and future viability, or do both. That means there is less incentive for the government to act fast.

THE PROCESS OF PRIVATIZATION IN CANADA

In C.D. Howe's time, the process of privatization was rather simple. Howe identified the candidates for sale. Howe determined the appropriate method of disposition. And Howe implemented the transaction.

Howe's spearheading produced generally good results at that time. But as some of you may remember, it got him and his government in serious trouble in the late 1950s when the same approach was used to handle loan guarantees to TransCanada Pipeline. Today, the structure and process which are in place to manage the privatization programme of the government are somewhat more sophisticated than in Howe's time.

In 1985, the Prime Minister appointed a Ministerial Task Force on Privatization. The task force was chaired by the Hon. Robert de Cotret, President of the Treasury Board, and it was mandated to carry out a review of the government's corporate interests.

In June 1986, the Prime Minister reinforced this structure through the appointment of the Hon. Barbara McDougall as Minister of State for Privatization and chairman of a full-fledged cabinet committee on privatization, regulatory affairs and operations. In August, the Deputy Minister, Dr. Janet Smith, was appointed, and by December 1986 a separate department—The Office of Privatization and Regulatory Affairs—was in place.

The process for privatization is now more fully centralized. The cabinet committee ensures that all relevant views are canvassed before proceeding with a transaction. There are also interdepartmental committees of officials to ensure that all the required work gets done. But management is clearly in the hands of one responsible department.

In January 1987, a privatization strategy was adopted to cover the entire review process from initial assessment through final sale. The process includes three principal stages.

First, there is an analysis of policy and financial considerations. At this stage, the government answers some basic questions: does the corporation still have a policy role; is it commercially viable; and is privatization feasible?

The second stage is in-depth review. It is conducted only for those corporations which the government believes are likely to perform better under private sector ownership. The review encompasses a broad range of consideration:

• the national and regional policy objectives;
• the financial situation of the corporation;

- the legal issues, including competition law and the regulatory framework;
- the concerns of the employees; and
- the appropriate method of sale, including the issues of foreign ownership and corporate concentration.

In order to conduct each review, the Office of Privatization and Regulatory Affairs assembles a working group of government and Crown corporation officials. Private sector advisers are added to the group to provide detailed analysis and advice on the financial and legal issues. Once this review is completed, recommendations are prepared and presented by the Minister of State to her colleagues in cabinet for discussion and approval.

The third and final stage of the process is the preparation and implementation of the sale. In this process, a key role is played by the Canada Development Investment Corporation to draw upon the extensive private sector experience of its staff and the board. This stage includes tabling the divestiture legislation, and the management of the bidding process or share issue.

The process which the government has put in place may at times appear cumbersome. But it provides the best guarantee that the relevant issues will be addressed, and that the transactions will benefit all concerned parties, including the employees, the consumers, and the taxpayers.

THE PROGRESS TO DATE

Thus far, the results of the Canadian privatization programme have been significant. In only two years, the government has completed eleven successful divestitures, for total cash proceeds of more than $1.3 billion. Some of these privatizations, including de Havilland, Canadair, and Teleglobe, have been high profile in their own way. Others, such as the Northern Transportation Company Limited and Fishery Products International have received less national attention but have been equally important for particular regions or sectors of the economy.

The privatizations realized thus far have produced tangible benefits for Canadians. The sale of Canadair to Bombardier has placed this important element of Canada's aerospace industry into the hands of a company which has the technical and marketing potential to make it prosper. The privatization of Teleglobe created a promising alliance between the entrepreneurship of Memotec and the experience, technology and market access of Teleglobe. The share issue in Fishery Products International provided employees an opportunity to own shares and hold a stake in the future of their company. In all cases the government obtained a fair deal for the taxpayer.

Until now, most of the sales have been to third parties. But the public is expressing growing interest in the possibility of acquiring shares in privatized corporations. In this regard, the investor response to the public share issue in Fishery Products International was very encouraging.

In order to address this opportunity, the government must develop experience in a broad range of new areas. It must look at the pricing of shares, the need for restrictions on ownership, and the means to market the issue. It must also take into consideration the securities regulations across Canada.

As for the future, Air Canada and Petro-Canada are still under review. Other candidates are the Radio-Chemical Company of Atomic Energy of Canada Limited, and Eldorado Nuclear Limited. The government, through the Canada Development Investment Corporation, is also looking into the possibility of selling its interest in National Sea Products of Nova Scotia.

In my view, the decisions on privatization will continue to be made on the basis of a thorough review of all the policy issues and interests involved.

CONCLUSION

My basic message is that the Canadian privatization programme should be viewed from the perspective of a tradition of balancing private and public sector initiative to provide the best possible benefits to the Canadian public. In the end, it is an exercise in management of government: doing the best with the tools available to achieve certain objectives. The environment changes; the objectives change with it; and so do the tools. Pure and simple. It is not a reversal of history. It is a pragmatic initiative which fits into Canada's public policy tradition.

The government has set in place a structure and a process consistent with this approach. The model is not a British one. It is not a French one. It is a Canadian model to respond to Canadian realities. I think the evidence shows that thus far it has worked rather well.

ROBERT W. POOLE, JR.

(Introduction by Michael A. Walker)

Dr. Robert Poole is president of the Reason Foundation, and in 1981 and again in 1985 and 1986 he was a consultant to the White House on the privatization of federal programmes. His book, *Cutting Back City Hall*, published in 1980, has been widely cited as a turning point in the attitude of public managers toward the privatization process. While the title of Bob Poole's remarks is "The Limits to Privatization," I want to forewarn you of what that might imply by reporting a few of the titles of his past publications: *Fighting Fires for Profit, An Efficiency Study of the Whatcom County Sheriff's Office, Privatizing the Airways, The Privatization of the Transportation Infrastructure, Air Traffic Control: The Private Sector Option*, and just to show how eclectic his outlook is, *The Objections to Privatization.*

CHAPTER 5

THE LIMITS OF PRIVATIZATION

Robert W. Poole, Jr.

A Privatization Revolution

I think it was very clear from this morning's discussions that there is a privatization revolution going on, and it is going on worldwide. You may well wonder, why is this happening? Is it the latest fad? Is it a flash in the pan, and three years from now everyone will be talking about something else and have forgotten about this? I don't think that's the case. I think what we're seeing in Canada, the United States, Britain and the rest of Europe, and in the Third World, is a growing recognition that the public sector has become greatly overextended during the last several decades. A great many things government is now doing are essentially business, commercial-type activities that are not done well at all by government—for institutional reasons dealing with the political process, the tendencies of civil service bureaucracies, access to tax money rather than having to obtain customers in the marketplace, and so forth.

With the successes of privatization in Britain and France and other countries, we are already seeing the ability of these techniques to cut the size and scope and cost of government without, at the same time, eliminating needed goods and services that people actually want.

I've been asked to talk today about the limits of privatization—how far can this process really go? When we talk about the kinds of enterprises we discussed this morning, basically commercial enterprises producing goods and services such as Jaguar, Conrail, Petro-Canada, Nippon Telephone, these are the sorts of things that obviously can be privatized. Numerous and in some cases the majority of known examples of those services —airlines and railroads and telephone systems—are well-functioning private enterprises. So that's not really at issue.

Public Service Privatization

The really interesting question is, how far can we go in the area of public services? When we apply privatization to public services, we're talking about shifting some or all aspects of those services to the private sector. That can mean privatizing only the financing of the services such as we do when we shift from taxation to support fire protection, for example, to a system of user fees. We have privatized the finance but not necessarily the delivery of the service. Contrariwise, if we privatize the delivery through competitive bidding but still fund the service through normal taxation, government becomes the purchasing agent acting for the taxpayers. We call that form of privatization contracting out, purchasing the service rather than producing it directly by government. Or we can divest the government of the responsibility for both producing and financing the services. A common example might be shifting from municipal garbage collection to an entirely private competitive marketplace for garbage collection. As you can see, there are various alternative forms of privatization in the public service area.

To answer the question of how far might this go, I'd like to draw on our experience in the United States. With fifty states and thousands of municipalities, we have a working laboratory for looking at the privatization of public services, which has been going on at a very extensive pace, particularly during the last ten years.

Through our Local Government Centre division, the Reason Foundation maintains a computerized data base of services that are privatized by state and local governments. At current count we have 28,000 instances of a specific service in a specific locality that has been privatized using one of a number of different forms of privatization, so you can see we have a large base of experience to draw from. The first large-scale national study that looked at how widespread privatization of services is (which was the main source for our data base) took place in 1983 and was conducted by the International City Management Association. It looked across the United States at all cities larger than 10,000 population and all counties bigger than 25,000 population. Nearly 2,000 of them responded, answering detailed questionnaires. ICMA looked at 59 different types of public services, everything from ambulance to zoning, as we say. For 13 of those 59 services, the 2,000 responding jurisdictions reported that the majority were using private enterprise for some or all of that service. In every one of the 59 types of services, there were some instances of privatization, even in police and fire services, which may surprise some people. The most commonly privatized of those services, with large majorities, were day care services for taking care of children, towing of illegally parked vehicles, community arts programmes, mental health programmes, para-transit programmes other than conventional regular line-haul transit, and residential garbage collection.

When we compare that 1983 survey with a less comprehensive survey that was done 10 years before and compare individual services, we find that the level of privatization has doubled or tripled over the decade from 1973 to 1983 in most cases. So, there is a very serious ongoing trend towards privatization right across the United States.

Why State and Local Governments Privatize

One important reason for this growing trend is that in contrast to our federal government, where there has been virtually no privatization other than Conrail earlier this year, state and local governments can't print money. They have to balance their budgets. In all but one state they legally have to operate with balanced budgets. We've had a growing tax revolt at the state and local level in the last decade. There's been strong resistance from citizens to continued support of a very rapid expansion of government spending, which is what we had in the '60s and early '70s. Fiscal pressure on local governments has been an important factor in promoting privatization.

The Stages of Public Service Privatization

We've identified three general stages in the trend toward public service privatization in the United States. The first stage, which is the simplest and easiest and least risky for elected officials, consists of contracting out normal municipal housekeeping services that don't deal directly with the public. Contracting out janitorial service in public buildings, park maintenance, trimming the grass in front of city hall, maintaining the city's fleet of vehicles and motor pool functions, operating city data processing services by a contract firm instead of with an in-house department, and to some extent, particularly in smaller cities, purchasing legal services, engineering services and other professional services from outside firms instead of maintaining an in-house staff is pretty widely accepted and hardly controversial across the United States.

Stage two, which is more complicated and has more direct public visibility, is contracting out or shedding to the private sector services that are delivered directly to the public—things that consumers consume and that voters therefore see directly in front of them everyday. This stage includes services like refuse collection, street sweeping, emergency ambulance service, and in a small number of cases, fire protection, park and recreation services and so forth. Some isolated examples of these types of services being done privately were well known even in the '60s, but by the middle to late '70s this trend really accelerated and we saw counties where the service had been traditionally provided for a long, long time in the public sector all of sudden starting to consider going out to bid, contracting it out, or in a smaller number of cases, divesting themselves of it altogether and leaving it to the marketplace. In particular, we saw this happen a lot in California following the passage of Proposition 13 in 1978 and in Massachusetts following the passage of Proposition 2 1/2 in 1981. These were both property tax reduction initiatives by the voters to force government to limit the extent of property taxes. That fiscal pressure led to a significant increase in both service shedding and contracting out in those two states.

Stage three in this public service privatization evolution started only a few years ago in the United States. It is quite an important development. This consists of going to the private sector for new, large-scale infrastructure projects. It's not privatizing something that already exists, although that same kind of thing exists in the public sector. When a city needs a *new* waste water treatment plant, or a state needs a *new* jail, or a city needs a *new* public hospital, instead of going through the traditional process of issuing their own bonds and building, owning and operating it, a growing number of communities are turning to private enterprise for a turnkey package. That means that private enterprise, usually a team of private firms consisting of an investment banking firm, a public accounting firm, and a large engineering construction firm, will form a consortium and offer to put together a package to finance, design, build, own and operate the entire project on a long-term contract basis. These contracts typically run between 20 and 30 years with cost control provisions built in. That length of time is necessary for the firm to amortize its investment in a major facility. We are seeing these types of deals in all the areas I mentioned. They were going even faster before last year's U.S. tax reform which made depreciation provisions less generous. Tax reform also greatly limited the use of tax-exempt bonds, so that has made some of the financial advantages less lucrative than they were. Many of these projects still make good enough sense, so they're still being proposed and acted upon. They can be done more rapidly and at lower overall cost in the private sector.

Advantages of Privatization

So far in this discussion I've assumed that there are some important advantages to privatization which make it a good alternative. Let me stop for a moment and talk about what those are. Basically, what we've grown to expect in the United States from public service privatization is better service at lower cost. Those are big claims. By better service I mean service that is more responsive to the needs consumers have and often service with important technological and managerial innovations. Lower cost means lower total operating costs to deliver the same degree of service and is simply measured on a fair basis, comparing apples with apples.

Why should this be true? In the first place, we're dealing with a vast difference in incentives between a private firm and the typical government agency that produces services on a monopoly basis with guaranteed access to taxpayers' money and no chance of any sort of competition. When we go to a contracting-out basis or open up an area like garbage collection to fully competitive service, we're substituting an entirely different set of incentives. We're substituting the profit motive. We're substituting the competitive spur of firms having to either win a contract from government or win customers in the marketplace directly by offering a cost-effective package of services. No matter how you try, it's very, very difficult in the public sector to duplicate that kind of operating environment and the competitive spurs to efficiency, given civil service and tax funding and so forth. It is extremely unlikely although not impossible. We do have some examples of highly efficient government agencies, but they're few and far between for understandable reasons.

Another reason we expect better performance out of the private sector, and this is probably a less important reason, is economies of scale. In the United States we have city and county governments of all different sizes as you do in Canada, ranging from cities of 3,000 or 6,000 population up to giant metropolises. Los Angeles has a population of 6 or 7 million just within its city limits and much more in the metro area. Yet all these different entities are trying to produce services that are delivered on the scale defined by the population and area of that unit of government. If you know anything about industrial organization, it has to sound a little bit bizarre that that would be efficient on all those different scales.

It turns out that there are obvious economies of scale that are different for different public services. Some, like garbage collection, have very little economy of scale. It could be done efficiently on an extremely low size small-scale decentralized basis. Others, like waste water treatment plants or refuse energy plants, have very significant economies of scale and only make sense on a very large scale. So you are more likely to get an efficient scale of operation if services are produced by competitive organizations in a marketplace. Even if you're talking about a contracting-out situation, a city that is getting ten services from private enterprise will be able to pick and choose. For a service with very low-scale economies, they might have ten contracts with ten different providers, each one of which is a sensible size for that service. Conversely, they might have one contract with a major firm for a service that has very large-scale economies, perhaps even on a shared basis with nearby cities. By using privatization, you are much more likely to get a sensible scale economy than you will when everything is done in-house.

Privatization Is Cost Effective

I've given you some theoretical reasons why we'd expect privatized public services to be more cost effective. What does the evidence actually show, and do we have such evidence? Indeed we have a wealth and growing abundance of evidence that these theoretical expectations actually pan out in practice. About ten years ago the National Science Foundation funded a nationwide study of garbage collection in the United States. It got data from about 1,400 cities and counties and found overwhelmingly that it was more cost effective to have garbage pickup done by private enterprise than by municipal departments. We're talking about a 50 to 60 percent cost savings when all costs are considered. One of the important findings of this study was that municipal agencies typically either don't know or can't report accurately what their true costs of producing a service are. When you ask them for their costs, they typically give you their direct operating costs, which even then may not include all of their direct costs. It will frequently leave out such costs as proportionate share of city overhead, employee fringe benefits, retirement programme costs, and capital costs. When you compare that kind of cost with what it costs private enterprise to operate, you are hardly making a fair, apples versus apples, comparison.

In the city of Los Angeles where I live I get billed $1.50 per month for garbage pickup for an unlimited number of cans, boxes and bags of whatever size I put out on the curb. Even their direct cost of picking that up can't be anywhere near that figure. It's got to be $5, $6, $8 or $9 a month. But people assume that because that's what is charged that is what the cost is to pick up garbage in Los Angeles. So, the first thing you have to look at is whether you have an outside, objective cost analysis that truly identifies what the costs are.

The National Science Foundation study in 1976 was the first major large-scale objective study that really looked at the data of public versus private, and it has changed the way the whole subject is discussed.

Incidently, the next speaker this afternoon, Jim McDavid, has done a similar study across Canada which found very similar conclusions. I won't try to steal his thunder by telling you any more about it.

A Comparative Study of Public Works Services

About three years ago a whole variety of public works services were studied on a systematic basis in southern California by a firm called Eco-Data. Southern California is a veritable laboratory in itself for privatization. Just in Los Angeles County there are about 85 separately incorporated municipalities. There are several hundred altogether in the three or four counties comprising southern California. They do an extensive amount of contracting out for public services. So when EcoData wanted a good study area to look at, they chose southern California. For each of eight different public works services they picked ten cities that produced that particular service in-house, with their own work-forces, funded by tax money, and ten cities that contracted with private enterprise on a competitive basis to get that service. With on-site field work and detailed cost data, they intensively studied these services. They were able to hold service levels constant and look at the comparative costs for a given level of service. They duplicated the earlier cost comparison on garbage collection, and then they went on to look at seven other services. Here were the cost results. For maintaining street trees, they found that municipal service was 37 percent more costly than competitive private enterprise. For street sweeping, they found that municipal service was 43 percent more costly. For grass maintenance in parks and median strips and so forth, they also found government 43 percent more costly. For traffic signal maintenance, basically repairing the lights that go out and cause traffic jams, it was 56 percent more costly to do that in-house than to contract it out. For building maintenance, ordinary janitorial service in government buildings, it was 73 percent more costly when done in-house. And for asphalt paving and repair work, it was 96 percent more costly in-house with the government's own work-force than on a competitive contract basis.

They looked in detail at the factors that led to those different outcomes, and they found things like a much more intelligent ratio of supervisors to staff. In some cases they found differences in pay scales. Usually, the pay scales weren't that significantly different but the fringe benefits were—much more generous fringe benefits and days off and so forth in the public sector. There was much less unexcused absenteeism in private enterprise than in government. It all boils down to what I said earlier—the difference in incentives between having a bottom line to satisfy versus having the kind of guaranteed annual income that is typical in the public sector.

Privatizing Fire Protection

Another very important and interesting study was done on private enterprise fire protection. There are private, for-profit fire companies in about 12 states in the United States. The best known example is in Arizona where about 15 different municipalities get fire protection from private enterprise, either on a contract basis where the city contracts for the service or on an individual subscription basis which tends to be in rural and low density areas.

In 1976 the Institute for Local Self Government went to Scottsdale, Arizona, a contract fire city, and compared it with three demographically very similar cities in the general Phoenix metropolitan area. They looked at measures of quality as well as measures of cost. They found that the average annual fire loss was about the same for all four cities. They found that the fire insurance rates homeowners paid were the same. They found that the response time getting to the fire was actually best in Scottsdale, the city with private fire. The bottom line was that the per household cost in Scottsdale, with private contract service, was about half what the average was of the three cities with municipal fire departments.

There was no particular magic about that result. The main cost in fire protection is paying people to sit around and wait for a fire to happen. What the private enterprise firm had done, and it has proven to work effectively over a 40-year period, is use a mixture of full-time people and paid reservists instead of using all full-time people. The paid reservists are on-call one week out of four. They have permission from their employer to leave their job when a fire call comes and respond to the fire, then clean up and go back to work. That mixture turns out to be so much more cost effective that it leads to these dramatic differences. There are some other differences, too, in terms of better use of new technology and so forth, but the main reason is simply a smarter use of personnel. Something anyone could have thought of, but it took the incentives of being in the private sector to actually do the job of thinking it up and making it work.

Sports Arenas and Stadiums

Another study was done last year by a professor at Pepperdine University, comparing public and private sports stadiums. He looked at 96 arenas and stadiums across the United States, about half public and half private. He compared the construction cost per seat in these stadiums and found that for hockey and basketball stadiums it was 46 percent more costly to do them in the public sector than in the private sector. Football and baseball fields were 142 percent more costly to do in the public sector than in the private sector. And, in terms of the incentives for cost-effectively operating them, he found these stadiums were used an average of 197 days per year in the public sector, compared to an average of 254 days per year by private enterprise. Again, having a bottom line and trying to get a return on your investment and get the most bang for your buck makes a difference. That's why the studies come out this way.

Transit Systems

The last comparative area I'll talk about is transit, where there have been a plethora of studies dating back over ten or twelve years. The most recent and probably the most comprehensive study comparing private versus public transit was published just last year in *Public Administration Review*. It was a nationwide survey. They looked at 595 municipal bus systems in the United States. Virtually all of these bus systems are subsidized. The differences among them are in the way they're operated and managed. The most conventional model is for some kind of municipal agency to own and operate the entire system. The second model is for the municipality to own the system but hire a management contractor to manage it—still with all government employees and civil service. The third model is to have the government responsible for funding the system but for it to hire a whole mix of private transit providers on a competitive basis to provide transit in the area. It turns out that the third model is the one that shows significant cost savings, on the order of 25 to 40 percent lower costs, thanks to that kind of competitive contracting. Simply hiring a management firm to operate a government-owned system produced virtually no statistically significant difference in cost effectiveness.

One study of express bus service in southern California showed that private enterprise could provide the identical level and quality of express buses for 50 percent of the cost. Early this year a study of one of the five supervisorial districts in L.A. County found that they could save about 30 percent by contracting with private enterprise instead of using the Southern California Rapid Transit District's municipal bus service. There have also been a number of studies overseas and in this country of the use of entirely private, decentralized jitney services that are based on 12- and 14-passenger vans. Our own assessment at the Reason Foundation is that the most cost-effective form of public transit for hire in most circumstances is going to be based on the 14-passenger van. Wendell Cox will probably be talking about these sorts of things, so I don't want to spend my limited time going into that any further.

The Cutting Edge of Privatization

I've given you some idea of the scope of services privatization in the United States. Let me talk about three areas now that are on the cutting edge today, to indicate how far it might go altogether. The first cutting edge area is jails and prisons. This has only been happening for a couple of years, and it's still very controversial. The American Civil Liberties Union thinks there's something fundamentally unconstitutional about having private for-profit firms running jails, even though they don't think it's unconstitutional for private for-profit brain surgeons to provide brain surgery. Be that as it may, it is not widely accepted yet as a proper thing to do. However, there are several dozen correctional institutions, ranging from minimum security up through medium security—maximum security is in the pipeline—currently being operated by private contractors. They have a good track record so far. The potential for this is extremely large. More than two-thirds of all state prison systems in the United States are under federal court orders charging unconstitutional conditions. So there is a great need for upgrading of prison conditions and building new prisons. The public sector does not have very many resources to do this. This turnkey model of private enterprise is providing a total package of financing, building, owning and operating, and it looks to have a great deal of potential. I expect we are going to see a great deal more of this across the United States in the next few years.

The second cutting edge area is education. This has not progressed very far yet, but I think it's coming. First, we already have a large private, for-profit market in day care services. We have chains like Kindercare and so forth that are all across the country and very well established. It's a natural extension for them to move into providing actual educational services. Secondly, we have demographic changes. Today a smaller fraction of the voting population has children in public schools than ever before, partly because so many people are living longer, retired people who are voting, and also because we have so many single people and childless people. The political support that automatically approves school bond issues is growing slimmer and slimmer, and there is going to be fiscal pressure on the public school systems for that reason.

At the same time, we have the maturing of the baby boom generation. Those baby boomers who have kids now have kids of school age, and they're very demanding consumers. With the recognized shortcomings of the public school systems, it seems very likely that this is going to be translated into a political demand for a more competitive system where you actually have a choice and get a better deal for your school tax dollars. The talk about education vouchers is heating up again in the United States. I wouldn't be at all surprised to see a serious education voucher programme adopted within the next few years in one state or another. We already have some contracting out going on in Minnesota. School districts are hiring alternative providers, groups of teachers organized as small companies, to provide schooling. I think this is just the tip of the iceberg of what is going to come over the next few years.

The third cutting edge area is highways and freeways. I used to get kidded about wanting to sell the roads. But it turns out that numerous studies have documented the gap between highway infrastructure needs and the money likely to be available from normal public sector sources over the next 15 years. Many people in the transportation field are concluding that if we're going to have significant additional capacity—especially in urban area expressways—built over the next 15 years, it is going to have to come from the private sector. Within the last six months we've seen very serious proposals. For example, a 10-mile extension of the Dulles airport toll road from Dulles airport to Leesburg, Virginia, has been proposed as an entirely private sector turnkey project—financed, built, owned and operated as a private, for-profit project. We have a second proposal in Colorado for a 100-mile private highway on a toll basis between Pueblo and Fort Collins that would have an 80 mile per hour speed limit because it is privately financed and not subject to control by the federal government. Despite California's traditional aversion to toll roads, both houses of the California legislature have passed a measure which now just needs to be tidied up and go to the governor for signature allowing our second largest county, Orange County just south of Los Angeles, to implement toll roads to meet the need for new freeways. They might actually be called "feeways" in southern California. Several major firms are just about to issue a press release which I've already seen, announcing their new joint venture to go into this marketplace and become the providers of private "feeways" for Orange County. A bill to do that state-wide passed one house of the legislature and may well pass in the next session, so I predict we are going to see a lot more of this.

Shifting Government Services to the Private Sector

I've given you some illustration of the range of public service privatization that is going on now in the United States. We haven't covered a few functions that government does. We haven't talked about welfare programmes. There is certainly some scope for privatization here. For one thing, in the U.S. there is quite a lot of competitive contracting with human service agencies, whether they're for-profit or non-profit, to provide various kinds of needed human service programmes such as helping retarded children and day care for old people in their homes. There is a lot of scope for expanding that.

Government is never going to be able to privatize the transfer of wealth from one set of taxpayers to a set of tax recipients. So long as people accept that as a public sector function, that will always be inherently governmental. But the actual provision of services to people who need them can increasingly be shifted to private providers. Government can also provide incentives through the tax system, as it does to some extent now in the United States, for motivating a greater role by private charity in providing the kinds of help to people in need that traditionally has been provided through the welfare state. For example, what do you suppose would be the impact on private giving for all sorts of good purposes if people were to receive a dollar-for-dollar tax credit instead of simply a tax deduction for contributions to non-profit human service agencies? In other words, instead of the dollar going to the government to do welfare, you could direct that same dollar to your choice of private non-profit human service agencies. One can imagine that there would be a tremendous explosion in private giving that could displace a great deal of what the government welfare system is now carrying out. That method hasn't yet been tried anywhere that I know of but is certainly conceivable.

Also, we haven't talked about what we call social security in the United States, mandatory government retirement programmes funded by taxation. You may be surprised to know that in Chile, despite that not being a very popular government around the world, about four years ago they set in motion what seems to be a very successful programme to privatize their state retirement system. Something like 40 percent of the population has already made the transition from the typical government compulsory retirement programme to a programme based on individual retirement accounts. You choose your own provider—you're still required to have a certain payroll deduction every pay cheque—and you put the money into a private provider plan that you select on the marketplace. That money is then invested for you and belongs to you in a way that most government social security retirement programmes do not. There is scope for doing that in other countries. Plans to that effect have been seriously talked about in Britain. Detailed programmes to make that kind of transition have been produced by the Heritage Foundation and the Cato Institute in the United States and are being talked about seriously by at least one presidential candidate, Pierre Dupont, who is a Republican.

I also haven't talked about police and courts. Here too there is some role for private enterprise. Believe it or not, there have been successful experiments with contracting out entire police services by small cities in the United States. We've documented a number of those. There is extensive experience with smaller cities purchasing their law enforcement services from an adjacent jurisdiction. In fact, I believe that the Mounties provide a contract law enforcement service to smaller communities in Canada. There is really no reason in principle why private security firms could not be allowed to compete in that market. As I say, a small number of examples of exactly that have taken place successfully in the United States, usually over the great opposition of the law enforcement personnel and their public employee unions. So it remains a very controversial thing, but it's not in principle impossible.

In addition, in the area of adjudication, we have a significant growth of what we call ADR, alternative dispute resolution mechanisms. These range from neighbourhood mediation centres to California's rent-a-judge programme, whereby according to a provision in the state constitution retired judges are able to offer their services to adjudicate and arbitrate contract disputes, divorce disputes and so forth in a way that is typically much, much faster than going through the civil court system where there are four year backlogs. It is much less expensive, and some very large-scale multimillion dollar suits, both commercial disputes and personal disputes, have been settled in recent years through that mechanism, thereby unburdening the civil courts to some extent and reducing the average delay times for everyone else who uses the court system. So even in police and courts there is some scope for partial privatization.

The Functions of Government

I'm certainly not saying there's no role at all for government. Making laws, protecting people's basic rights—these are basic functions of government and I presume always will be. Of course, in the United States today we're even trying to privatize foreign policy with Oliver North, but I'm not so sure how good an idea that is. Most of the public services government is providing today, certainly at the state and local level in the United States and the provincial and municipal level in Canada, are things that can be done in the private sector. We know they have been and are being done well in the private sector, generally a lot more cost effectively than typical government agencies do them. I think that is really what privatization of public services is all about.

DISCUSSION

Edited by Michael A. Walker

Question: From the Canadian perspective, the United States seems to be a very different kind of country. You seem to do things quite a bit differently. For one thing, you have more democracy. How transferable is the U.S. experience to other countries? Do you know what's happened in other countries? And, finally, how important is ideology?

Answer: That's a very good question. I think it's highly transferable, and I think ideology has had very little to do with it in the United States. In the first place, the same sort of local services contracting out and service shedding has been happening in Great Britain since about 1980, as Madsen Pirie could tell you. There has been a significant contracting out revolution throughout Britain in the last six years that's been motivated partly by ideological reasons but significantly, also, simply for good fiscal responsibility reasons of getting the job done cost effectively.

There is a fairly significant amount of contracting out of municipal services in Switzerland and West Germany. We are in touch with a research institute in West Germany that studied it extensively there. We only learned a couple of years ago that this sort of municipal contracting out of services is extremely common in Japan. It's been a traditional way of doing things for a long time in Japan, at least since World War II. John Pepper Marlin, of the Council for Municipal Performance in New York, has produced a couple of detailed reports on the contracting out of public services in Japan. It's well established. It's not on any ideological basis at all, but simply a sensible way of doing things.

Companies make make-or-buy decisions all the time; it's a normal thing to do. Can we do this more efficiently in-house or more efficiently by purchasing it from outside? There's no reason at all why municipal governments shouldn't do exactly the same thing—see where their comparative advantage really lies and where they can get the most bang for the buck.

In the United States we're now finding that a number of Democratic mayors are becoming big advocates of contracting out, including one example I know well, the mayor of Phoenix, Terry Goddard, a former union person who is an enthusiastic advocate of competitive contracting out simply because it's a cost-effective, good deal for the taxpayers. It need not have anything to do with ideology at all.

Question: Municipally operated services, for example waste disposal, are income tax exempt, whereas private companies must pay corporate income taxes. Why cannot municipally operated services do better in the marketplace?

Answer: You'll hear this a lot. People will not only cite the fact that private firms have to pay income taxes but they also have to pay property taxes on whatever property they have. They have advertising expenses that the public sector typically doesn't have. They also have to have something left over for the bottom line for a profit. In the very static mentality way that a lot of union people look at the situation, here are three or four extra costs that private enterprise has on top of all the same costs that government has. So, how on earth could private enterprise do the job at less total cost?

What that static way of looking at things ignores is the role that incentives play in figuring out what your costs are going to be. Costs are not a given; costs are a function of how entrepreneurs look at organizing people and equipment and systems to get a given job done. As the example I gave of the private fire department in Scottsdale, Arizona, should indicate, getting the same fire protection with half the full-time manpower and no reduction in quality is simply a function of entrepreneurial insight that says: "No, our costs are not the same; our costs are dramatically different because we've thought smarter and figured out a better way to do the job." That's what you try to aim for by having competition for the provider of a service.

Question: Is the process of privatization simply a matter of de-unionization?

Answer: No, hardly. In fact, this is also a misleading impression that many people have. It's not a de-unionizing or anti-unionizing process at all, although the leading opponents of municipal privatization are public employee unions. We don't have any real statistics, but I would say that many if not most of the privatized municipal services in the U.S. are run by unionized employees. The Teamsters Union is very big in running privatized services.

Unionization is not really relevant at all except in terms of the process of opposing the move to privatize. Private enterprise deals with unions all the time. Most firms have unions, and most privatized public services are done by unionized employees. It's simply a case of getting the most service for the dollars.

Question: Is economic development ever a significant rationale for the privatization of public sector operations, that is, as opposed to better service at lower cost?

Answer: Economic development is sometimes talked about as part of the rationale, but usually cost savings through privatization come about over a period of several years through using fewer people to do the same job, often, as in the fire example, using a mixture of full-time and part-time people where it was all full-time people before. So, in terms of job creation, the short-term effect of privatization often means fewer people employed to produce the same amount of services. So, in that kind of short-term sense, it's negative.

On the other hand, when you look at it from the society-wide standpoint, what kind of sense does it make to employ 300 people to pick up garbage if you can get the same job done with 200 people and have those other people producing other goods and services. In a longer term, broader perspective, it's very pro economic development because it means that the resources of society are being used in more productive endeavours overall instead of being wasted by being used inefficiently.

Question: Which group or factor is the greatest barrier to privatizing services?

Answer: I think I mentioned that in practical political terms today in the United States, public employee unions are certainly the only significant organized opposition, although the general inertia and attachment to the status quo of managers and civil servants is also a significant factor. It's not well organized, but it can provide a significant delaying factor or an outright dig-in-the-heels opposition because it's comfortable not having to operate in the more competitive style of private enterprise. It's unsettling for people in government to have to learn to deal with entrepreneurs, to think like entrepreneurs or even to leave government and become entrepreneurs. So that is another source of resistance.

Question: Are you aware of creative alternatives to firing employees when you contract out services?

Answer: Yes, we now know a great deal about how to deal with those employee transition processes, and I'll point to the Los Angeles County government as one of the real experts at smooth transitions. Ever since 1979—the year after Proposition 13—Los Angeles County has had an extensive programme to contract out services, particularly expansions of existing services. Instead of simply adding more government employees when an area is growing, they do all the new service with contracting instead of with government employees. They've had a strict "no lay-off policy" in all their privatizations. Do it slowly and gradually such that either attrition will take care of it or you can afford to transfer any employees that aren't needed in the new operation to some other branch of county government and still keep them employed—if they're willing to transfer, obviously. But there has been a strict policy of no involuntary lay-offs.

Many municipal governments in this kind of process require the bidding firm to at least make employment offers to all the current municipal employees as a condition of winning the bid. That doesn't mean they have to keep them forever. They can use their normal performance-based personnel evaluation systems thereafter to decide whether they're carrying their own weight. But they have to offer to employ them all as a transition measure. That kind of thing really does tend to make the process go much smoother and less disruptively.

Question: How do small- to medium-sized municipalities protect themselves from the problem of a service supplier getting a contract with a low bid one year and then jacking up the price in the second contract?

Answer: That's a very common fear. There's no single answer to that. We now have a number of detailed handbooks on how to write contracts and structure bidding processes and so forth. Very seldom do you offer only one-year contracts. Typically, you would offer a two- or three-year contract, even for ordinary services like street sweeping. You may have a formula built into that for the second and third year costs, which provides for an increase tied to the CPI or something like that.

The other answer is that when you go out to bid for the next go-round, you hold a truly competitive bidding process again, whereby the incumbent firm that's had the contract for the first three years is on an equal playing field with all the bidders from outside. You don't build in any advantage for them. You keep the process honest and above board. For a small city that's never done it before, it is not obvious how to do that well. Sometimes they do it poorly and get taken advantage of, but there's no excuse for not learning how to do it right. There are thousands and thousands of successful examples and lots of how-to books now available.

Question: How are service levels monitored and maintained?

Answer: Part of writing a good contract is to define measures of performance and allocate some city staff function to actually keeping track of what those performance levels are and, obviously, having an open line for citizen complaints as well as the service that the citizens themselves can directly see and monitor. One of the surprising benefits of privatization has been that when a service is contracted out, it's often the first time that anyone has thought about quantitative performance measures. That's not always true. Some cities do have performance measures now, but it's much more common than you think that nobody's ever tried to quantify what municipal performance is. What is good garbage collection? What is good fire protection? Often, the process of putting something out to bid is the first time you define what it is that we're actually supposed to be getting and how do we measure it and how do we know we're getting our money's worth? It's a very constructive and healthy thing to do.

Question: Are you able to comment on the U.S. versus the Canadian experience regarding medical costs and services?

Answer: Unfortunately, I'm not, because I'm not that familiar with the Canadian experience. I say that kind of apologetically, because we are neighbours and Americans should pay more attention to Canada. But with 50 states and thousands of municipalities to try to study and keep track of, we really have our hands full just trying to be experts on American experiences. I'm sorry.

Michael Walker: If I could perhaps expand a bit on the question that's come from the audience, we in Canada see that medical costs in the United States have been going up much more rapidly than they have in Canada. I guess some of that is because we don't actually have as good a medical care system in the sense that we're not getting the same services. To what extent are medical services provided on a market-oriented basis in the United States?

Answer: The costs of medical care are very high in the United States, and they're still going up. However, the rate of increase in the last four years or so has slowed down significantly compared to what it was in the previous ten years. My own assessment is that the biggest single factor causing the very rapid growth and build-up of medical costs has been the government hyping the demand artificially with the medicare and medicaid programmes that for too long were a blank cheque to doctors and hospitals to continue to provide services with no real limit or cost consciousness. They're now being much tougher on the provision of what costs will be reimbursed, and that's partly causing a slowdown in the rate of growth of costs.

Also—I don't know if this is true in Canada—we now have a doctor glut in the United States. The medical schools have been cranking out people at such a rate because it's been so popular to go into medicine, that we now have doctors chasing after markets—chasing after patients. This has led to the growth of a much more competitive marketplace in medicine in the last five years or so.

We now have lots of different types of medical services that didn't exist before. We have drive-up emergency rooms in shopping centres—the so-called doc-in-a-box concept—where simple procedures can be done at a lower cost than in a regular doctor's office and definitely at lower costs than emergency rooms in major hospitals where they're trying to cover a big part of their overhead through the emergency room. You strip away all that and you have a free-standing emergency room that can do a much more competitive job. Also, now that doctors and hospitals are legally permitted to advertise, you're seeing aggressive competition starting to come into the medical marketplace.

It's too soon to say how much of an effect this is going to have, but the rate of cost growth and the share of GNP going to medical care has definitely slowed down in the last three or four years at the same time that these competitive mechanisms have started to come into play. I think there is a cause and effect relationship there.

Question: Several years ago you wrote an article in *Policy Review*, "Objections to Privatization." What are the problems with privatization?

Answer: We have talked about some of these things. One of the objections was, how could private enterprise possibly do it cheaper, given it has these extra costs? And I explained that—the costs are not fixed; the costs are a function of the entrepreneur's judgement and skill. Secondly, you avoid the problem of getting locked into a buy-in situation where they bid low and then jack-up the price later by more intelligent contracting.

One problem that hasn't come up is the idea unions very frequently raise, that there are a lot of scandals and corruption associated with contracting out—firms will make pay-offs to elected officials in order to get a contract and keep it—so you don't really have a fair process. The taxpayers end up getting ripped off because they'll get the thing under the table and then they'll give them all kinds of supplements to the contract later on to make up for the low initial price and so forth.

The people who make that argument about corruption being inherent in the process are mostly from one union—the American Federation of State, County and Municipal Employees, ASCME. They've written four books attacking contracting out in the last ten years, and in each book they come up with another dozen or so anecdotes about specific cases where privatization has gone wrong—sometimes with corruption, sometimes just a mismanaged firm that leads to higher costs. They then try to generalize from the new dozen examples that they see that this is typical.

We've been studying privatization for more than ten years at the Reason Foundation. We've collected a data base of 28,000 known cases. We've been analysing scientific studies looking at large samples, comparing public versus private, and we don't come up with anything like that. My guess is that if ASCME were able to do a scientifically valid study with large numbers of cases, showing there was a positive correlation with corruption and mismanagement going along with privatization on any significant scale, they would certainly have published it by now. Yet, all they come up with is a handful of cases each time, from the many thousands that we know of where privatization has been successfully implemented.

Either our reporters and investigative journalists are completely asleep at the switch and are not catching these things when, in fact, they're widespread, or they simply aren't happening except as isolated bad examples, which I strongly suspect is the case. Therefore, I think we can say that while there certainly is a temptation to have under-the-table deals and corruption, the evidence is that it is not a widespread problem at all.

JAMES McDAVID

(Introduction by Michael A. Walker)

We've been hearing a lot about the international experience with privatization, both in the privatization of assets and of services. In this penultimate session for the afternoon, we're going to consider some Canadian experience with privatization.

We're very fortunate today to have with us Professor James McDavid, an associate professor of public administration in the School of Public Administration at the University of Victoria. He holds a B.A. and M.A. in international relations from the University of Alberta, and an M.A. and Ph.D. in political science from Indiana University. I don't think it's an exaggeration to say that Jim is the most knowledgeable person in Canada about the comparative costs of public and private service production in the municipal sector.

He is the custodian of a unique body of data which he has collected from municipalities across Canada and which provides information on costs, service levels, production methods and environmental conditions. These are linked to the production of fire and police services as well as the collection and disposal of solid waste.

His research has been published in the *Public Finance Quarterly*, the *Canadian Public Administration Journal*, the *International Journal of Public Administration* as well as the *International Journal of Comparative and Applied Criminal Justice*.

CHAPTER 6

PRIVATIZING LOCAL GOVERNMENT SERVICES IN CANADA

James McDavid

INTRODUCTION

Provincial and federal efforts to privatize Crown corporations and departments of their ministries have attracted most of the public attention in Canada to date. Certainly, these initiatives are important, but the attention given to them overshadows a well-established privatization tradition in Canada at the local government level. I will focus on efforts to privatize local government services in our country and will present findings from research that has examined the cost and productivity differences between public and private producers of the same services.

Before I begin, it's worth pointing out that local governments in Canada spent 30 percent of all moneys expended by all governments in Canada in 1983. That fact makes local government a big business in Canada. Further, the range of services provided by the large numbers of local governments across the country provides us with many opportunities to see if privatization really works.

DEFINING PRIVATIZATION

It is clear from the presentations made thus far that privatization means different things to different people. There are at least five different ways that the term "privatization" has been used in discussing local government in

Canada. I would like to list them for you and point out which one I am using.

Privatization can mean:

- Contracting out a service (or part of it) to one or more private profit-oriented companies. This is the most common definition in Canada and the United States, and the one I'll be using.

In addition there are four others that are worth mentioning:

- Contracting out a service, but doing so with a private non-profit organization. Social services are contracted out in this manner in some localities.
- Franchising a private company to produce a service exclusively in a given geographic area. Examples include electrical distribution or water distribution for municipalities.
- Giving grants to private non-profit agencies to provide services. This is done less frequently than other means of privatizing.
- Getting out of providing a service altogether. An example would be selling off all solid waste collection vehicles and making residents in a community responsible for hiring their own private collection company.

As has been mentioned in other presentations, privatization can also mean the selling off of state-owned corporations as has been done in Britain. Here in North America we have also seen examples of privatizing which involve giving the consumers vouchers and allowing them to pick the agency (public or private) from which they buy a service. Education services have been marketed in this way.

PRIVATIZING LOCAL GOVERNMENT SERVICES: EVIDENCE FROM TWO NATIONAL SURVEYS

Survey of Municipal Managers

In 1981-82, I conducted a cross-Canada survey of municipalities with populations over 10,000 persons. The survey was targeted at municipal managers, and several of the questions looked at contracting out services. About 200 surveys were mailed out, and by the time follow-ups had been completed 136 managers had responded.

Figure 1 shows the results of one question that asked managers to list the services contracted out in their municipalities. As you can see, the two largest groups (with 26.4 percent each of all contracts) are ones we might

Figure 1

Types of Contracts as Percentages of All Contracts

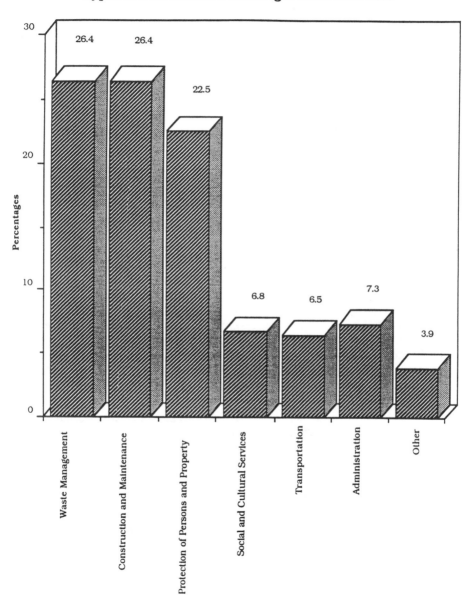

expect—namely, solid waste management and construction/maintenance activities.

Waste management includes solid waste collection, disposal, sewage treatment and landfill site supervision. If we look at dollars expended for some of these functions, Statistics Canada reports that in 1983, $528 million were spent by local governments across Canada on solid waste collection and disposal alone. That is a lot of business for the agencies involved in this service.

In the construction and maintenance areas, services like road construction, road maintenance, snow removal, sanitary and storm sewer construction and janitorial services are included. In 1983, local road construction was a $3 billion item and snow removal cost local governments $400 million across Canada.

Other services contracted out included those involved in protecting persons and property (police, animal control, and pest control); social and cultural services (libraries, food concessions, tourism and convention services, day care, elderly housing, recreation services); transportation (public transit, parking); administrative services (planning, computing, accounting, engineering, tax billing, secretarial services); and a category called "other services" that picks up contracts like water supply agreements and miscellaneous service contracts.

It is important to keep in mind that the statistics reported in figure 1 can only give us a rough idea of the services actually contracted out in Canadian local governments. Asking a municipal manager to list all services contracted out often results in an undercounting problem. Generalist managers may not recall all instances of contracting out that occur in their operations. Thus, to get more accurate and detailed information on contracting out municipal services it is necessary to trade off breadth for depth. In other words, to obtain the information necessary to conduct comparisons between public and private producers of municipal services, it is necessary to focus on a limited number of services and ask questions of the people involved in providing each service.

Survey of Municipal Engineers and Solid Waste Contractors

A second cross-Canada survey was completed in 1981-82, and it focused on residential solid waste collection services provided in municipalities over 10,000 population. The questionnaires were mailed to city engineers, and in cases where the service had been contracted out, follow-up surveys were sent to the private contractors involved with those cities.

Of the 200 municipalities surveyed, responses were received from 126. This is an excellent return rate (63 percent) for this kind of survey and indicated at the time the widespread interest in the results of the study. Municipalities in Quebec were not surveyed because the Ministry of Municipal Affairs in Quebec City indicated it did not want surveys mailed directly to its municipalities. Efforts to negotiate a compromise proved to be very costly and had to be terminated for lack of time and funding.

The pie chart in figure 2 shows how residential solid waste was collected in Canadian municipalities in 1980. As you can see, the largest percentage of municipalities surveyed (42.1 percent) had privatized their residential collection operations. Another 37.3 percent used a mixed collection system wherein private companies collected part of the residential wastes (usually from apartments and condominiums) and the rest was collected by municipal crews. About 21 percent of municipalities used their own crews exclusively. If we look at the populations served in each of these three types of collection, however, it turns out that exclusive municipal collection accounts for about 30 percent of the total population served.

In privatizing any local government service, cost considerations are often a key factor. Prior to my survey, little comparative cost data had been collected in Canada that allowed people to see how public and private service costs compared.

One reason for the lack of research comparing costs is the difficulty in translating municipal budgeting procedures, which sometimes don't fully account for service costs, into a form that renders them comparable to private company figures. It is common for public budgeting procedures to leave out components of service costs—examples might be administrative overhead or fringe benefits.

In my research, I designed the questionnaire so that people filling it out were asked to break down reported total costs into components. By adding the components, it was possible to tell whether the total cost reported contained more items than listed, or (in a few cases) whether the total cost was artificially low (where total costs were less than the sum of component costs). Components included in the survey were salaries, fringe benefits, vehicle maintenance, fuel and lubricants, capital expenditures, building rent and utilities.

In cases where particular municipalities omitted a cost component, econometric techniques were used to impute a cost figure for that component. In addition, vehicle depreciation costs were added to municipal

Figure 2

**Residential Solid Waste Collection in
Canadian Municipalities (1980)**

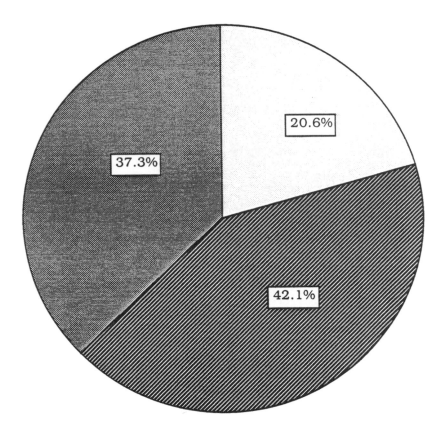

Municipal (Own Forces) Collection
(N=26)

Private (Contract) Collection
(N=53)

Mixed Collection
(N=47)

costs to bring them as close as possible to a fair comparison with private company contract costs.

Figure 3 shows the key comparison of costs per household of residential solid waste collection in each of the three types of systems. As you can see, public collection costs are considerably higher than private contractor prices. In fact, municipalities that collected all of their residential solid waste in 1980 were 51 percent more costly per household than contractor prices (plus contract monitoring changes) for municipalities that had privatized the collection service. Public crews in mixed systems are about 12 percent more costly per household than situations where the entire service has been contracted out.

To refine the cost comparisons in figure 3, it is important to account for differences in collection systems (other than public versus private) that could explain cost differences. For example, municipalities that enjoy twice a week collection will have higher costs than those with once a week collection. Differences in service levels can obscure comparisons between public and private collection costs.

To account for this problem, and the problems created by differences in geography and climate as well, a multivariate analysis of cost differences was calculated, controlling statistically for frequency of collection, location of collection, total tonnes collected, population density and annual temperature variation.

Once costs are adjusted, the big difference between public and private remains. Public costs per household are now $42.14 compared to $29.88 for private contracting. This is still a 41 percent difference.

RESULTS OF PRIVATIZATION: TWO CASE STUDIES

If we look at the experiences of particular municipalities, we can better understand the process of privatizing and get a clearer look at the results. Before/after comparisons of costs and productivity are useful in assessing the results of privatizing municipal services.

I'll focus on the experiences of two Canadian cities, one on the west coast (Richmond, B.C.) and one on the east coast (Halifax, Nova Scotia). Both cities decided, after efforts to negotiate productivity improvements with their unionized work forces, to contract out their residential solid waste collection operations to private firms. In the next few minutes, I'd like to summarize their experiences.

108

Figure 3

**Residential Solid Waste
Collection Costs**

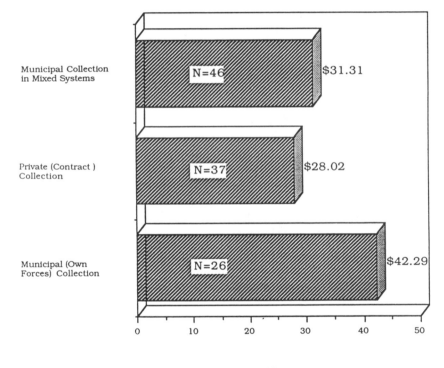

**Cost per Household
(Dollars)**

Richmond, B.C.

Richmond decided to contract out its solid waste collection operation in early 1983. Prior to that decision, the City Engineer and his department had tried repeatedly to alter existing work arrangements to increase crew productivities. A key event in Richmond's history was the area-wide strike of the Vancouver region locals of CUPE. That strike, occurring from January through March 1981, escalated collection costs rapidly as the effects of a substantial salary increase were figured over the subsequent two years.

Efforts to modify crew numbers (principally reducing the number of residential collection crews in the winter months) eventually resulted in a breakdown in negotiations in the fall of 1982. Richmond Council decided to contract the service out in January 1983 and affirmed that decision in February. The contractor began work in March 1983.

Figure 5 summarizes key before/after comparisons for Richmond. The statistics in the table were obtained from the City Engineer's records and pertain only to residential solid waste collection in the district. Collection costs from 1980-82 include all major operating costs: salaries, fringe benefits, vehicle maintenance, fuel and lubricants, vehicle depreciation and overhead charge. Costs for 1983 include the price of the contract to the municipality, a contract monitoring cost ($43,000) and an overhead charge on the contract monitoring cost. As you can see, public collection costs per household were much higher in 1982 than in 1983 when collection was privatized. In fact, costs in 1982 were 66 percent higher than in 1983.

Why the big differences? The explanation boils down to differences in crew productivities. The same size of crews were used in 1982 as were used by the contractor in 1983 (two-man crews) and the same vehicles were used in 1983 (the contractor purchased the municipal collection fleet and used it to service the district). Thus, the 65 percent difference in crew productivities shown in figure 5 is due to contractor crews working more efficiently.

Two other indicators (not shown in figure 5) also support the productivity differences. In 1982, the average number of trucks used per day was 8.4. The comparable figure for 1983 was 5.3 trucks per day. In 1982, the average tonnes/truck/day was 12.4 tonnes. That figure increased to 20.5 tonnes/truck/day with privatization.

Richmond is due to rebid its contract in 1988, and indications are that the municipality will continue to contract the service out to the private sector.

Figure 4

**Tonnes of Solid Waste Collected Per
Crew Person Per Hour**

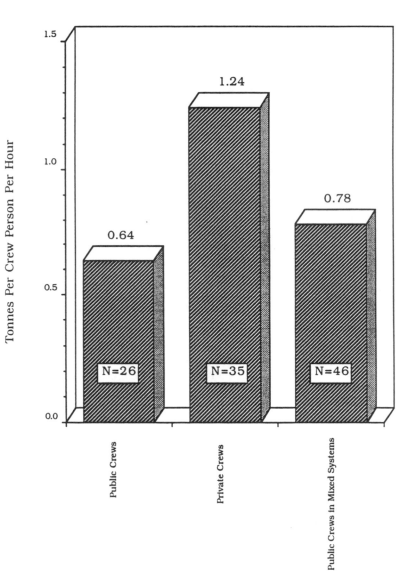

Figure 5

Costs and Productivity Levels in Richmond Before and After Privatization

	Before Privatization			After Privatization
	1980	1981	1982	1983
Cost Per Household	42.71	52.27	52.71	31.72
Total Households Served	25,007	25,456	25,731	26,141
Total Tonnes Collected	24,772	19,438	24,985	26,232
Tonnes Per Crew Person Per Day	5.29	5.79	6.20	10.25

Halifax, Nova Scotia

Halifax also decided to contract out its solid waste collection operation in 1983. That decision, like Richmond's, was made after repeated attempts to improve crew productivities. As early as 1980, the Engineering and Works Department had implemented a task system, which gave collection crews the rest of the work day off (with pay) once all the routes were finished. On the average, crews were working six-hour days.

That level of slack was not viewed as a problem because projections of population (and solid waste volumes) into the mid-1980s indicated that crews would be collecting greater volumes over time. Unfortunately, a regional recession in 1980-81 changed the growth picture and crew slack actually increased to four hours per shift on some days as solid waste volumes diminished.

In 1981, Engineering and Works decided to reduce the number of collection crews from nine to seven, keeping three men per vehicle. This change would have saved the city about 20 percent of its 1982 collection budget.

The union was informed of the proposed changes and told they would be implemented in January 1982. From the first day of implementation, problems began. The seven crews were unable to complete their routes in an eight-hour day. In effect, a work slowdown occurred, and crew productivities actually declined by 54 percent. To complete the routes, unionized crews were initially paid overtime, but that threatened to wipe out the savings anticipated by reducing the number of crews. The city hired a private contractor to complete the overtime collections and realized a saving over public crew overtime costs.

Labour problems continued so that by July 1982 the city decided to hire a contractor on a full-time temporary basis to collect all solid wastes. The contractor employed seven two-man crews and was able to complete all routes in an eight-hour working day. In effect, the contractor crews were fully one-third more productive than city crews even if the proposed route reduction had been implemented smoothly.

The city council liked the results and decided in late 1982 to contract out the collection operation for three years. Bids were solicited and the winning bid was 46 percent less expensive than the projected cost of municipal collection in 1983 (even allowing for the reduction in the number of city collection crews). Unionized employees were invited to bid, but refused to reduce their demand that nine routes with three men per vehicle be a condition of their employment. Their bid turned out to be nearly double that of the winning contractor.

Role of the Unionized Employees

In both cities, the unions resisted privatization strongly. In Richmond, for example, the union organized a petition that was presented to city council in their February meeting. The petition had 17,000 signatures on it. Council members were lobbied intensively, with phone campaigns targeted at those five persons who voted for privatizing the collection operation.

Similar pressure was brought against council members in Halifax. Union members warned the public about the prospect of deteriorating service with a private contractor. Once a contractor was hired, the city would be unable to bargain effectively because it had gotten out of the business. Halifax decided, in fact, to sell its collection vehicles but keep the money in a fund that can be used to purchase trucks should the city decide to get back into the business.

In both municipalities, the union used the legal system to try to prevent privatization. In Halifax, the union filed a grievance in January 1982 objecting to the seven-route plan on the grounds that it violated existing work practices. The city filed a counter grievance accusing the union of a work slowdown, hence an illegal strike. Arbitrators found for the city of Halifax and the city was awarded damages in a subsequent hearing.

In Richmond's case, the union took the district to the B.C. Supreme Court (May 1983) with a petition to invalidate the by-law authorizing contracting out. The court turned the petition down. Later that year (October 1983) an arbitration hearing denied the union's claim that contracting out violated a contract provision protecting the union against unilateral technological changes.

Summary of the Two Cases

Perhaps the most important point about these two cases, aside from the clear cost savings due to privatization, is the fact that both municipalities viewed themselves as having alternatives to own-forces provision of the service. When bargaining over productivity improvements reached an impasse with the union locals, the cities exercised the option of choosing a more efficient alternative. Having the choice, and using it if it benefits the municipal taxpayers, is really the key to capturing the benefits of privatization.

CLOSING COMMENTS

I'd like to generalize the findings I've reported thus far and then point to a couple of trends that I believe will be important in the future.

My findings are quite consistent with those reported in research cited earlier today by Robert Poole. American studies, and studies done in Europe and elsewhere overseas, consistently point to the fact that privatizing solid waste collection services saves money without sacrificing quality. In Richmond's case, for example, the contractor agreed to provide the same level of service at 40 percent less than the municipality had been charging it residents the year before.

Solid waste-related findings can be generalized to other municipal services. Robert Poole reported the findings from Barbara Steven's study in Los Angeles County. She concluded that in seven of eight services studied, privatization saves money without sacrificing quality.

Here in Canada, research in services other than solid waste collection is yet to be done, but municipal managers and elected officials are acting on their instincts and using privatization to cut costs.

Two brief examples will illustrate my point. In 1981, the town of Drayton Valley in Alberta realized that its revenues could not keep up with expanding service costs. The council, on the recommendation of the mayor, decided to cut back the number of employees but maintain the services by contracting out. Sharp cuts in staff (nearly 50 percent) were coupled with schemes to encourage employees to start their own businesses and contract with the town. Currently, Drayton Valley has a balanced budget and continues to rely heavily on contracting as a means of providing services.

In 1984, Metchosin, B.C., was incorporated in the Greater Victoria region and is one of very few municipalities in Canada that is dedicated to the objective of providing *all* services through contracts and service agreements. Currently, the municipality (population 3,500) operates with three full-time employees: a manager, a secretary and an accounting clerk. All its services are provided through contracts (public and private producers are both involved) and service agreements.

One general trend, supported by examples like Drayton Valley and Metchosin, is for municipalities to rely more on contracting out. The recession in 1982-83 had an important effect on municipal budgets and the attention paid to service costs. In Greater Vancouver, for example, two municipalities had contracted out their solid waste collection operations prior to 1981 (Delta and Surrey), but from 1981 through 1983 four other communities privatized this service. Private contractors now serve residents of West Vancouver, Richmond, North Vancouver City and Coquitlam. Collectively, private contractors now service 39 percent of the residential solid waste collection market in Greater Vancouver.

Related to this trend is one that is critical to the success of the municipal privatization enterprise as a whole. Over time, municipal officials are becoming more aware of the existence of alternatives in the provision of services to taxpayers. The prospect of municipal employees providing services (and the attendant problems of managing unions) is now being balanced against the alternative of hiring private firms to provide the service, on contract, for a specified price and with written assurances of service levels and service quality.

In effect, municipal officials are encouraging competition by being more open to alternatives. The benefits that flow from this attitude are suggested by another example from the Vancouver region. In 1982, West Vancouver's privatized residential solid waste collection costs were $44.80 per household. That figure is a substantial saving over the 1981 public collection costs of $53.34. But in 1983, Richmond contracted out its residential collection operation for $31.72 per household—a much lower figure than West Vancouver's 1982 contract price.

Why the big reduction in Richmond one year later? Service levels were the same in both municipalities. It is true that West Vancouver is more difficult to service due to its topography, but it is unlikely that that factor alone would account for the 30 percent reduction in costs.

An alternative explanation is that between 1981 (when West Vancouver negotiated its five-year contract) and 1983 when Richmond tendered its collection operation, the market had gotten much tighter in Greater Vancouver. Private firms were openly competing with each other by offering unsolicited bids to municipalities that operated with municipal crews. And municipal officials were openly using those bids as bargaining chips in productivity negotiations with their employees. Municipal officials had learned that competition is beneficial and works to their advantage as they look at alternative ways of efficiently delivering services.

The theme of competition is also involved in my final remarks. A trend that may emerge (and that I am encouraging) is to foster competition between public and private producers by setting up situations *within* municipalities where municipal crews do the same jobs as contractor crews.

I'll give you an example from the West Vancouver District. In September 1982, the district needed to hire additional staff to complete the annual fall ditch cleaning operation. The district has 30 miles of open ditches, and about 20 miles are cleaned each year on a rotating basis. Rather than hire more employees, the municipality hired a contractor to do the excess work. In effect, municipal crews and contractor crews were both doing the same work. The results were instructive. Both sets of crews finished their jobs in less time than had been true in previous years. Further, the municipality saved money by contracting part of the job out.

Since the work was comparable, officials in the Engineering Department decided to try the same scheme next year and compare costs and productivity levels. Again, total costs were lower than expected. But municipal crew productivity did not move as quickly as expected in the direction of contractor crews'. Thus, in 1984 the municipality, having experimented for two years, decided to contract the whole job out. The district continues to contract the service out to this day.

By splitting the work up, the Engineering Department was able to directly compare its crews and contractor crews. The district had also created several alternatives for itself:

- It could continue to run a mixed public/private operation, fostering competition while maintaining its own hand in the game.
- It could have reverted back to municipal crews if it had wanted to. This option gave the municipality an extra measure of security.
- It could (and ultimately did) choose to contract the whole service out.

Developing and maintaining alternatives is the key to how West Vancouver benefitted from its "experiment" with ditch cleaning. More generally, as municipal officials realize that there are alternatives in many services to having their own forces do the job, they will discover that competition is the tool that makes it possible to realize efficiency gains and make municipal budgets go further. The research results strongly suggest that when municipalities tap into the private sector where competition is the norm, they benefit substantially.

It takes political courage to tackle the "obstacles" to privatization, but increasingly, municipal managers and elected officials are realizing that the longer term benefits to taxpayers of privatizing ultimately outweigh the short-term inconveniences.

DISCUSSION

Edited by Michael A. Walker

Question: What kinds of municipalities pick which kinds of service production, and is there a pattern? What is the relationship between the different kinds of collections?

Answer: Based on my research, it turns out that the largest municipalities are least likely to contract out services like solid waste collection. For a variety of reasons, they prefer to maintain their own crews. That seems to be a pattern that exists right across Canada.

As municipalities get smaller, there's a greater tendency to rely on contracting out. Obviously, it would have been interesting to look at municipalities with under 10,000 population but that was not possible in my data collection. In terms of an informal number of anecdotes and stories and in talking to people, it appears that the use of contracts in small municipalities is actually very widespread in Canada.

Question: Does that imply that, although according to the pie-chart only 20 percent of contracts are by municipalities themselves, that might represent a very large percentage of the total population?

Answer: Yes. That's an excellent point. Even though it is 20 percent of the municipalities, if I had put up a pie-chart showing population, it would have been a very much larger section of the population that is served by public agencies alone.

Question: Were the Richmond solid waste employees laid off? Did the unions seek relief or seek to impose collective agreement provisions on the private contractors?

Answer: The answer to the first question is, yes, some employees were laid off. They had a bumping provision within their contract with the municipality which permitted solid waste collection employees to bump other employees. I believe a total of four employees were affected by the contracting out move.

There is something else that I should have added. The municipality was concerned with the lay-off situation, and basically instructed the winning bidder to interview all the employees affected by the contracting out and offer them first right of refusal to work for the contractor. It turned out that very few of the employees actually chose to go to work for the contractor. Significantly enough, one of them actually ended up being an owner-operator within the operation that served the municipality from that point on.

Regarding the second question, I'm not aware of any effort by the union to impose succession rights on the municipality. That didn't emerge in the aftermath as an issue that was decided either by arbitration or any other part of the legal process, so I'm assuming it never reached that point.

Question: You spoke of the number of incentives reported in public, private and mixed operations. Could you give some examples of the types of incentives you found?

Answer: The principal incentive, as I mentioned, is the use of a task system that involves providing an incentive for people to work faster. That incentive is used widely in the public sector, and virtually every municipal operation that's interested in productivity improvement implements one version or another. Incentives that are available in the private sector are often much more flexible and individually targeted than those in the public sector, for civil service union reasons. In the private sector you typically have productivity incentives that are based on crew productivity rather than whole operation productivity. Although I can't think of any specific examples, there are bonus systems that I'm aware of that private companies routinely use to top up the salaries of their collection crews.

Question: You've talked about solid waste. What other services have you studied, and do you show similar patterns or results?

Answer: The main one I've studied, of course, is residential solid waste collection. By way of answering the question, I'll say something about the nature of that service. It turns out that solid waste collection is similar to other municipal services that are fairly easy to count, and it's relatively easy to tell how good a job is being done. For example, when you're talking about garbage collection, you're basically talking about numbers of tons collected or number of households served. You're talking about quality, frequency of collection, consumer complaints about missed collections and so on.

Other services that are frequently privatized are ones that have similar characteristics, namely, ones for which there are agreed upon standards and ways of telling how well the job is being done. The ones that are more difficult to privatize and are much less frequently privatized are things like social services, where the way the job is done is important but it's not easy to measure how well the job is done. It takes a lot more effort to measure how well the job is done. Hence, municipal managers prefer not to contract out those services because in contracting them out you're really not shedding any of your managerial load. In fact, you're increasing it by trying to manage it at arm's length.

Question: Given the heavy union counteractions when privatization is discussed, how should a municipality initiate the change to minimize antagonism and problems?

Answer: I think municipalities have learned a great deal about relationships with their employees over the last three or four years. I've seen an evolution in my research. Initially, when privatization became important—and this was really about 1982, when a lot of municipalities were interested in it at about the same time—there was a great deal of concern about balancing budgets. There was an immediate need for some sort of fiscal cutbacks and, hence, the need to actively consider laying people off. So, at the very point in time when this new way of producing services for taxpayers was being implemented, it was also clear that it was going to have lay-off potential for municipal unions. So, municipal unions dug in their heels, assumed from that point on that contracting out or privatization would involve damaging their numbers, and resisted it very strongly.

Since that point in time, it has become much clearer that when you're dealing with municipal employees, it's a much more reasonable strategy to try to deal with them so that they're not going to be threatened by lay-offs. Instead of laying off employees, find ways of reducing the complement of municipal employees through attrition. It's a much slower process; it doesn't solve your short-term fiscal needs, but in the current fiscal environment it's much more feasible and a lot more politically palatable than lay-offs.

Question: Why did you not deal directly with the municipalities in Quebec? Surely there is no law against surveying them.

Answer: At the time, I was concerned about the acceptability of my research. Keep in mind that to my knowledge at that point in time no one had endeavoured to actually look at the issue of costs and productivity, comparing public and private production of local services on a Canada-wide basis. It was clear, even as I was doing my research, that it was going to be controversial no matter what happened. People warned me that because of the nature of my research, very few people would co-operate with me.

When I got my feedback from the ministry of Municipal Affairs in Quebec that they preferred that I didn't deal with the municipalities, it was a case where I was going to have to expend considerable resources in order to get those municipalities. In addition to that, I was going to have to deal with negative PR at the provincial level, which could have affected my response rate. I decided at the margin that I should spend my resources somewhere else.

Question: In spite of the growing spector of municipal tax revolts, many municipal governments continue to ignore privatization as a productive solution to their fiscal problems. How does one stimulate action in unresponsive municipal politicians?

Answer: I'll be quite blunt. Privatization takes political guts. If you don't have the political leadership at the municipal council level—if they're not onside and willing to stay onside—it doesn't matter if the administration is gung ho, has all the evidence, and is willing to line up all the evidence for the city council. I emphasize that point of staying onside because of the case of one municipality in Alberta. They initially decided to contract out one-quarter of their solid waste collection operation and run a five-year experiment. This would have been the first time in Canada, to my knowledge, that a municipality would have actually had an opportunity to do that. They decided to do it, and then in a last minute vote, with a couple of the people who were supporters missing, they reversed the decision and the whole thing came to nought.

People at the political level have to be willing to take a leadership role and have to be willing to take some flak. It is not going to be easy sledding. The hardest part is getting people to the point where the service is actually privatized. From then on, you can enjoy the political benefits, but it's convincing yourself that you're going to be a winner when everybody is telling you that you're costing yourself votes as long as you support this heresy that's difficult.

CHAPTER 7

PANEL DISCUSSION

Edited by Michael A. Walker

Madsen Pirie: My first observation is that it's obviously long after the time when you should be privatizing. Here we are still talking about it, years after other countries have already begun. I don't think anything has emerged which shows that Canada is uniquely different. So, if one hundred nations can privatize successfully and turn Crown corporations into profitable private enterprises and boost their economic wealth in the process, nothing has emerged to make me think Canada is any different. I think it's a learning process and, as you do it, you learn how to do it better. My advice is basically get doing it.

Michael Walker: Again, completely serendipidously, sitting next to Madsen is Ken Stein. You've been sitting here all day listening to various presentations. What conclusions do you draw for Canada? Do you agree with Madsen?

Kenneth Stein: No, clearly I don't. From the point of view of the federal government and provincial governments in Canada, I think they are doing the kinds of privatizations they want to do at a pace they feel is appropriate. I don't detect a great upswelling of populist capitalism among Canadians. Canadian share ownership is already high. Certain provinces have put in place stock participation and incentive plans that have led to more stock ownership by Canadians. The kinds of things being done at the federal or provincial level are being done on the basis of decisions as to the policy role a corporation serves. Judgements are being made on that basis.

I think Canada has been privatizing since we began 120 years ago. The first book on privatization was published by the Fraser Institute in Canada, so I don't think the rest of the world has to push us. What the British have done is quite impressive, but you don't have to run down Canada just to say that the British are impressive.

Madsen Pirie: I would like to make one point about the social role of Crown corporations, taking this issue head-on. I don't really think that running businesses through government is a very efficient way to achieve social goals. If you want to achieve social goals, it's much more efficient to buy them. A government should say, we want these goals fulfilled—transport services provided for outlying regions; airports served with a weekly service or whatever—and invite the private sector to bid to provide that service for the least subsidy. You get a much clearer picture and government can control the service quality much more accurately than by going into the whole business of running corporations and trying to do the mixed job of running them efficiently to make a profit and achieving social goals as a kind of by-product. It's a very poor and inefficient mixture.

Robert Poole: I can second that thought and point out that for the last fifteen years or so that model, unfortunately, is exactly the way municipal transit systems have been run in the United States. The whole system has been run as a welfare programme, making transit services available at about a third of what they actually cost, with the idea that it's justified to have the public sector provide transit because some people are transit dependent or poor and can't afford to own a car and therefore need the system.

Demographic studies, particularly of rail systems like the Washington Metro and San Francisco's BART, show that very significant fractions of the ridership of rail systems, particularly, are upper-middle class professionals. Yet, they're being provided with a highly subsidized service run as a welfare programme. If government is going to do those things, it would make far more sense to price it at the market price and run it on a free market basis. If it is deemed desirable to subsidize transit-dependent people, directly subsidize those people.

Neither Canada or the United States provides food to the poor by nationalizing grocery stores and making all the food available at subsidized prices because some people can't afford to pay for food at market prices. Instead, we simply subsidize those who are deemed to meet those requirements and let the market do the rest of it. Why should we provide transit or other services on a welfare basis for everyone when we certainly can run those things as market services and simply subsidize those who are deemed to be in need?

Oliver Letwin: As outsiders, in a way the most interesting point which has come out today is the difference between the way in which the two gentlemen on my right view this matter. During lunch in what was, I thought, an absolutely admirable example of a civil servant protecting every possible avenue of criticism against his minister.... Really, when I get home I will make representations for this gentleman to be employed in the British civil service—I can't think of a more perfect case of hedging one's bets. What underlies that performance at lunch time, I think, is the thesis that there ought to be some viewpoint from which you can look down on nationalized industries, judge how many of them are or are not suitable instruments of policy and how far privatization would or would not be conducive to the achievement of certain policy goals and so on.

I don't think that's the viewpoint that Madsen Pirie or I or several others would take. The reason I wouldn't take it is that I don't think it exists. I don't think there is a dispassionate position from which you can view government or nongovernment ownership and ask yourself which is the better of the options. All of the policy objectives you could achieve through government ownership you could also achieve through other means—subsidy, regulation, control of particular industries, legislation and so forth.

It seems to me that the underlying question is, do you, on the whole, trust or distrust the ability of civil servants to control companies in a way that will maximize economic efficiency? In the provision of local services or even perhaps government services in general, you can make sensible comparisons because you have large numbers of cases of both kinds—very similar, as we've been hearing here this afternoon. In the case of large trading organizations, you have no such ability. There simply aren't enough comparisons which are anything like comparable to make such judgements. So, you have to ask yourself a priori, "which do I believe is most likely to work?"

Let me give you one example, although many such examples could be adduced, which persuaded me and I think persuaded the British government originally that one ought to favour in principle non-state ownership. The example is the budgeting process for British Telecom before privatization and after it. An economist was brought into BT in the last two years for the specific purpose of doing their budgeting. At a meeting in Venice that I went to, he was giving a marvellous account of just how it looked before and how it looks now. Before, the Treasury set a thing called the external financing limit, which told how much money they could suck up each year from public and private sources and bond issues and the like. They went to ministers and argued about this amount. Once they got it, they sat down with their engineers and said, "draw us up a list of your favourite projects in order of preference, please. We will fund up to the limit of our external financing limit. When we've finished we'll go back to the Treasury and ask for some more. If we don't succeed, we'll try again next year." That was how it was before.

Now, they look at the net present value of each investment. They look at the internal rate of return of each investment. They try to judge whether the internal rate of return is or is not justified in terms of the weighted average cost of capital to the company, in other words whether shareholder value is ultimately being increased or decreased by a specific investment.

Two utterly different attitudes to investment in an industry where investment is 80 percent of the determinant value—almost inevitably different, because you couldn't ask the same kinds of questions in a public corporation with any meaning. Having asked, you'd still be subject to the external financing limit set by the Treasury. You couldn't conduct a budgeting process in the private sector the way you can in the public sector, because your shareholders would sooner or later desert you, your stock price would fall, and you couldn't raise any capital.

That kind of example can never be conclusive—you can't prove, ultimately, that BT is a better company as a result— nevertheless, it persuades many of us that the initial preference is towards being in favour of privatization. I think that initial preference for that kind of reason is missing in Ottawa at the moment, and for what it's worth, my guess is that until it's present, no amount of analysis will actually lead to any action. I think the restrictions on the provincial governments are quite different in Canada, and I expect that your provinces are going to be way ahead of your federal government in this respect for many years to come.

Kenneth Stein: I guess I should make one simple response to all that. I don't see the objectives of Crown corporations as necessarily being social objectives. How a particular society wants to run things is a matter of choice. For example, Alberta has a provincially-owned telephone system and Bell Telephone serves Ontario. To tell the people of Ontario or Alberta that they have a better or worse telephone system is not really the point. Alberta has chosen to manage it in a certain way, and Ontario in another way. It's hard for anyone to say that you get a worse or better kind of service in those two provinces. The social objectives for telephone service are probably much the same in both provinces.

Usually, when Crown corporations live beyond their time, it is because they go beyond the monopoly situation into a competitive situation. Then I think it's clear that they should be in the private sector and on that basis they should go. I think that is a general thrust of the government. The key is deciding when you feel comfortable with that kind of situation.

QUESTIONS FROM THE FLOOR

Michael Walker: Ken, there are quite a number of questions here for you. There is one which is kind of impertinent, in a way, but given what has been said today about the process of privatization it may be relevant. You may pass it up, but if you care to answer it, I think it would be interesting. It says: "You work for the ministry of privatization, but you don't seem to be much of an enthusiast. Shouldn't you resign?"

I'm sure Ken realizes that it is partly tongue-in-cheek. But it raises an interesting question about the role of public servants in the privatization process, and I hope others who have been public servants will comment after you've had your shot at it.

Kenneth Stein: I'm sorry if I come across sounding not very enthusiastic about it. I think the government is quite enthusiastic about privatization. Perhaps as a bureaucrat one doesn't charge up with enthusiasm. I think the government and the Prime Minister would be a little bit surprised. They feel that over the last two years, through a lot of difficulties, they've moved on certain problem areas. I think we are at a crucial point in terms of deciding what to do next.

A list was put up on one of the slides today, and Canada wasn't on the list of $200 billion worth of sales to be made. The American share was about $4 billion. With what we have on our list now, Canada could do that in the next year. Everybody here is saying, do it. As officials, we've done the planning. It's for ministers to decide how to proceed now. I don't feel in any different situation than a lawyer providing advice to a client in these circumstances. It's for the client, whose feet are going to be to the grill as to the success of the programme, to make the fundamental decisions, and I recognize that.

Oliver Letwin: I absolutely agree with that. I don't think it's the role of civil servants anywhere to determine what policy ought to be. It's a temptation which every civil servant must have because you're asking intelligent people, otherwise, to not have an opinion, which is a difficult thing for them to do. A good civil servant tries to resist that. In the end, politicians should never blame civil servants, because they always have the option to move them or to change their own minds. If it's not happening and it ought to be happening—which, as an outsider, it's not for me to say—then it's the politicians that are to blame and not the civil servants. I think people ought to be very clear about that. It's a nasty thing for politicians to claim that it's not on their own shoulders. If you have the political will, in the end you can do it.

Question: Why are you the only one doing significant research in the area of privatization of municipal services?

James McDavid: I'm not sure. Certainly, I don't have a monopoly in this area. I've corresponded with people across Canada who are ostensibly interested in privatization, and they always ask me for my data or my results and that's about as far as it goes. I'm waiting for someone to either branch out into other services or corroborate the research I've done, but it hasn't happened to this point in time. I presume that it's a matter of time, and if there really is interest, at least in the academic community, there will be some additional people doing the research. It may well be that there isn't a great deal of enthusiasm for privatization in the academic community even though there is growing enthusiasm for privatization among the people who are actually involved in producing and providing services. That may be more a reflection on my colleagues than it is upon the state of privatization in Canada.

Question: Ken Stein's list of priorities on which to base a privatization programme started off with "the need to consider federal and provincial policies." Surely the reasons should start off with the need to assess "the benefit to the taxpayer."

Kenneth Stein: Yes, that's part of that. It goes without saying that the benefit to the taxpayer is the ultimate measurement. Mrs. McDougall has said that time and time again. She's looking at a fair deal for the taxpayer, and she is looking for improvements in the services Crown corporations provide.

James McDavid: I wonder if I might just make a comment on that. We can all piously say that the bottom line is to serve the taxpayer, but at least in local government in Canada I know that this individual we refer to as the taxpayer is very often the last individual who is taken into account in the process because that individual is not organized. He or she does not have representatives who are financially and organizationally capable of standing up and repeatedly intervening in any kind of policy-making process. Although we all claim to be on the side of the taxpayer, I think it is realistic to say that unless the taxpayer does something like what was done in California in 1978, the taxpayers' interests are going to be no more representative than a lot of other anonymous players in the game.

Question: What percent of the population held shares in the United Kingdom in 1979? What percentage holds shares now?

Madsen Pirie: It depends whose measure you follow. If you look at the figures for last year, which pre-date the privatization of British Airways, Rolls Royce, and British Airports Authority, 3.5 million individuals held shares in 1979 and slightly over 8 million individuals held shares in 1986.

Oliver Letwin: I think an important point to add relates to the future rather than the past. A very large number—no one is quite sure what percentage, but it may well be over 75 percent—of the new shareholders entering the market hold one or two or at most three stocks. A quite surprisingly large number—again, uncertain, but perhaps over 50 percent—hold just one. Those are people who come into the market because of privatization and have retained all or some of what they bought. There is going to come a time when the present bull market turns into a bear market, and those shares are going to get less valuable rather than more valuable. I know you've had your own experiences in British Columbia with BCRIC, and the experience was particularly vivid because shares of BCRIC dropped so fast—like a brick, one might say. But it will happen in the U.K., too, and in France and other places where there are millions of shareholders.

A very interesting and open question is what will happen as a result? What kind of market volatility are we going to experience when there are four or five million shareholders, perhaps by then 10 or 15 million, each holding just one or two stocks trying to climb out of their stocks very rapidly? What's going to happen politically when they see the shares dropping, particularly if the same government is still in power that sold them to them? Those are open questions that have yet to be settled.

For myself, I actually believe that in the long run it will be constructive rather than destructive. I think there's a grave danger of people believing that shares are a kind of magic: you invest in them and produce profits without thinking about it. They have risks as well as rewards attached, and it's about time that ordinary people—may of whom are employees in large corporations—realize that when the economy as a whole performs badly there are attendant risks for a group of people who are not anonymous or unimportant but are themselves, namely, shareholders. So, I think it could be extremely painful in the short term, and perhaps extremely constructive in the long term. Whether we get over the potential short-term pain remains to be seen.

Question: Actually, I have to ask the question again, because I'm not sure we got an answer. What percentage of the population holds shares in the U.K. in 1987?

Oliver Letwin: Roughly speaking, a twentieth of the population held shares in 1979. Roughly speaking, a fifth or a sixth now hold shares.

Madsen Pirie: That's counting children as well. That's the whole population.

Question: The other part of the question is to Ken Stein. What percentage of the populace held shares in Canada in 1979 and now?

Kenneth Stein: People from the audience can correct me—it varies quite extensively, of course, by region—but it is felt that the investing public is close to 20 percent. The structure may be a bit different from other countries. You may not agree with this, but the savings rate in Canada is quite high. The number of people who have savings in mutual funds or registered retirement savings plans or the Quebec Stock Savings Plan, et cetera, is quite extensive. If you have people investing in mutual funds, do you count that as being a stockholder? If you do, you can drive the percentage up quite a bit. Generally, I think the standard is 20 percent of Canadian individuals.

Madsen Pirie: You get a higher figure in Britain then, obviously, comparing like with like.

Kenneth Stein: It varies by exchange and by survey.

Madsen Pirie: It's not just shares in Britain. Do remember privatization of the state houses. The proportion of people who own their own houses in Britain has gone from 48 percent in 1979 to two out of three today. It's the privatization programme that's been responsible for a very large proportion of that increase. So, it's not just people investing in stocks and shares; it's people investing in property as well.

Oliver Letwin: This is an extremely interesting point. Is it really true that roughly 20 to 25 percent of Canadian adults hold shares?

Kenneth Stein: Yes, including mutual funds.

Oliver Letwin: Then the opportunities for an immediate, wide distribution share offering here, I think John would agree with me, are immense compared to what they were in England.

Kenneth Stein: I think that's what every investment dealer I've ever met says.

Madsen Pirie: We had to start by teaching people what stocks and shares were.

Kenneth Stein: I should just make one thing clear though, share ownership in Canada is regionally quite disparate. With the Fishery Products International offering, I think we must have increased the number of people who owned shares in the province of Newfoundland by a significant amount. In Toronto there is a higher percentage. A significantly lower percentage of people owned shares in Quebec, but I understand that has doubled or tripled in the last three or four years with the Quebec Stock Savings Plan. (The latest survey is that carried out by the Toronto Stock Exchange, published in December 1986.)

Question: Please explain recent developments in the United States in which antitrust legislation may be used to spur privatization.

Robert Poole: In 1983 in a case involving a cable television franchise, the U.S. Supreme Court ruled that municipal governments are not automatically exempt from the application of antitrust laws, which meant that granting a legal monopoly was potentially actionable as a restraint of trade. That led to quite a furore and a number of lawsuits in cases involving things like ambulance service and garbage pick-up where exclusive franchises or the municipality's own directly provided service as a monopoly had been the norm for many, many years.

The National League of Cities went to Congress very quickly to try to get that situation changed. If I recall correctly, their initial attempt, which was to have a federal law passed that would nullify that Supreme Court interpretation and explicitly exempt cities from any application of the antitrust laws, failed. What they did get through was a provision that says, in the event that a city is sued under antitrust laws for such types of monopolistic activities, the normal antitrust provision for treble damages does not apply. The city would only have to pay ordinary damages. That provision did pass. That has significantly reduced the incentive of parties to file antitrust challenges to city-type monopolies, so there have not been a great number of those suits pursued since that time. But it is a potential lever to use in opening up tight situations.

Taxi-cab licensing ordinances that strictly limit and restrict the number of cabs or the number of cab companies which can be franchised, which are very common in American cities, can be acted against. Exclusive municipal monopoly and provision of servicing and so forth can be acted against. In fact, during the last five or six years the Federal Trade Commission, which is another federal regulatory agency, has been in the hands of relatively free market-oriented directors. It has actually gone to court against some city governments, charging that their taxi licencing is an antitrust violation and attempting to open up those markets. Usually, those cases have been settled out of court with the cities agreeing to at least loosen up their regulations and allow new firms to enter.

Question: Is this an option in Canada?

James McDavid: I don't know if it's an option in Canada. I don't know of any legal cases that would even compare to the kind of situation Bob is talking about. I'm aware of situations where taxi-cab restrictions have been challenged by private companies but have not been challenged on the basis of a violation of antitrust laws. They have been challenged on different grounds. There was a case in Victoria, for example, where a company wanted to break into the taxi-cab business and didn't have the proper licencing. Nevertheless, it proceeded to run taxi-cabs and was eventually prosecuted by the municipality for breaking the regulations. The case was essentially decided in favour of the municipality on the understanding that the company concerned could in fact obtain a licence if it applied at some point in the future.

Herbert Grubel: Mr. Stein mentioned a first criterion by which desirability of privatization should be assessed: that is, is it consistent with national and regional policy objectives. Mr. Letwin took this to mean social policy interests. I think what is missing here is actually the motivation that I would call the public policy choice interest. In fact, the consistent policy concern of politicians is asking whether or not it will get them re-elected. This is not necessarily the same as some social objective, as Mr. Letwin interpreted it.

I would like to make one other brief point concerning the question of competition. Again, Mr. Letwin raised it; the other speakers did not mention it. I'm worried about the fact that once the now privatized firms, their workers and their management begin to realize they are sitting on a monopoly, they will eventually use this monopoly position to pay themselves very nice salaries and get slack in their management policies, knowing full well that even if they make losses the government is not ever going to let them fail. They will be bailed out again and will eventually become renationalized. This is exactly what happened in Yugoslavia.

The workers' councils were supposed to end the conflict between labour and management because the workers own the firm. How many of them are holding one share? How much is it worth to them? One hundred pounds, fifty pounds? Relative to what they can get over the rest of their lifetime in higher earnings, they don't care if their share becomes worthless. This is not a matter of conjecture, the Yugoslavians have not avoided the problems of state involvement with worker ownership. You must try to combine the privatization with some way of ensuring that there is viable competition.

One last quick point in relation to what you call semi-privatization in New Zealand. I'm worried about this because there is no way in which the threat of a takeover by a private firm or others presents an incentive for the management to be efficient. That's exactly what ails BCRIC. They ensured that BCRIC could never be taken over by anybody. Therefore, the managers remained subject to political influence and never had the incentives to become efficient.

Oliver Letwin: I'll take your point about monopolies first. Four things go against what you're saying, though fundamentally I agree that monopolies are less satisfactory by far than some form of competitive arrangement.

The first qualification is that almost no monopoly, even though it may be a natural monopoly within its own sphere, is entirely monopolistic from the point of its financial performance. For example, British Gas, which is as near a natural monopoly in its distribution system as you can get, competes—over the very long term, admittedly—aggressively against electricity for almost all its activities. So, it's by no means the case that the management can just absolutely go to sleep without affecting their own pay packets in the long run.

Secondly, the chance for management to go to sleep decreases as the stiffness of regulation increases. The drive for economic efficiency—not service efficiency but economic efficiency—through the "X" component of the "RPI-X" formula is pretty stiff. I admit that it's not as tough as in the case of fullblooded competition, but it's much tougher, for instance, than the kind of competition which IBM faces. So, it's by no means a negligible tool.

The scale of shareholding of the minor employees may only be one hundred pounds, but the scale of shareholding of the senior executives in some cases is now beginning to make their salaries look pretty paultry. So, you shouldn't under-rate their interest in the long-term financial performance of the company.

The final point about these monopolies is that there can well be two or three stages to this process. It may well be that in England ten years from now we won't be talking so much about privatization, which may still be continuing but will be taken for granted, but rather about the need to introduce tough anti-monopoly legislation and determine Sherman Antitrust Acts and things like them which we don't have at the moment. So, it may well be that this is a two-stage process at least.

On your public policy choice point, I agree with you. When ministers talk about public policy considerations dictating whether they do or don't do something they are in the end democrats, and the overriding consideration for that in their minds is whether or not the thing will be popular in the long run. Political courage doesn't consist in doing things which will never make you popular, but rather in doing things that will make you popular not tomorrow but the day after because people will come to see the benefits. That's the kind of courage politicians require to engage in privatization. It's difficult before you've done it. Once you've done it, it can prove extremely popular.

Regarding management efficiency in New Zealand, I agree with you. There are dangers if you don't have the capacity to be taken over. Incidentally, that doesn't just apply to partial privatization; it applies to almost every major privatization in the world at the moment. The formula that provides for the special share or the golden share, or whatever you call it, in effect prevents takeover. It enables government to exercise a veto against anyone who is agglomerating too great a concentration of shares. Yes, there is a danger that maximum efficiency will not be subjected to Jerry Goldsmith or Lord Hanson taking it over.

With large scale public utilities, I'm not sure that takeover was ever a feasible option in any case. So, I'm not sure that the New Zealand partial privatization is in either respect particularly worse than normal privatization. What is needed in New Zealand is a two- or three-stage process, where increased competition is introduced later on. That competitive pressure rather than the pressure of potential takeover is what I think will keep those firms efficient in the very long run. In the meanwhile, just having to live in the private sector is, I assure you, already doing wonders for the way in which those managements go about deciding things.

Both John and I have had some experience dealing with managements in New Zealand, and it's quite impressive how the mere exercise of valuing the company for the purchase and sale agreement and then having to live in the private sector has transformed their attitudes. You're talking about keeping that transformation going over twenty or thirty years, and I agree that may need more medicine yet.

John Williams: I agree with everything Oliver just said. It's quite interesting to try to relate what you have said with my experience with BT and the other big privatizations and the change you saw in the management style and approach as they got near privatization. The last thing they'd want would be to ever get anywhere back near the state sector; that's anathema to them. It had a galvanizing effect throughout BT certainly, and I'm sure it will with British Gas as well.

Madsen Pirie: Sometimes you have to privatize a monopoly if you're going to get it privatized at all. But once it is in the private sector, its monopoly is vulnerable. It is not sustained by the legislative process. It's vulnerable to technological innovative and to alternative types of service. When the threats do come at a later stage, the legislative clout which kept its monopoly as a public corporation is gone.

Robert Poole: I wanted to raise a critical point about the conflict on the part of governments such as the Thatcher government when it comes to privatizing monopolies such as British Gas and British Telecom. The net asset value—the value as a going concern of selling it as a monopoly—is going to be a lot higher in the short term, at least, than selling it as a competing firm suddenly opened up to competition. So, there's tension between the goal of raising the maximum amount of money from the privatization and using that for cutting other government expenditures—cutting the rate of income tax and so forth—versus the goal of accomplishing the best for the interests of consumers. These are very difficult public policy choices.

In a study the Reason Foundation just finished on privatizing the U.S. Postal Service, we did a balance sheet assessment and concluded about a $10 billion net worth for the U.S. Postal Service as a monopoly. Then we tried to estimate the value—if you simultaneously deregulate and open up the market to competition at the time that you privatize. Our first cut best estimate is that that value might be cut in half to $5 billion. So, you have a real dilemma between competing goals of serving the public better as consumers versus getting the maximum dollars for it as a monopoly.

Oliver Letwin: That's absolutely right, and we have yet to see which way the government will come down on that in the case of electricity. I don't think the contrast need be as stark as half if the thing is skillfully designed and the right bits are open to competition, but it's inevitably going to shave 10 or 20 percent off the value.

Question: From what sources do you see opposition arising to privatization, and what steps do you suggest to diffuse such opposition?

Kenneth Stein: I think the opposition varies for each particular Crown corporation. How people feel about privatization relates more to the policy area involved. Therefore, in the example of the privatizations of the fisheries companies—Fishery Products and National Sea—I couldn't see any opposition at all. It was pretty much a set thing. When Parliament passed the Fisheries Restructuring Act in 1983, it was unanimously supported by all three parties.

On the other hand, in the area of transportation, Mr. Ouellet, the opposition transport critic said in the House of Commons on June 17, "The battle the Minister had to fight to get Bill C-18 through is nothing compared to what he should expect if he ever tries to privatize Air Canada. We are going to oppose such an initiative systematically and relentlessly, because we think that public interest dictates that we keep this Crown corporation." Mr. Turner, the leader of the Liberal Party, has said he is opposed to the privatization of Air Canada, so there is probably some modicum of an indication that there will be a bit of a battle.

The difficulty on Petro-Canada will probably be that that oil company was created about 15 years ago, during a minority government, and was very much part of the New Democratic Party's energy policy. Therefore, the New Democratic Party would probably take a very strong view on the Petro-Canada privatization.

Generally, you see opposition in particular policy areas rather than in an overall sense. I haven't heard many Canadians say that they're opposed to the concept of privatization in total.

Question: To what extent are public sector managers trained and educated to prepare, manage and evaluate contracts? If not, what needs to be done?

James McDavid: To this point in time there's been very little systematic training in managing, writing, monitoring and evaluating contracts. A lot of the "training" that goes on is essentially learned by example. That's not necessarily a bad way to do it. It turns out that municipalities learn a great deal from each other. In greater Vancouver, for example, once a couple of municipalities paved the way regarding the wording and structure of garbage contracts, the contracts were virtually copied by subsequent municipalities in their dealings with contractors. Since nobody has had any problems with the contracts, it appears to have been a pretty good move. Municipalities do that kind of thing with respect to by-laws and a lot of other things.

That doesn't mean training isn't important, but to my knowledge that is something that's going to be down the road a long ways yet in Canada.

Question: The University of Victoria's School of Public Administration is one of the finest schools of its kind in the country. Do you have a programme or a course which trains public administrators in how to do these things, or is privatization even mentioned in the courses they are getting their diplomas or their degrees in?

James McDavid: Several of us have an active interest in privatization. We offer workshops from time to time to people who are interested, and we will continue to do that in the future.

Question: But it's not a part of the curriculum?

James McDavid: It's not a regular part of the curriculum except that it gets into the courses that several of us teach.

Question: How does the Labour Party in the U.K. deal with the success of the privatization programme?

John Williams: I think the Labour Party's position on privatizations has shifted from the classic nationalization/privatization confrontation that there used to be. During the last election, the Labour Party talked about social ownership rather than renationalization of the privatized corporations. It's not quite clear what they meant by that but some kind of continued participation by people in privatized companies, maybe some kind of non-voting equity. But the kind of "we are against privatization" stance that characterized their position has now been modified. I think they have come to accept the inevitability of the benefits of privatization.

Oliver Letwin: Just to put a gloss on that, the Labour Party is tearing itself limb from limb at the moment. In my recent election campaign I fought the first female, black, Trotsky-ite candidate. Quite seriously, the far left of the Labour Party has gone. They are now trying to explain that Mr. Kinnock has completely betrayed the principles of socialism, by which they mean Marxism, by going in with social ownership. They're trying to bring it back to clause 4 of the Labour Party Constitution, which still exists, and which suggests that they would take into public ownership the commanding heights of the economy. The other wing of the Labour Party is explaining that they're never going to win another election unless they give up any idea of removing these shares altogether. So, there's an interesting political battle going on there, and the longer it goes on the happier Conservative politicians are going to be.

Question: What about the council houses?

Oliver Letwin: The Labour Party has given up on Council houses completely. That policy is so popular and so widespread in its popularity that they've simply agreed that they'll go on privatizing council houses. Incidentally, they have not opposed the new policy for the creation of tenant co-operatives, which I think is going to make the council house sale policy look small. I bet, here and now, that there will be something like 3 million more sales of dwellings—when I say sales, I mean transfers of dwellings to tenant co-operatives—over the next four to five years. I think that's going to become a major plank of Labour Party policy pretty rapidly.

Question: How were people in the U.K. chosen to provide advice on privatization? Were they chosen on a tender or bid system?

Oliver Letwin: Yes, very much so indeed. It's called a beauty parade system. It involves a very large amount of expenditure of time and effort on the part of investment banks, and we resent it extremely. But it's the right way to go about it, there's no doubt. The presentations are now extremely professional printed documents. People spend a lot of time working out most of what they would do if they were actually doing the job beforehand and then go along and get grilled by civil servants who are now pretty expert in this. Then there's a fee-bargaining session, which makes buying a horse from a gypsy look like an easy ride. The whole process is extremely active and effective. I'm afraid to say that other countries are starting to take this up. Going into the act now is like having an exam when you've been a recalcitrant schoolboy and failed three times already. You tend to get asked questions like: "The mistakes you've made have been horrendous; what would you do to correct them in this instance?" It leaves you somewhat gasping.

However, there are countries that haven't yet designed such elaborate systems, and I'm entirely in favour of that. We have to hope that there will be more of those in less well-developed countries as time goes on. I'm surprised, however, that in a country as sophisticated as Canada there wasn't, so far as I know, an international appeal for advisers through a tender system. We'd be happy to tender, as I'm sure John would, at the next available opportunity.

John Williams: Let me tell you something about the U.K. system. It's very fair and competitive, and the emphasis is on it being seen to be fair—but the same old banks get appointed.

Oliver Letwin: The truth is that there are about four or five expert banks, and it's extremely difficult to guess which one of those will actually do it better than the others. I'm going to have to admit that. But there is a clear group of people now who really have very wide experience. By coincidence you actually have the two leading banks present. Between John's organization and ours, we account for more than half, perhaps almost two-thirds, of the total bulk of what's been privatized in the U.K.

Question: This is actually titled "an unfair question." Why didn't the Canadian government go to tender and/or a bid system to "hire" some organization to look at the question of privatization and provide advice to government on the issue?

Kenneth Stein: We haven't actually gone through an underwriting process. The only underwriting we've done is on FPI, and we left that to the board of FPI in discussion with others. The board of Fishery Products went through the beauty show, as my minister hates to hear it called, in terms of selecting an underwriter. They selected a group of four Canadian underwriters.

For our planning process we established a bidding system in February. We called in about fifteen investment houses—both Canadian and non-Canadian but with operations in Canada—to give us advice on three privatizations: Air Canada, Petro-Canada and Radio-Chemical Corporation of Canada. For Air Canada we selected Dominion Securities, Levesque Beaubien, and First Boston Corporation. Air Canada selected Wood Gundy and Morgan Stanley as their advisers. On Petro-Canada we had McLeod Young and Weir and Pemberton, and on Radio-Chemical we selected Merrill Lynch. We still have a list of others. The CDIC used a competitive bidding system for advice on National Sea Products. So, we are running an open bidding system for financial advisers.

PART TWO

INSTITUTIONAL AND POLITICAL ASPECTS OF PRIVATIZATION

THOMAS KIERANS

(Introduction by Michael A. Walker)

Our second speaker this morning is a very distinguished Canadian and a person who has had careers in many areas of public life. Tom Kierans was educated at McGill University and at the University of Chicago where he studied finance, economics and political science. He has been vice-president and director of Nesbitt Thomson and Company, senior vice-president of Pitfield Mackay Ross and also is currently president, director and a member of the executive committee of McLeod Young Weir Ltd. He has been an adviser on financing and aspects of management to the World Bank, the Premier of Ontario, the Prime Minister and the Government of Canada and to many other governments and corporations. In addition, he also has been an academic and is the past chairman of the Ontario Economic Council. Currently, he is director and chairman of the Investment Committee of the Institute for Research on Public Policy and is a member of the editorial committee of the IRPPs journal, *Options*. He is also an advisory committee member of the Howe Research Institute.

CHAPTER 8

FEDERAL GOVERNMENT POLICY ISSUES AND CURRENT PRIVATIZATION INITIATIVES

Thomas Kierans

OBSERVATIONS ON SOME POLICY ISSUES

I have a bit of a pot-pourri, but I thought I would begin by discussing some policy issues and then relate some anecdotes around immediate past and current privatization initiatives at the federal level.

In terms of some ruminations on the thoughts I heard yesterday, I found quite a contrast, of course, between Madsen Pirie and Ken Stein. On the one hand I hear our British friends saying that we Canadians are long overdue—privatization is a good thing, a proven commodity, get on with it. On the other hand I heard Ken saying that this is pretty much business as usual for us. We did this under C.D. Howe, and we're going to do it again as required—adopting an examination of commercial Crowns where they're redundant, making sure they don't get in the way of various policy sets.

In my humble view, I don't think either of those views correctly encapsulates the true approximation of reality that exists in Canada. When examining the issue of privatization in economic terms, I think it is important to remember that the concept is to strengthen the market at the expense of the state. So, in that context, let's call a spade a spade. Privatization is a relatively minor economic policy subcomponent of a much larger policy set.

Making the Market Work

To put it into context and to indicate some of the larger policy sets associated with making the market work, I would note that this government took the initiative in terms of bilateral trade relationships with the United States. If successful, that initiative would eclipse any number of privatization policies in terms of having a priority on making the market work at the expense of the state. I would point out that this government dismantled the National Energy Programme, which was without question one of the most pervasive intrusions into the private sector that we've ever seen in this country. The government is committed to a market-oriented hydrocarbons policy.

I would also comment that when the government unloaded de Havilland and Canadair it was doing much more than examining its portfolio of commercial Crowns for redundancies. It was much more explicitly renouncing the previous government's industrial interventionist policy stance to ensure a Canadian presence in either the so-called commanding heights or the so-called infant-industry groupings. That was a major "let's make the market work" policy initiative itself.

Further, I would observe that if anyone had paid any attention to capital and portfolio flows into this country and related it to the dismantling of FIRA—itself one of the great barriers to making the market work—one would have come to the conclusion that the overall policy set is alive and well. Under the previous restrictive environment four or five years ago, it would have been inconceivable that Amoco would be bidding for Dome or that British Industries would be taking out Maple Leaf Mills.

Finally, while the Air Canada decision is not yet taken, substantial progress has been made in terms of getting the sectoral policy framework for the privatization of Air Canada right. Substantial progress has been made toward the deregulation of air transportation and the improvement of competition in that industry. Obviously, if privatization is to strengthen the market at the expense of the state one has to get the sectoral policy objectives in place correctly or you might wind up doing something as unheard of as privatizing a monopoly into private hands.

Dealing within a Federal State

Also on the subject of privatization but away from policy, I would point out that the act of privatization itself is a very narrow, specific, political effort which impinges—unlike broader policy sets—on specific consumers and specific labour unions and specific groups of people and specific regions of the country. Those specific interest groups can mobilize an awful lot of support. The delicacy of approaching that kind of thing is compounded in Canada by the fact that, unlike the United Kingdom, we're not a unitary state. We have constitutionally empowered voices from coast to coast which can authoritatively be raised to block such initiatives.

It's obvious that any first term government is going to approach this issue very gingerly, but so, of course, did the United Kingdom. One could certainly applaud Mrs. Thatcher's determination in her second term while respecting very much her care and her need to understand the full extent of the complex issue that she undertook in her first term.

Canada Differs from the United Kingdom

I'm appreciative of others' solicitousness about what we're doing here, but I think in turn they have to appreciate two things. The situation here is quite different from that of the United Kingdom. Canadians own their own homes; we don't have to turn that clock back. Direct individual participation in the equity capital markets of Canada is incomparably greater than is the case in the United Kingdom, so I would not expect that we would have our Queen appearing on paid television announcements flogging the Canadian equivalent of British Telecom. I don't think our securities commissioners are going to quite go for that.

Finally, I would observe that by the end of this government's first term, if one cumulatively looks at provincial initiatives which will have been put in place, it will have shown a fair measure of progress. I'm thinking about Cambior in the province of Quebec, UTDC in Ontario, Sask Oil and other developments in Saskatchewan, and then load on top of that Fishery Products for the feds and Teleglobe and others which I think are going to come. The government's heart is very much in the right place.

A Privatization Policy

I'm not suggesting that the federal government has a coherent privatization policy. It's still pretty ad hoc. I always feel badly when public servants have to appear in situations like this, taking the place of the Minister. Ken Stein understands the issues thoroughly, but it's not his job to acknowledge any incompleteness of federal policy nor our place to say to him what we might say to a minister or the Prime Minister.

We have to concede that if they don't have this subcomponent of the policy sector quite right yet, they do have the process right, now at long last. The wheeler dealing, the stumbling, the outright chaos of the early years has been replaced by an orderly, co-ordinated and duly considered process. That, in and of itself, will provide initiatives and achievements.

Municipal Privatization of Services

Just one final intervention. I certainly want to congratulate the Fraser Institute and Michael Walker for an emphasis which I haven't seen at conferences before—I've been at a lot of them on this issue and contributed to the literature—and that's the whole issue of municipal privatization of services. Having gone through the audience, I can see that there's a great deal of interest in that. That's highly desirable because at this time, of course, we are living beyond our means as are the Americans and lots of other people. At some point, the federal government is going to download a large part of the expenditure problem onto the provinces, who in turn will offload it in part onto the municipalities. Since the municipalities are not in a position to print money on the one hand and certainly don't have the borrowing capacities of the provincial governments on the other, that's going to be one of the early areas where the rubber is really going to meet the road. It's heartening to see research being done on the efficiencies and savings that can be affected there. I think those sessions yesterday were among the most interesting that I've attended.

SOME CANADIAN PRIVATIZATIONS

At this point I'm going to doff the policy hat—I wasn't invited here for that anyway—and don my practitioner's hat to discuss five or six deals, anecdotally. Specifically, I have in mind discussing some of the practical aspects of privatizing Fishery Products, National Sea, Petro-Canada, Air Canada and Radio-Chemical where individual investors and the capital markets are involved. This is going to very much be a "gently on my mind" discussion, because some of the issues I'm going to raise are reasonably disputable among reasonable people. Some of them are very thorny.

Fishery Products

I'll begin with Fishery Products, which may not be all that well known out here. Going back a few years, basically for social policy reasons, the federal government nationalized the bulk of the Atlantic fishery. In a nutshell, through bad management and fragmentation of the industry and very bad labour relations, the Atlantic fishery had over-extended itself. The whole industry was essentially bankrupt. There were two components to that nationalization. For simplicity's sake I'll say that half the industry was based in Newfoundland and the other half was more or less based in Nova Scotia.

Fishery Products had been totally nationalized by the federal government. It had a very peculiar setup. Unlike other privatizations I will be discussing this morning, the board of directors of Fishery Products was formed by the federal government but selected only from the private sector—a very esteemed group of private sector businessmen—and had the specific responsibility for privatizing this company. So, it's not exactly a perfect model for some of the other things we will be talking about because in those cases the federal government may have the mandate. In this case the board had the mandate, and it made some differences.

In terms of privatizing this company, the capital structure was restored to the company through infusions of federal and provincial equity contributions. Further, management was able—and I'll come back to this—to restore a measure of labour stability. Finally, with the removal of the interest burden on the one hand, with the application of more intelligent management on the other, and the recovery of the industry itself, it became possible to anticipate privatizing this entity sooner rather than later.

There are a number of objectives that the board and management wished to put in place. First among those was an objective that doesn't really meet strict economic criteria. The board and management were of the view that this was an indigenous Newfoundland business. If it was to be managed as a division of Canada Packers out of Toronto or Labatt's out of London or whatever the case might be, inevitably the measures taken to restore a sense of economic stability to the enterprise would go down the drain. Right off it was established that this company could not be taken over. That was done by implementing, through an act of the Newfoundland legislature, a 15 percent limit on the holding of any one person. There are a number of interesting aspects to that because no differential voting shares were contained in the capital structure, so corporate democracy could still prevail. If management is bad, there is nothing to stop individual and institutional holders from getting together in a proxy situation and tossing management out. But it did preclude either a foreign or a mainland corporation from controlling this company and moving the management of it away from the island.

There were other factors set out to be achieved in this offering which were relatively unique. First and foremost, while the capital markets of Canada may be very sophisticated and very broad indeed from an individual participation point of view, in fact, few Newfoundlanders and only a very small elite actually owned common shares. The government wanted to have a "Newfoundland first" option in the offering so Newfoundlanders would be able to participate in what essentially was an indigenous enterprise. In addition to that, the company implemented a very powerful profit-sharing programme as well as an employee share-ownership programme as part of its improved relations with labour.

Prior to the privatization of the company, employees were offered, received and took up shares.

The company and its board of directors was very keen that there be no ongoing influence from government. So, to all intents and purposes, the entire government interest was put on the block at the same time. This led to an offering of approximately $150 million which, for a small company and a hitherto unknown industry, turned out to be quite large.

Another factor had to do with the pricing aspects of the situation. A series of angles of perception might have been adopted here. For example, the federal government was negotiating the sale, and I have no doubt that the federal government could have gotten a better price for its shares had it negotiated the sale of the shares through a specific trade or industry single purchaser. That was a policy that was eschewed by both the federal and Newfoundland governments. The second pricing consideration came down to the fact that this was a new company by any measure. It was an untested, unknown entity in a highly cyclical business. So the governments and the board of directors were determined not to fully price the issue.

The issue was priced at $12.50 a share. It could easily have cleared at $13.50 to $14 a share, and all parties knew that at the time. Subsequently, those observations proved out when the shares opened and were recycled in the $14 range. As you may have heard, they are now $19, but that was a long time after. A lot of other factors have intruded since then.

Other factors were of interest. There was a desire to set up a kind of testing mechanism whereby Canadian institutions and retail investors who didn't know very much about this industry might not in effect hold us hostage to get the lowest possible price. As a consequence, we had an extensive road show offering in the United Kingdom and on the continent. Europeans are extremely knowledgeable about the industry and follow it with a great deal of interest. We couldn't go to the United States, quite simply because we couldn't get through the SEC because of their inability to bend on filing requirements pertaining to a company that had been reorganized and had no history and which absolutely required forecasts to be incorporated in the prospectus. We would have had a very good reception in Boston and New England had we been able to file there.

Overall, it was a spectacularly successful offering. I think I agree with Ken Stein that the orderliness of the process has been much superior. I think the Fishery Products deal got privatization off in a fairly intelligent and positive way, which will have a good bearing on future issues.

National Sea

A second issue which the federal government is looking at, to which I am not privy, is the disposition of the remaining minority interest in National Sea. That was the Halifax side of the restructuring of the Atlantic fishery. There wasn't complete nationalization there. A couple of families in the private sector in Nova Scotia exerted influence and retained a private sector influence in that company. Also, the company has a small market for its shares. At this point in time, the government is a distinct minority shareholder. The families to which I have alluded are the controlling shareholders. The government is looking at disposing of the remainder of its position. In the aftermath of the Fishery Products deal, that is a straight no-brainer in the sense that investors now do understand quite a bit about the fishery industry. They know how to value these shares, and $40 million or $50 million worth of stock coming through the market is certainly not going to prove troublesome.

There is one problem related to the role of governments in looking at these types of things. National Sea has a differential voting structure. The government is going to have to consider what to do about that issue in terms of the fact that these families will wind up in absolute control, through multiple voting shares of this company, although they will have a distinct minority of the equity in the company. This raises all the issues of corporate accountability and democracy in Canada today. It also raises the issue of whether the government should care or not. That's a fairly troublesome thing.

Air Canada

The third one which I'll talk about briefly is Air Canada. I have relatively little to say other than to note that this is an extraordinarily difficult decision for the federal government at this point in time. On the one hand they do have a meaningful sectoral policy in place. They have implemented some measures of deregulation. There is competition with Canadian International and to a lesser extent with Ward Air. But the airline business is also a very tough business. This particular company is in for a very challenging future in terms of capital re-equipping and the capital costs associated with it, with regard to its labour relations and to the uncertainty associated with the new regulatory and competition environment within which Air Canada will be operating, both from the point of view of foreign carriers and the newly enhanced and strengthened domestic flight carriers.

My own view on this situation—I'm not privy to the government's view at all—is that these things argue for the government privatizing the whole thing in one fell swoop if possible. Otherwise, you just have the worst of both worlds when the difficulties come. Alternatively, do none of it. If the government were to conclude that it was prepared to privatize all of it, it has to recognize that they are privatizing a high risk investment. People may lose money. The government is going to have to come to a conclusion as to whether that matters or not. Also, the prime minister has had a problem since early in his government when he appeared to promise Quebec labour leaders that Air Canada was not for sale.

They are very much caught between a rock and a hard place. If they don't privatize it all, Canadian International Airlines and Ward Air are correctly going to raise the deep pockets argument, particularly with such a massive re-equipping programme down the road. Secondly, the government doesn't need that kind of drain on its cash requirements, and the government risks being embroiled in future labour disputes should Air Canada decide that the new economics of the business require take-backs and a different labour climate within the company.

Petro-Canada

The fourth issue I am going to talk about is Petro-Canada. Petro-Canada has done a very good job of grooming itself to be privatized. The market certainly would be highly receptive to an offering of Petro-Canada at this time. In my judgement, Petro-Canada could easily raise a billion to $1.5 billion in Canada alone from investors only, without attempting to broaden it to people who don't normally invest.

Petro-Canada, of course, is also replete with a whole series of difficult issues and tradeoffs. There is the question to which I just alluded—whether you try to broaden it to raise as much money as possible with the view that because this was a creature of the consolidated revenue funds, all Canadians should be offered an opportunity to purchase it. My own view is that that is probably not a wise decision.

Petro-Canada is not a utility. It's not British Telecom, for the sake of example, it's an oil and gas company. Oil and gas stocks go up and they go down, and they do so with considerably greater volatility than utility stocks. Broadening the participation beyond seasoned investors—through post office offerings or whatever we would do—doesn't seem to me to be a very good idea.

A second difficult notion that the government is wrestling with is the notion of the policy instrument status of Petro-Canada. With the possible exception of the NDP, I think few observers are of the view that Petro-Canada need any longer have a policy instrument mandate in which the government could order it under certain conditions to advance beyond economic notions: drilling in the Beaufort or Hibernia or any number of things. Even if such a requirement did exist, the government can cause anybody to do that through regulation and tendering mechanisms. One doesn't need a specific policy instrument for that purpose.

Unfortunately, in Canada oil and gas is a commodity like no other because we make it so. My economist friends go nuts when I make this observation, but it's not like copper. Canadians tend to look on it differently for a lot of reasons, so it's a tough decision for the government to make. Obviously, we don't want to privatize a $1.5 billion offering into the individual capital markets of a company that the government will then turn around and start issuing orders to. So, it's something that has to be resolved before it can go ahead.

Another tricky problem, and the British have certainly looked at this very thoroughly, is the government's "right" to continue to monitor its ongoing investment. Petro-Canada is worth $5 billion, so if you do a $1.5 billion offering you are still going to have the federal government with a very large investment in the company. Does it get its pro rata number of directors? Does it influence business policy decisions through those directors and those kinds of things? These are all under close discussion and obviously would have to be released in a prospectus in the event that the government decides to proceed.

Another problem, although it doesn't strike me as particularly troublesome now, is oil market uncertainty. While the price of oil is $21.50 or some such thing like that today, there is no God-given assurance that it won't go back to 17, which is to say that the climate for oil stocks won't change. That takes me back to the issue that it is an oil stock, and you ought not to privatize it pretending that the thing is a utility.

As one looks at Petro-Canada, another factor is that it's going to have substantial capital expenditures in years ahead and will need future offerings. What will the policy be vis-a-vis the government being able to unload additional secondary shares, as opposed to the company, and the new shareholders need through the company, to raise additional treasury capital.

Radio-Chemical

For those of you who know anything about Radio-Chemical, it's kind of a neat little company. It ought to be privatized, because existing as a division of sorts within AECL, and therefore within government purview, it is in many ways precluded from expanding and behaving in a timely and dynamic fashion, in a way that's necessary for it to expand its business. The trouble is that a small part of its business is associated with irradiated food, which is now the subject of enormous dispute among less-informed people. I'm always amazed that scientists discuss these matters calmly and with a great degree of certainty, but the farther away you get from actual technical and scientific knowledge the more people seem to be assured that there is something wrong here. Having said that, it makes it rather difficult to contemplate privatizing this company through a broad public distribution to investors. Here I would concur with Oliver Letwin's remark yesterday, that if one has to sell to a trade purchaser, do that only as a last resort. That would be a great pity, but that is what it looks like now.

SOME ADVICE AND A WARNING

Keep It Simple

There is another issue which is very germane to politicians and public policy makers and public servants looking at the issue of privatization per se. My own view is that they ought to "keep it simple, stupid". Fishery Products was a fairly low level, fairly containable, fairly controllable way of dipping your toe in the pond. You want to build up some experience and some expertise, and you also want to build up a reasonable climate. Air Canada is about as complex as it gets. The government is going to have to trade that off against the possibility that if they were to go with Air Canada first it might impair the climate for Petro-Canada. A lot turns on a Petro-Canada offering.

If I was asked—and I haven't been asked and I doubt that I'll be asked—my advice to the government would be commit itself to the sale of one hundred percent of Air Canada but defer it for a year and go with Petro-Canada first. The real problem about announcing the intent to privatize something and then deferring it—and I think we saw this with the British Airways situation going back to the early '80s—is that you tend to set up a situation in which the entity to be privatized tries to create a competitive environment to its advantage. I don't think that will be the case with Air Canada. I think the competitive and regulatory environment has already been set in place. The ability of the company to determine or influence these exogenous events is not very great. The balance of judgement might be that the government would be best advised to proceed with Petro-Canada and do Air Canada later, but as I said this is very much a "gently on my mind" situation because they're tough issues.

Not an Entirely Healthy Notion

I'm going to close with one parenthetical observation on the whole question of timing. As we move along, in terms of anticipating and effecting privatizations, timing is going to get particularly tricky. Mrs. Thatcher's government was extremely fortunate in the sense that they really began this process in earnest at the beginning of what is now a five-year sustained bull market. That has led to a number of things. The British have done the process extraordinarily well. They have also done it with a view to broadening the individual shareholder's commitment to the private sector of the economy in the country, so pricing in some instances has been done with that in mind. Finally, as I said, it's been a good market. So what's grown up is the not entirely healthy notion among investors that if this is a privatization I can buy it because I'm "guaranteed" 15 or 20 percent on the upside. That kind of attitude is an accident looking for a place to happen, and it's particularly troublesome from the point of view of policy makers.

DISCUSSION

Edited by Michael A. Walker

Question: Is the difference between the U.K. and Canada really structural or is it political? Is it a matter of leadership in Canada?

Answer: That's a fair question, and it's a tough question too. Leadership certainly plays a factor. There is no one in the western world who provides the inherent consistency of leadership that Mrs. Thatcher does. Having said that, as we have seen on the free trade issue in Canada, Canadians are somewhat different from the following point of view. When Mrs. Thatcher came to power, in my judgement, there was a lot more evidence that specific policies weren't working and a broader and more pervasive willingness to try something else. In Canada, you have to be reasonably sophisticated to understand what is working and what isn't working and to understand the costs associated with what isn't working. Canadians are still, to a significant extent in my judgement, on the entitlement curve that we all began in the '60s. So I think it's probably a tougher thing to do here, but it is a leadership issue as well.

Question: If shares in Petro-Canada are not offered to all Canadians, in your opinion who should have the opportunity to buy? Why not an initial offering similar to that of Alberta Energy Company?

Answer: The problem I have with offering it to everybody is twofold. The fact is that it is an oil stock, the world price of oil could drop from $21.50 to $16.00 on very short notice. Oil stocks which are now trading well, through what we regard as intrinsic value, would get badly hammered. Petro-Canada would stand to do so at the same time. If you want to sell it to everybody, I suppose you could pretend it's really not an oil company and offer a kind of special share with an enhanced dividend. The fact of the matter is that if Petro-Canada is going to operate in the private sector, it ought to have its discretionary cash flow available for the reasons that other people do. I don't think there's much point in trying to confuse people who are not sophisticated enough to buy it. I think they ought to understand that it's an oil stock. I hope the government would understand that there are enough sophisticated investors used to buying oil stocks, so that we wouldn't seek to put five shares in the stocking of everyone who has never owned a stock before.

Question: Would you agree that Canadians tend to research items like privatization into the ground rather than taking positive action?

Answer: I, of course, have argued that we have taken positive action, given the fact that we started late and keeping in mind that Mr. Trudeau's government was a very interventionist government. The function of the CDIC at that time was not to privatize. The function of CDIC was to make sure that those Crown corporations ran better, which is a big difference. This government has not been in power that long. It takes time to study these issues. I think some progress is being made, and I think more shall be made.

Question: If Petro-Canada is worth $5 billion, why only have a $1.5 billion offering? Why not sell the whole thing?

Answer: That's really a political question more than anything else. I'm going to treat it as such. You might sell the whole thing if you did an international offering, including the United States and got it through the SEC. You could only do so by shifting the majority of the equity interest outside Canada. I don't think any political government is prepared to bite that bullet.

Question: Comments at yesterday's session indicated that the privatization process in the U.K. and in other countries had an effect on the capital markets institutional development in those countries. Please comment on the policy implications for capital markets of privatization in Canada.

Answer: We have very broad individual representation in our capital markets. Our capital markets are extremely efficient and compare with the best anywhere in the world. So we don't have that goal, although it's an extremely worthy goal. When one looks at countries like Argentina or Chile, where privatization is the order of the day, it's very difficult to do those privatizations without having a capital market. My partner, Pierre Matuszewski, will be speaking at lunch about the implications of that vis-a-vis Cambior in Quebec.

Question: What is the situation with regard to Canadian National Railways?

Answer: To my knowledge, and I don't have any direct knowledge, that is on the back burner and is not one of the government's priorities for the foreseeable future.

GRAHAM WALKER

(Introduction by Michael A. Walker)

Graham Walker has over 30 years of extensive experience in the investment industry in Saskatchewan, primarily in the sales and investment banking areas. He became deputy chairman and director of Pemberton Houston Willoughby Bell Gouinlock Inc. upon the merger of Houston Willoughby and Pemberton Securities in 1983. Previous to the merger he served as the chairman and chief executive officer of Houston Willoughby Ltd. In addition to his involvement with Pemberton Houston Willoughby, Mr. Walker is a director of Cairns Homes Ltd., Co-Enerco, the Potash Corporation of Saskatchewan, Saskatchewan Oil and Gas Corporation, the Atlantic Council of Canada, and the YMCA. Mr. Walker is chairman of the Crown Management Board of Saskatchewan, the holding corporation which directs the affairs of all Saskatchewan commercial Crown corporations. In this capacity he has advised Premier Grant Devine and his government on all matters relating to the development and implementation of their public participation and privatization initiatives, including the development of an overall strategy for the province.

CHAPTER 9

CANADIAN SUCCESS IN PRIVATIZATION

Graham Walker

PRIVATIZATION IN WESTERN CANADA

I am pleased to be here today to speak on a topic very close to my heart: privatization in the west. When I say close to my heart, I mean real close to my heart. Believe me, you don't make a livelihood in the investment industry in Saskatchewan, commit yourself politically against socialism and *not* take more than just a passing interest in privatization in the west.

Thomas Kierans has just spoken eloquently and insightfully about the federal government privatization thrust. I will try to broaden the privatization context by discussing the privatization experience here in the west. This is not a new topic here, you know. Like always, we in the west seem to be a few years ahead of our federal counterparts. Mr. Kierans spoke of Air Canada. Here in the west, we recollect with fondness the privatization experience of Pacific Western Airlines. Mr. Kierans also spoke of Petro-Canada. Again, we have more than just vague recollections of the roots of Alberta Energy Company and Sask Oil.

I will focus my presentation on some of these western privatization precedents, with specific mention of certain common threads that weave among them. I will also discuss briefly the approach to privatization taken by the Saskatchewan government, which I feel has been of significant merit and is worthy of consideration elsewhere.

Privatization of Alberta Energy Company

In the province of Alberta there have been two major privatization initiatives in recent years: the Alberta Energy Company and Pacific Western Airlines. Both have been extremely successful.

Alberta Energy Company's origin was in the form of a joint participation arrangement between the public and private sector, with the Alberta government maintaining a majority ownership interest in the company on predominantly the same terms and conditions as the investing public.

The Alberta Energy Company was incorporated in 1973 pursuant to a special act of the Alberta legislature. The act enshrined the mandate of AEC to stimulate, advance, and strengthen the industrial resource base of the Canadian economy, particularly in Alberta, and to encourage and enable Albertans and other Canadians to participate in the development of Alberta's industrial and resource potential. The act specified that:

- the company would be at least 50 percent owned by the province of Alberta until it reached certain levels of maturity and size;
- at least 75 percent of the board of directors would be residents of Alberta;
- the province could appoint no more than four of the directors;
- no shareholder, other than the Province of Alberta could own more than 1 percent of the company's outstanding shares.

The government of Alberta clearly stated that its nominees to the board of directors would be in the minority and that its intention was to participate in the ownership, not the management, of the company.

At the time of the AEC's initial public offering of common shares, the corporation had no meaningful business history but held various energy sector assets with a total book value of $77 million. The plan for the distribution of common shares to the public, which would reduce the ownership interest of the government of Alberta to 50 percent, allowed an initial two-week period during which Alberta residents (including resident corporations and financial institutions) would be given priority in subscription. During this period, applications to purchase more than the total umber of shares were received from over 50,000 Albertans. Larger orders were cut back and the issue was placed entirely in Alberta. Almost 3 percent of the province's then population subscribed for shares, to raise $75 million.

The issue was generally regarded to be highly successful and this was attributed to a number of key factors:

- the issue was placed on an agency basis by a broad distribution system comprising government offices, investment dealers, trust companies and chartered banks;
- the issue had strong appeal to a sense of provincial "patriotism"; and
- there was a widespread opinion that the offering had a bargain price and that the corporation had very good prospects, which were perceived to be enhanced by the continued support and ownership of the provincial government.

AEC has enjoyed a history of success and growth in its emergence as a major Canadian industrial and resource-based company. Assets grew from $196 million in 1975 to over $2 billion today. In this same period, revenues grew from $5 million to $546 million. AEC is now engaged directly or indirectly in oil and gas, petrochemicals, pipelines, coal, steel and forestry operations.

Although the government of Alberta still retains a 37 percent interest in AEC, its business operations are perceived by investors and industry participants to be free of government influence. At present, the government nominee directors (all from the private sector) total three of the company's 10 directors.

Pacific Western Airlines Is Privatized

The Pacific Western Airline privatization, undertaken in 1983, was in many respects similar to the AEC privatization. It too was privatized pursuant to a special act of the Alberta legislature with specific provisions promoting broad ownership subject to certain imposed share ownership constraints. However, there was one important differentiating factor in the PWA experience: the PWA privatization resulted in the province of Alberta reducing its ownership to that of a minority interest.

The PWA privatization involved the offering of common shares owned by the province of Alberta together with the offering of additional treasury shares of the corporation for a total offering size of approximately $108 million. Of the offering, 70 percent was sold to individual investors, 40 percent of which were Alberta residents; 30 percent of the offering was sold to Canadian institutional investors inside and outside Alberta. As a result of the offering, the province of Alberta reduced its holding in PWA to approximately 15 percent of the outstanding voting shares.

The offering successfully accomplished a twofold financial purpose, first, providing PWA with sufficient capital to maintain a competitive position in the marketplace; and, second, generating the province of

Alberta almost $40 million for its divested equity interest. Several aspects of the offering are of note:

- the offering consisted of a conventional underwriting, but priority was given to western Canadian distribution.
- a special act respecting PWA promoted broad ownership and ensured against future threats on control by prohibiting any one shareholder, other than the Province of Alberta, from holding more than 4 percent of the issue voting shares.
- there was an extremely strong demand for the shares among both retail and institutional investors. Prior to the offering, a maximum issue size of $75 million was perceived to be a lofty objective for a successful issue.
- the issue was successful without the support of a high profile marketing campaign by the province of Alberta.

In September 1984, the Province of Alberta sold additional common shares on an agency basis to further reduce the province's shareholding to 4 percent of the outstanding shares of PWA, the maximum allowable to any shareholder.

Since 1983, PWA has emerged as a major Canadian and international airline presence, now guiding the controls of the Canadian Pacific fleet under the new name Canadian Airlines International.

In retrospect, the Alberta privatization experience has brought about two very significant and expanding companies to the benefit of Canadian business and the province of Alberta. Ask yourself if two Crown corporations could have accomplished such sweeping success in such a short span of time.

PUBLIC PARTICIPATION IN SASKATCHEWAN

In Saskatchewan, privatization, or as it is called there "public participation", is also alive and well, having been resurrected, if you will, from the smothering pillows of prairie socialism. And, yes, there are many who have been converted, many who can actually say, "by golly, there can indeed be life outside of a Crown corporation."

Upon taking political office in 1982, the Saskatchewan Conservative government was determined to privatize a portion of the Crown enterprises which had been established by the NDP administration. The concept of privatization posed some particular political and investment concerns for the Conservative government:

- the Saskatchewan Crown corporations had clearly encroached upon the commercially competitive aspects of the Saskatchewan economy in such a way as to impede private sector development in the resource and financial sectors,
- the Crown corporation approach to the Saskatchewan economy was firmly routed in NDP tradition. Any privatization initiative would strike a major political debate, and
- Saskatchewan lacked an experienced investment base to access capital for any localized privatization initiative.

In Saskatchewan, the privatization thrust has been interwoven with the objective to encourage the development of a provincial capital market. Why finance Crown corporations with external funds when within the province there are enormous savings to be tapped for internal public participation?

Saskatchewan's Approach Is Noteworthy

A Deliberate, Long-Term Programme

The Saskatchewan government realized that for any privatization process to succeed it must be done in a deliberate, orderly manner. Any one privatization initiative has many distinct and conflicting interests, and it is paramount that each contemplated transaction be viewed as a particular component in a broader, evolving programme. One bad experience, particularly a bad political experience can easily prejudice even the noblest of notions. As we well know, emperors, whether they be prime ministers, premiers or privatization ministers, do not like to be caught without their clothes.

A Centralized Decision-Making Process

Saskatchewan centralized its privatization programme through the Crown Management Board, the holding company for the Saskatchewan Crown corporations (of which I was formerly the chairman). Since the Crown Management Board of Directors is comprised of senior cabinet ministers (including the premier), as well as prominent private sector businessmen, there is a productive fusion of politics and business directing the privatization process. Although each Crown corporation is not precluded from making its own assessment of its possible privatization, any such activity undertaken by a Crown is only done with the full knowledge, support and co-ordination of the Crown Management Board. Such control is essential in any politically and financially sensitive endeavour.

Preparing the Investor

In addressing the issue of privatization or public participation, the Saskatchewan government was concerned about the investment preferences of the Saskatchewan public. Investment data showed that Saskatchewan residents were not equity investors. To address this concern, the government implemented a deliberate investment programme which progressively educated prospective investors.

The first programme implemented was a series of offerings of Saskatchewan Power Corporation savings bonds, intended to increase the profile of the Crown corporations as an investment vehicle for Saskatchewan residents. These offerings have been and continue to be very successful. The Sask Power savings bond offering was then followed by a Sask Oil participating bond issue, a security having the safety and income features of a traditional bond issue together with a participation feature somewhat similar to an equity instrument. However, no voting shares were offered to the public. This offering was also very successful, selling out immediately. The government was now confident the public was responding favourably to the opportunity of investing in the Crowns and not merely in a traditional savings bond manner.

Another important step the government took was to implement certain equity programmes, such as a venture capital programme and a stock savings plan, to facilitate a stronger equity focus among the Saskatchewan investing public. The next and perhaps most important step in the privatization process was the outright offering to the public of equity in Sask Oil.

Sask Oil was established in 1973 as a special act Crown corporation. The act was amended in 1985 so Sask Oil would cease to be a Crown corporation and become a corporation with share capital to facilitate public participation. The participation was achieved through $110 million public offering of units, consisting of common shares and convertible preferred voting shares. The combination of common shares and dividend bearing preferred shares appealed to the conservative Saskatchewan investor. It was also politically attractive in that it had the effect of broadening the investor base. The preferred share component of the unit was designed to also minimize market price depreciation in the event of a falling world oil market. Although oil prices did indeed fall dramatically after the offering, the Sask Oil unit value did not experience the same severe price declines as other oil and gas common share equities.

The offering was first sold in Saskatchewan through a broad range of financial institutions and then subsequently across Canada through the investment dealer network. Within Saskatchewan, a strong marketing campaign throughout the province preceded the offering of the issue. Almost $60 million (approximately 54 percent) of the offering was sold to Saskatchewan residents. There is no question that the strong investor acceptance of the issue in Saskatchewan did much to muffle any political attack by the opposition. There was only modest debate in the legislature. It was clear the privatization process in Saskatchewan had moved beyond the planning process and was now into a successful implementation mode. As a result of the initial Sask Oil offering, the Province of Saskatchewan's voting interest was reduced to 58 percent of the voting shares of the corporation.

Moving under the 50 percent threshold is a very important step in any privatization process. To the extent that this can be accomplished in the initial privatization, so much the better. Sask Oil is a case in point. Although the government made clear its intentions to remain only a passive shareholder and not interfere in management affairs, it still initially retained ownership in excess of 50 percent. Therefore, in the minds of some political critics, Sask Oil was still a Crown corporation and, consequently, still subject to political debate. When Sask Oil recently acquired an Alberta-based oil and gas company for $66 million, the opposition was quick to run a full page ad in all the papers crying shame to the Tories for letting one of its Crowns spend $66 million in Alberta, while at the same time doing away with the dental programme and other programmes in Saskatchewan—hardly a proper and fair comparison by any means. In fact, a clear blow below the belt. But, as we all know, any politics packaged properly can be effective.

However, hopefully such nonsense can now be put to rest. Sask Oil is just now completing an additional $50 million offering of treasury shares, which is scheduled to close next week. This offering will reduce the government's ownership interest to approximately 46 percent of the voting shares.

As in the case of the AEC and PWA privatizations, specific share ownership restraints were established through the Sask Oil Act. Any investor, or group of associated investors, other than the Province of Saskatchewan, is prohibited from owning more than 4 percent of the voting shares of Sask Oil. In addition, the holders of voting shares must be Canadian residents. The ongoing relationship between the government of

Saskatchewan and Sask Oil is quite similar to the relationship between AEC and the province of Alberta. The government of Saskatchewan has indicated that it intends to participate in ownership, not management, of Sask Oil and that it does not intend to vote its shareholdings, although it retained the power to do so. The act permits the province of Saskatchewan to appoint members to the board of directors in proportion to their share voting percentage.

Another Privatization Stirs Criticism

Sask Oil is not the only example of privatization in Saskatchewan. Last year, the government sold its Crown pulp and paper company, Papco, to Weyerhaeuser of Canada. This too stirred much criticism in the opposition ranks. However, the opposition to Papco has also quieted of late. With not yet a year having passed since the closing of the Papco sale, Weyerhaeuser has already commenced construction of an expansionary paper mill operation constituting $250 million dollars of additional capital investment and 215 new jobs. I can assure you that the previous Crown-run Papco would not have shown such enterprising initiative.

Future Trends in Saskatchewan

I am not a spokesman for the Saskatchewan government but based on a report in 21 July 1987 *Globe and Mail*, I think it is safe to say that we can expect Saskatchewan to remain very active in the area of privatization or public participation. The premier was quoted as saying "the general philosophy is that the resource companies should be in the hands of the public, through public-share offerings ... joint ventures, or just outright put into the private sector." Mr. Devine said in an interview, "we wouldn't have nationalized them in the first place."

However, none of these initiatives can take place overnight. The public often tends to become impatient about this subject, not fully appreciating the demanding and delicate process that must take place between concept and realization. Yet it is very important that a government does not succumb to this public impatience. I think the government of Saskatchewan has prudently understood that. Do it. But do it right!

BRITISH COLUMBIA PRIVATIZATION EFFORTS

In British Columbia, I think it is quite obvious, especially to those of us who have participated in or attended this conference, that a prudent and deliberate privatization is well under way. We all had the good fortune to hear the Hon. Stephen Rogers this morning. It was the second time that I have been fortunate enough to hear Mr. Rogers speak on the issue of privatization. My impressions are that things certainly seem under control in the privatization front in B.C. It makes eminent sense to me that the issue of privatization be centralized within the responsibilities of one ministry. Without such centralization nothing would ever get done. In Saskatchewan, they have come to understand this. I am not being facetious when I say the government of British Columbia may have accelerated their privatization process by as much as five years simply by centralizing the activity centre.

The government of British Columbia has also chosen to look before it leaped, lest it subject itself to the proverbial fate of the road-runner. Mad enthusiastic dashes are fine within the controls of a Walt Disney director. In politics and in privatization there is no Walt Disney. In politics and privatization, you cannot continuously fall from the top to the bottom of the Fraser Canyon and be no less worse for wear. Maybe a few times, if you are lucky. Sure people are impatient. That has been and will always be the voters prerogative. *Hell, if it were any other way we might have politicians who think long term.* What a strange world that would be.

Seriously though, when it comes to privatization, I think the people will be patient provided they have a reasonable expectation that they will in due course see the product. And I think the recent efforts of Mr. Rogers and his government have sufficiently established that reasonable expectation in the people's minds. The minister has mentioned a number of privatization candidates in British Columbia. I don't think it is appropriate for me to comment on those prospective candidates.

The BCRIC Privatization

It is hard to talk about privatization in British Columbia without talking about BCRIC. Much has been said about the province of British Columbia's privatization of several government enterprises in 1979 through the creation of the British Columbia Resources Investment Corporation. Most people are aware that BCRIC, as an evolving entity, has been criticized. However, there is one aspect of BCRIC that forever will be acclaimed, that being the extraordinary sales success of its initial public offering.

I have a strong recollection of BCRIC being privatized. You must appreciate the setting. I am out in Saskatchewan, the Riders are well into their 20-year losing streak, business is poor, and what little taxes I am paying help support the NDP nationalization efforts. And there, out past the Rockies, towards the Pacific, we hear of this glorious event called BCRIC. I can still hear the echo of my then competitor Bob Wyman telling me how business was suddenly booming in B.C. "Graham, you wouldn't believe it. It is just so huge. And only in B.C., Graham. They are only selling it in B.C." Thank you Bob.

Well, BCRIC was huge. Staggeringly huge. If there was ever an example of the B.C. capitalist spirit, it was clearly seen in early 1979. The offering, as most of you remember, consisted of the gifting of five shares of BCRIC to all residents of British Columbia. In addition, there was a concurrent offering of BCRIC shares at $6.00 per share. The results were phenomenal—170,000 B.C. residents bought, I said *bought*, shares in BCRIC, with an average size order of approximately $2500. About 5,000 individuals bought the maximum of 5,000 shares. The total value of the new issue was $487.5 million. This was no passing matter in 1979. In fact, it was then the third largest common share offering in North American history. All in British Columbia. No wonder Bob Wyman was smiling.

We out in Saskatchewan had to wait to buy BCRIC shares in the aftermarket. Like a lot of people, I bought them as soon as the opportunity arrived. I have made a few investment decisions which I have grown to regret. However, I do not include BCRIC among them. Yes, I would even do it again. Believe me, if you have lived all your life a strong believer in the capitalist spirit, and have spent the largest part of your life campaigning against socialism and nationalism in action, you'll understand what I mean when I say I would do it again.

Closing Remarks

In closing, I would like to reiterate to the minister that the investment community in British Columbia and, to the extent that they are allowed, the investment community outside British Columbia, are looking forward to the next opportunity to facilitate the transfer of capital resources from the public sector to the private sector for the enduring benefit of British Columbians.

DISCUSSION

Edited by Michael A. Walker

Question: What three Crowns do you think will be the next to go private in western Canada?

Answer: I don't know the answer to that. I think B.C. will probably privatize a Crown first, but I don't know which one it will be.

Question: Do you not think that the restrictions on holdings—1 percent, 2 percent, or even 4 percent—will lead to a bad result, as it will allow management to entrench itself and it may not allow the free market forces to operate?

Answer: There are three examples of restricted ownership in western Canada: AEC, which is only 1 percent, PWA and Sask Oil. I don't think any of those have been affected. The most important thing is to get the government down below 50 percent. My friends at AEC say that the 1 percent restriction does not affect the market values of their shares, but as soon as the government went below 50 percent of AEC the financial institutions across Canada and, in fact, worldwide showed a greater interest because they didn't like the government to have that much impact. In the last issue of Sask Oil, 40 institutions bought Sask Oil that didn't own it before. That's mostly because it's an attractive company, but in addition to that the government ownership went down below 50 percent.

Question: I think the gist of the question is that private sector firms are disciplined, in part because of the fear that somebody can accumulate shares and turf out the existing group and put in a new group by taking an ownership position. In your view, does the existence of these limitations expose the privatization process to a bad result?

Graham Walker: I don't think it exposes the privatization process to a bad result. We have to remember that in moving the company from the public sector into the private sector there is a sensitivity of former ownership protection by the government. Ultimately, perhaps, these ownership restrictions could be removed, but they'd have to be removed by legislation. The matter of the ability to accumulate a sufficient number of shares to take over the company—I don't know how to answer that.

Thomas Kierans: I'll give you an economic answer which is theory in the aggregate and not necessarily applicable to theory in the particular. The theory in the aggregate is quite simple. Where such blockages exist, the market efficiency will be encumbered. That's not an issue. When you apply that to specific instances, however, you're really stretching. There is still corporate democracy, which is to say that you can get a lot of institutions and a lot of individual investors together and, if you think management's not running things properly, turf them out by a proxy war. Finally, when looking at that kind of restriction, look at the AEC experience of 1 percent. That's far too low. You want it large enough to be able to attract a large number of institutional owners.

Question: When did you sell your BCRIC shares?

Answer: Much later.

Question: I'm surprised at the reference to 50 percent, 40 percent or 30 percent ownership, referring to the government block. These are very large blocks and indicate the possibility of government control. Please comment.

Answer: In the case of Sask Oil, the provincial government minister of the time wrote a letter which appears in the prospectus that said in effect the government would be an owner not a manager. Yes, they have control. There's no question about it, but they deal with it in that manner. The same thing happened in Alberta, and it has worked very well. Some people feel comfortable with a government/private sector ownership combination.

MICHAEL C. BURNS

(Introduction by Michael A. Walker)

Michael Burns has some unique experience as both an observer and a participant in Crown corporations. He has a background in the private sector with IBM and in education at the University of Manitoba. He has served on the boards of five major Crown corporations and a dozen of their subsidiaries. One has been privatized; UTDC in Ontario was sold last year. Others, such as BCDC and AECL are going through privatization processes. He was chairman of the Manitoba Cabinet committee on automobile insurance, which studied and recommended privatization of the Manitoba Public Insurance Corporation. One Crown which he initiated from the first Order in Council, Expo 86 Corporation, is approaching its sunset, one of a very few to have come full circle. He may be the only Canadian to have established a joint venture company between a People's Republic of China Crown corporation and a provincially owned Ontario company. He closely observed the privatization of B.C. Systems Corporation and the ICBC General Insurance Division as an adviser to the B.C. government.

CHAPTER 10

CONSIDERATIONS IN PRIVATIZING A LARGE CROWN CORPORATION

Michael C. Burns

CROWN CORPORATIONS ARE POWERFUL

I am speaking to you today from a perspective quite different from most of the other speakers. I have been involved as a creator of Crown corporations, an operator of companies and as a privatizer of Crown corporations in Canada. I have served with five major Crown-owned corporations and about a dozen subsidiaries. I initiated two of them from the ground up, one of which was Expo 86. The most unique Crown was a subsidiary jointly owned by an Ontario Crown and the People's Republic of China. I have seen Crowns in almost every flavour. In my 20 years with IBM, our biggest clients were Crown corporations.

As a general management consultant, I find myself and my clients dealing with major Crowns daily. I have respect for the Crown corporations and what they have accomplished in Canada. Whether this could have been done by the private sector is not clear. But whatever the good and bad of Crown corporations, they are a powerful and unique breed of semi-commercial entity with a unique attribute—unlimited funding and legislative back-up when required.

The Privatization of Crown Corporations

I have encountered privatization in many forms, and I favour it in most cases. The Urban Transportation Development Corporation, an Ontario

Crown, was sold in 1986. I observed this as a board member both before privatization and after, in the shell that was left behind.

I developed a proposal for the privatization of a major part of British Columbia Development Corporation. With the Bennett government I observed the difficult privatization at B.C. Systems Corporation and ICBCs General Insurance Division and have been able to observe the progress of the privatized companies.

A Failed Privatization

My most intense experience was as chairman of the Cabinet Review Committee on the Manitoba Public Insurance Corporation. As Michael Walker has asked me to use this as the model for my presentation today, I should briefly explain the circumstances.

The Manitoba Public Insurance Corporation is one of three very similar major general insurance companies owned by the provinces of Saskatchewan, Manitoba and British Columbia. All have their roots in Saskatchewan where the SGIO was established some 40 years ago. All were instituted by CCF or NDP governments using basically the same senior strategists led by Jim Dutton and Norm Bortnick.

The Conservative government of Manitoba recruited me and a team to review the corporation and recommend a future course for the corporation. We studied the matter for six months. In the course of this, we became very familiar with this corporation and its sister companies in Saskatchewan and British Columbia, as well as the industry in Canada. My examples will be drawn from all three of these Crowns.

We provided the government with a detailed plan by which this industry (which is what it was) could be returned to the private sector. It was a good plan but for reasons of political timing was not implemented.

THE AUTO INSURANCE INDUSTRY IS UNIQUE

Why discuss a failed privatization attempt? There is good reason to look at this general insurance industry because it is unique. Three major provinces have nationalized the industry. All three have survived free enterprise governments. And more importantly, while all the privatization talk goes on, it is the one major industry under threat of further nationalization.

As we speak, Ontario is seriously contemplating the institution of a provincial auto insurance scheme effectively nationalizing this billion dollar industry in Ontario. For this reason, the Canadian auto insurance industry is an interesting microcosm for privatization studies. Just when you thought the tide was turning, here is an industry on the defensive against a non-socialist government.

I will use examples from this industry as the base to establish three main themes. First, that Canadian Crowns are driven by a complex mix of commercial and public policy objectives. This makes them hard to privatize. They are, as Sterling Lyon described them, a socialist omelette.

Secondly, there are unique and innovative approaches which can make that omelette palatable and privatizable. And finally, while there is a shortage of competence available to privatizers and buyers of Crowns, such talent can be organized to successfully conclude privatization.

FACTORS THAT BIND CROWN CORPORATIONS

As we have said, Crown corporations are a complex mixture, an omelette, held together with several sticky substances. They intertwine diverse public policy objectives with purely commercial ones. Three groups of factors bind the omelette together, particularly when threatened with privatization:

- The melding of public policy with the commercial enterprise;
- The advantages of the convenience of the monopoly;
- The seconded self-interest that creates the affection for the corporation in the public.

These are the elements that a privatizer or those that would take over the Crown corporation must deal with if they wish to be successful. To ignore these elements will give both the privatizer and the buyer an enormous amount of grief and defeat the purpose and possibly even prevent the completion.

Public Policy and Commercial Enterprise

I will describe each of these groups and share some of our experiences in the auto insurance case with you. First, melding public policy with commercial enterprise is one of the most difficult elements to deal with. It is put in place by politicians and bureaucrats when these organizations are established for good reason:

- it expands empires;
- it protects the entity from interference because it provides them with two measurement standards.

Each Crown will have a set of commercial parameters and when pressed on these, one can revert to the public policy standard. This is not uncommon among Crowns no matter what industry. I am sure we have all heard an unnamed federal Crown corporation that would say: "Of course we lose money on commercial television; but who can put a price on bringing Canadian culture to the North?" The dual objective it provides is a moving target which has become very convenient. This dual set of objectives also allows Crown corporations to bribe the public with its own money, providing motherhood services and taking credit for them under a public policy guide.

Specifically, in the auto insurance field, we found this melding of commercial and public policy to be quite broad. Aside from offering commercial products, the government-owned insurance corporations were charged with significant public policy missions and responsibilities. From their creation and to this date they have the mission to keep rates down. The impression is that these corporations are providing an essential service at close to cost. Secondly, they were to provide universal rates without discrimination which was considered to be a public good. The third example is their mission to keep uninsured vehicles off the road. All of those popular public policy objectives were sold hard by the corporation when there was a threat of privatization.

If left unanswered, these objections will provide serious difficulty to a privatizer and to the industry taking over. They need to be addressed intelligently and unique solutions found to them. We found some of those approaches and solutions in the insurance case in response to Pirie's third law, "devise a plan to gain more advantage."

With regard to pricing, it was determined that public perception of low prices or "service almost at cost" was somewhat of a myth. The accounting and statistics that were used in support of this myth would make a Howe Street commando blush. We identified subsidies totalling $90 million or 20 percent of the total revenue in the period studied. This did not include the theoretical subsidy of income tax exemption and some reserve requirement costs. Still, the corporation had the courage to compare its published rates to those of the private sector and claim victory over capitalism. A privatizer stepping into this mine field would surely have to explain and convince his public that the subsidies did indeed exist and were adding to his actual rates through taxation. In future, these costs would appear in his insurance rate and not in his tax bill.

In regard to universal rates, Crown insurance companies had acceded to government pressure to eliminate many of the premium rating factors which would require the industry to throw away the actuarial tables and offer the same rate to an eighteen year old muscle car driver as to a ten-year accident-free driver. This, of course, was sold and accepted as an element of public policy. This was a social policy. The examples used to prove the point were not the eighteen year old with the five-litre Mustang but the brush-cut kid who used the Gremlin to drive to choir practice. A public sold on these kinds of embedded policies is not going to be easily converted to a standard commercial approach to rating automobile drivers.

Innovative approaches had to be found if Pirie's third law was to be observed: "devise a plan to gain more advantage." The recommendations we made allowed a melding of the perceived public benefit of the current policy with the realities of the new commercial ones. In this particular case, an approach which included a take-all-comers feature and a standard differential matrix for rating all risks was recommended.

Aside from the operational aspects that directly interfaced with the public, other elements of public policy are woven into the structure of government-owned Crown insurance corporations. A claim to high ratios of local investment was successfully embedded in the mind of the public. Corporations said, in effect, "we don't invest for the highest return (to make your insurance policy the best commercial contract), wherever possible we lend to schools and municipalities in the province. If we were privatized, who would lend money to our schools, cities and towns?" Here we have another insidious mixture of perceived good—a public policy completely intertwined with a commercial undertaking.

When we looked closer, first we found the perception was not always true. Companies that claimed to have high local investment records really ran lower ratios than the commercial companies in the same type of business. Once again, our privatization recommendations had to reflect this perceived advantage and were not purely commercial. They did involve some requirements for mandatory local investment but at the same time we pointed out that the public must be informed that there was an adequate market for school and municipal debt instruments and that the financing would not come to an end on the privatization of the corporation.

Each of these elements of public policy had a perceived benefit established by long use in the community. Had they not been dealt with in a sensitive way, in a way different from one that would handle a commercial sale of a business, it would provide the opportunity for the public to believe they were significantly less well off in a privatized environment.

We approached these in our recommendations with unique and workable solutions which we think could be applied elsewhere. They included a sensitivity for the political reality and intelligent use of opinion research and advertising.

The Convenience of a Monopoly

A second major area of impediment was dealing with the convenience of the monopoly. This is a siren song which provides a strong defence against privatization of Canadian Crown corporations. Again, it involves Pirie's first law: "never cancel an advantage." Commercial transactions inter-tied to systems of government provide an efficiency in a monopoly that is very attractive to the users.

In the auto insurance case, for instance, a single form of licence and insurance is a very real efficiency. Embedded in this system are cross-subsidization of the motor vehicle agencies and compulsions under law which are difficult to transfer to a commercial situation. Here privatizers must be clever to design a system with the right mix of regulation and accommodation from government systems that assures the major elements that the conveniences of the monopoly are not lost.

Cutting the insurance programme loose without providing these conveniences would have doubtless brought great disrepute to the privatization and likely serious impact on the government proposing it. We recommended a central registration system for licensing and insurance run by government to retain the single form of licence and insurance. We also recommended the requirement of a first party settlement system and an agency which would facilitate and co-ordinate activities of operating companies.

It was clear that these solutions were feasible and could have been implemented by the industry itself working in a free enterprise environment *before* the government entered the field with a monopoly. This kind of co-ordinated activity was undertaken by the industry in Quebec. Many of the conveniences of the monopoly were embedded in the system and the industry protected from nationalization. These thoughts, no doubt, are going through the minds of Canadian insurers as the Ontario government debates the merits of nationalizing that industry at this very moment.

Seconded Self-Interest

The third area of impediment that we observed was the seconded self-interest that Crown corporations have developed over the years of operation. We identified this in several areas: body shops, the employee union, insurance agents, and the public themselves. Here, the threat of privatization created some opposition, and Pirie's second law, "make friends of your enemies," came into effect.

With regard to the body shops, there was a close, almost paternalistic, relationship between them and the insurance corporation. Our analysis indicated that the corporation was paying 14 percent more than comparable rates in other provinces for the service of the body shops. The body shops themselves openly complained that if the insurance corporation went away, they would suffer on two counts. First, the government-owned plan paid much more promptly than the companies. And secondly, they would be required to compete on price among themselves—a terribly onerous thing.

The absence of competition was so complete that when auto glass replacement firms offered clients the refund of the deductible on their glass replacement, the corporation moved strongly to oppose it and prevent this kind of competition. The close relationship was further identified in another instance where a company was providing business management training for the owners of body shops in order that they could all be equally profitable. As one might imagine, body shop owners were not in favour of a privatization and were prompt to say so. Once again, innovative approaches to making the transition with this group of suppliers was necessary for the potential success of the privatization by making friends of enemies.

With regard to the union, unique circumstances are created with a large monopoly Crown. In this particular industry, only a small percentage of general insurance workers are organized which, of course, created a level of concern on the part of the union. Further, a large number of employees are grouped in a single union. In a new environment, these would be scattered among a number of companies and possibly different unions. For this reason, the union was certainly vociferous in its opposition. The union situation was further complicated by the fact this was a public sector union which would be making transition into the private field. The reality of this difficulty was experienced in the privatization of the general insurance portion of the Insurance Corporation of British Columbia. With the benefit of the British experience, it is clear that some application of employee share participation would have been most helpful.

The insurance agents in this experience were, of course, happy to be receiving commissions at almost commercial scale and having to deal with only one set of policies and companies. They had been very much brought onside through cross-selling of general insurance and auto insurance and had good reasons not to be entirely thrilled about privatization. Finding an equitable means to include them in a similar way, but with higher administrative activity in the new environment, was another of the unique challenges that we were faced with in our recommendations.

Finally, the public had been seconded in its own self-interest as well. They understood that they had ownership in one of the largest financial institutions in the province. They had bought and paid for this, and how were they to get their money back? They were right, of course. There was real value in what had been built for them. However, because it was based on government regulation and coercion in the monopoly, the value would be difficult to recapture as these attributes would not be available in a privatized industry.

Again, we were forced with identifying a unique approach to make the transition in the face of this problem. We looked at all the available approaches. We looked at bricking it, stoning it, gassing it; finally, we decided to mute it. That is, we recommended that the unique solution for this particular enterprise would be to mutualize the insurance company, effectively turning the ownership of the corporation over to its policy holders.

This had a number of positive aspects. First, we were fortunate in that there had been a long and successful tradition of mutual insurance companies in Canada and, therefore, the precedents and conventions were set. Secondly, we need strike no price for it, establish no value at which it was to be sold. We had no selling expenses, and finally, the value stayed with the people who had created it.

THE POLITICIAN CONFRONTS REALITY

With these few examples then, it can be seen that there are real impediments to be faced in privatization, and living up to Pirie's law is not easy. What looks easy when it is done right, will require skill, knowledge and a commitment on the part of those planning it. It requires innovative political skills added to the traditional commercial expertise.

Particularly, in the monopoly setting in Canada, there is no highly developed sense of dissatisfaction among Canadians as Canadian Crowns (excepting a few) are by no means intolerable. When the politician comes to face the reality, as was done in this case, he is confronted with little good news.

Prior to getting on with the job of privatizing an agency such as this, he must:

- Reveal the subsidies.
- Plunge his electorate into the cruel reality of market rates from which they have probably been shielded by tax subsidies.

- Strive to maintain the effect of an integrated monopoly and the conveniences it provides.
- He is up against a bureaucracy schooled in the protection of the entity.
- A public conned and bribed with their own money to a large degree, and
- Unions and suppliers in some cases with sweetheart deals.

As he approaches this dilemma, he is often forced to rely on inexperienced advisers and analysts to evaluate and implement his programme.

Facing these challenges, the privatizer finds few people with any firsthand experience in converting such a corporation. With respect to my fellow panel members, only a few outside this group have any real experience in evaluating or implementing privatizations in Canada. Therefore, governments will often turn to the traditional business brokers, to investment houses accustomed to selling commercial businesses.

But as we have seen, these Canadian Crown corporations are somewhat different. They are often not businesses which can be sold as it. There may be a whole new regime to be created if these entities are to be passed to private hands. A different and expanded set of skills may be required before the broker can exercise his craft and secure the best price for the entity.

A Centre for Privatization Expertise

If the government wishes to survive the privatization process and indeed gain some credit for it, it must plan carefully and consider some of the difficult areas which I have briefly described. As a result of this experience, and with the increased interest in privatization, I recommended in September 1984 that a Competence Centre for Privatization be established. Such a centre would bring together the traditional disciplines such as valuation, general management, stock and money market specialists, tax experts and audit specialists, but in addition, would add the unique disciplines required to deal with the transition of Crown-owned entities.

Providing these skills and preparing the political and public climate for a privatization is our business at the Sentinel Group. We provide some of those bridging skills not normally required in a business sale, linking political reality to commerce. We understand and use techniques of modern business practice but also the tools of public policy such as opinion research, political strategy and regulation designed to tune the political elements of the issue to the commercial reality. Our involvement never displaces the investment banker or business broker but enhances the product for the seller and the buyer.

Let me make that point clear. There is as much need for political sensitivity and opinion research on the buyer's part as on the government's side. Well-designed purchase bids can help immensely to improve the success and viability of a privatization. These need not be solicited bids. With the application of such skills, better bids will be put forward from buyers which will be both profitable and smooth the transition, and privatizers will be able to respond to the needs of the situation and the buyers.

Any jurisdiction considering privatization should look to identifying such a Centre of Competence or recruiting a team of its own. Buyers who are anxious to submit successful bids should seek out such well-balanced teams to assist in these esoteric areas. I am pleased to say that a firm with which I and a later speaker, Mr. Schwartz, are associated—Deloitte, Haskins & Sells—has formed such a group to assist its clients. Pirie's fourth law states, "hire the expertise to maximize your chance of success." So call us early and often.

DISCUSSION

Edited by Michael A. Walker

Question: Are provincial Crown corporations to some extent just a response to federal taxation legislation and policy?

Answer: In terms of a province responding to an opportunity presented for avoidance of federal taxes, clearly some of those factors are at work. In the insurance case, I think it was more a response to the industry being fragmented and failing to provide, in a very serious way, the requirements of the public that wanted a more convenient, more equitable, lower cost system. I don't see that as a response in that particular industry.

Question: In terms of the minority Liberal government in Ontario and its attitude toward insurance, do you think the Liberal government has been influenced by the NDP, who suggest moving to a government controlled automobile insurance industry? Would they pursue this when or if they were to have a majority mandate?

Answer: I'm absolutely certain they've been conditioned to it by the NDP government. It's interesting to notice, though, that the Davis government did a study on the same subject. Really, the root of this is coming from public pressure. I think there may be an opportunity for the insurance companies in the political sense in Ontario as Peterson tries to break away from the NDP in the next election, which he certainly will. This may be one of the things that hits the cutting room floor. If I were advising that industry, I'd be pressing hard for evidence that he had broken away as a political strategy. I'd be doing the things that the same insurers did in Quebec to solve the problems Peterson is trying to solve with nationalization.

Question: Why was the privatization of B.C. Systems a failure?

Answer: I don't think it was a good project to privatize; it's as simple as that. It's a computer utility imbedded deeply in a government. No one has ever done one successfully that I am aware of; it's just too deeply imbedded in the government to make good sense. There are so many inter-ties you have to leave in that it was just an odd duck to try to privatize.

Question: To whom was the recommendation made, and what happened to the recommendation to establish a centre for privatization?

Answer: It was made to both the federal and provincial governments. I think it failed for lack of assembly of people who would serve in it. I think that was chiefly conditioned by the fact that there wasn't a highly-focused perception that they were intent on doing privatization. It was going to take a very serious commitment by various senior and experienced people who had a lot of other exciting things to do.

Question: What is your assessment of the current political environment for privatization in British Columbia?

Answer: As Stephen said, I think Mrs. Thatcher has made it a very popular political element everywhere. Not only is it positive, but it's now being demanded of every government in office. It's not an option any more; it's a mandatory item of public policy. I think all governments are going to be measured on their performance in it. It has been elevated to an absolute must in western governments.

Question: Under mutualization of Manitoba Public Insurance, would competition have been permitted? If not, why not?

Answer: Absolutely. The purpose was to throw the corporation in its present form into the marketplace and let it survive or fail on its ability to compete. In doing that, it was very difficult to build a level playing field for the other companies. But we think we've succeeded. The whole object of the exercise was to take away the monopoly and the government ownership.

Question: Is not the holding of a large block of shares by government a dangerous situation in the event of a change of government, for example, an NDP win in Saskatchewan or Alberta or in Canada?

Answer: We attempted to unscramble the omelette, so there was no possibility to rescramble it. It was similar to the approach that Madsen Pirie discussed—put the ownership in enough electoral hands, and you'll have a hell of a job pulling it back together. We were putting the ownership, de facto, into the hands of half a million policyholders, and I think that's one of the best shark repellents anyone's thought of so far. We've never seen it assailed yet, so we won't know whether it works until there is a change of government in a privatized environment. I'm pleased to hear that five years later that's an approach thought to be effective in Britain.

Question: What strategies did you devise for dealing with the unions?

Answer: Our strategies for dealing with the unions weren't particularly good. That was an area where we had nothing but blood, sweat, toil and tears in front of us. If we had had the experience of the British approach to employee share ownership, I think we would have rounded that out rather nicely. That would have solved many of the problems we hadn't found a solution for in that exercise.

Question: How would you privatize Canada Post?

Answer: I think I might buy every business in the country a "Fax" machine.

PIERRE MATUSZEWSKI

(Introduction by Michael A. Walker)

Our guest speaker today has come to tell us about privatization developments in the province of Quebec where some very interesting things are happening. Pierre Matuszewski was born in London, England, came to Canada via Vancouver, and settled in the province of Quebec. He was educated at Stanislaus College (Montreal), Laval University and McGill University. He then joined the firm of McLeod Young Weir, where he is currently vice-president and director in corporate finance in Montreal. His particular credentials from the point of view of the subject under consideration at this conference are that he was the person responsible for and in charge of the first ever public privatization by the government of Quebec, that of Soquem/Cambior in 1986. He will focus his remarks today on the success of that experiment and what it has to tell us about how we might proceed in the rest of Canada.

CHAPTER 11

PARTIAL PUBLIC PRIVATIZATION IN QUEBEC SOQUEM/CAMBIOR

Pierre Matuszewski

INTRODUCTORY REMARKS

It was one year ago today that a final prospectus for an offering of securities of Cambior inc. was filed across Canada for a domestic as well as an international issue totalling $157.5 million. It was the first and so far the only public privatization of the Quebec government. McLeod Young Weir was the global adviser on the transaction, and I was the project manager. I would like to tell you about this case of partial privatization.

I assume that most of you are not familiar with the name SOQUEM. It stands for Societe Quebecoise d'Exploration Miniere or the Crown corporation responsible for mining exploration in Quebec. I hasten to add that most Quebecers did not know who SOQUEM was either, nor for that matter did they care. This was no high-profile Petro-Canada or Pacific Western Airlines.

For many an observer of privatizations and the privatization process, the partial privatization of Soquem should have been an obvious and easy process. How can the privatization of an unknown Crown corporation be difficult? Yet, this company had $146 million of assets and employed 525 employees as of its last year end. Secondly, a corporation that drills a few holes in the ground in Northwestern Quebec and only operates two mines: a money-losing salt mine off the east coast of the province and a niobium mine near Chicoutimi can hardly be considered to be running an essential service like the post office, for instance. Nor was it part of the national security infrastructure. Its one single point in common with many other Crown corporations is that in 1986 it was losing money, and that is where its problems started.

This privatization should have been a shoe-in, a non-event. This has turned out to be one of the major public privatization successes in Canada recently, one that saw $157 million raised in Canada and in Europe—the first time, to my knowledge, that a Canadian public privatization offering was formally made outside the country.

First, I will briefly give you the background on Crown corporations in Quebec as well as an outline of the current government of Quebec's privatization platform. The second part will deal with the partial privatization of Soquem. I will touch mainly on issues such as the need to privatize, structuring considerations, marketing and pricing issues and life after privatization. Finally, I would like to outline what lessons can be learned from this case of partial privatization: issues such as the need for political will, how to deal with management, what to do with the residual Crown corporation and attitudes after privatization.

PRIVATIZATION IN QUEBEC

A Definition

Before getting into the thick of the subject, let me define what I mean by partial privatization. My definition of partial privatization is the selling off of a large part but by no means substantial portion of a Crown corporation's assets to the private sector. In this definition, the Crown corporation retains some activities after the privatization and may or may not own a residual interest in the privatized assets.

Crown Corporations in Quebec

Like most other provinces, over the years Quebec has developed a network of provincial Crown corporations. If one excludes Crown corporations or agencies that deal in education and social affairs matters, a couple of years ago Quebec had approximately fifty Crown corporations.

These fifty Crown corporations can, in turn, be classified into three categories. The largest category, comprised of thirty companies, are in effect corporations whose purpose is to administer subsidized activities such as ferry operations and industrial expansion activities. Another category is comprised of seven corporations that are in effect monopolies such as Hydro-Quebec, the Liquor Board and the Lotteries Board. Finally, the last category is comprised of ten corporations whose activities are essentially commercial and/or industrial in nature.

The activities in which these latter corporations are engaged include iron and steel making, mining, forestry, oil and gas, fisheries, and transportation. Of these ten Crown corporations, five were created in the 1960s, as was Soquem, created in 1965 at a time when the rallying cry in Quebec was, "master of our own destiny." It simply meant that we wanted to establish control over our resources and our economy to provide an outlet for our entrepreneurs and students. The basis of the creation of those Crown corporations was not dogma. It was economic nationalism and nation building. No province, nor the federal government, nor for that matter can any country deny any action it has taken based on such a principle.

That was twenty years ago. Since then much has changed. A generation has come of age and has gained experience. It is now ready to take over its industry and face the competitive world without the omnipresent protective shield of big brother, the government.

In 1985, the time was ripe for a Quebec government to tackle the matter of privatization. Elected on December 2, 1985, the current Quebec government was indeed ready to tackle privatization. Its campaign platform already included detailed steps it would take in such matters. On December 12, ten days after its election, at the swearing in of cabinet, a minister was appointed specifically responsible for privatization. To the people in the know, this nomination meant two things. First, that the government was or appeared to be serious about privatization. Secondly, that there was to be one man in charge of this process. The nomination seemed to indicate that the government didn't want this process to become a political football between ministers as had been the case in some instances before in other jurisdictions.

Two months after being sworn in, Minister Pierre Fortier tabled a 70-page document titled, "Privatization of Crown Corporations: Orientations and Prospects." After reviewing the Canadian and British experiences and the status and performance of Quebec Crown corporations, the minister laid out the guiding principles of his government vis-a-vis Crown corporations and their privatization. He also set out the process which was to be followed. In retrospect, it is fair to say that while this document had the proper intent and indeed the proper content, it had little impact. The opposition was in disarray after a stinging defeat. The media were more interested in other economic news, despite occasional attempts to launch political balloons. Generally, the February doldrums had settled in.

Nevertheless, this document contained good news. For people like myself who believe in the general principle that less government is better government, this was excellent news. This was not only a confirmation of the process going ahead—it contained a message of pragmatism. It was, in effect, "privatization if necessary but not necessarily privatization," to quote the title of a paper delivered by Tom Kierans in 1984.

Let me briefly summarize for you the guiding principles set out by the minister. First, a general bias towards the private sector taking charge of procuring goods and services. Second, that the structural objective—the benefit for the Quebec economy—prevail over financial considerations. Third, that the approach be a case-by-case approach, a pragmatic one. Fourth, that the privatization process be made transparent. This was a partial answer to the critics who say that a Crown corporation belongs to all taxpayers, therefore all taxpayers have a right to know. Fifth, was a statement that employees, communities and suppliers would be treated fairly. And lastly, that the remaining Crown corporations would have to comply with rigorous production and competitive criteria.

I draw your attention not only to the meaning of those six guidelines but to the fact that they were presented as government policy. This was a sign of political will, and also of political openness. Half the battle was won.

Before addressing the core of my topic, I would like to add one comment still on the topic of the government's platform. At the same time Minister Fortier was delivering his document, an advisory committee of prominent businessmen and businesswomen was being set up to guide the government in its privatization efforts. Their report was tabled in June 1986. Amongst other recommendations, they suggested that all ten commercially oriented Crown corporations be privatized.

What Was Soquem?

Soquem was created in 1965 by a special act of the National Assembly. Its purpose was twofold. First, it was to conduct mining exploration. Secondly, it was to seek, develop, and transform mineral substances. In order to reach its objectives, it could do so in conjunction with others. In any event, Soquem had to aim for profitability.

From 1965 to 1977 Soquem was increasing its exploration activities while living off government equity injections and the small cash flow that came from its niobium, copper, zinc, lead, silver and gold operations. Late in that period, Soquem discovered a gold-bearing property that would turn out to be one of the largest open-pit gold mining operations in Canada, that of Doyon. Soquem took in Lac Minerals as a fifty-fifty partner. Lac was also to be the manager of the site. Revenues started shooting up. At the same time, gold prices were rising to historical price levels. From revenues in 1978 of $5.9 million, they became $14.6 million in 1979, $15.5 million in 1980 and then $45.9 million in 1981, $40.4 million in 1982, and $42.3 million in 1983. The bottom line was as dramatically affected if not more so in 1981-82 because of the increase in the price of gold.

However, during the same period, Soquem had another challenge. In the late 1970s it had discovered a salt deposit in the Magdalen Islands off the east coast of the Gaspe Peninsula. It made the recommendation to its shareholder, the government, to go ahead and develop a salt mine but under very specific assumptions including a proper capital structure. As you can imagine, the project was already financially marginal at best but politically very attractive. Whereas the original $65 million cost was to have had a portion financed by a fresh equity injection, bad luck, an accident and other delays almost doubled the costs to $125 million. Worst of all, Soquem was told that the whole cost of the project had to be financed by internal cash flow and debt. In three years, 1982-84, Soquem borrowed $75 million. By the summer of 1986 at the time of the privatization, its debt had ballooned to $100 million. Soquem was in trouble financially.

The Need to Privatize

During the nine-year period 1977 to 1985, the average return on equity of Soquem was 1.42 percent. In 1984 it showed a loss of $6.2 million; in 1985, $5.0 million; and in 1986, $9.9 million. Things could not get better. In the meantime, the Doyon mine was planning to go underground at a substantial cost. The salt mine needed still more money to be turned around. The status quo was not a solution financially for Soquem nor was it an economically viable solution for the province. Indeed the lack of money meant that the two job-creating projects Soquem was involved with, Doyon and the salt mine, would see their expansion curtailed or terminated. On the exploration front, budgets decreased dramatically during the same nine-year period. While Soquem had spent $70 million in exploration from 1965 to 1985, it spent only $1.2 million in 1985 and $800,000 in 1986.

When analysing the options open to Soquem, we came to the conclusion that not only was Soquem in financial dire straights, but that its mission had been accomplished. Through tax incentives, the private sector had taken over exploration in the province. Privatization was thus one of the solutions. Other solutions included extra capitalization from the shareholder which was out of the question. Selling some assets was another solution but was unappealing for two reasons. Short of selling the Crown jewel, the 50 percent interest in Doyon Mine, or selling or closing the salt mine, no other asset would have dramatically helped Soquem's financial position. More philosophically, given that Soquem was a nation-building exercise, it would have been political suicide to sell these assets lock, stock and barrel to a specific private party, especially if the buyer were from out of the province. Therefore, privatization was retained.

The Bride's Basket

Before leading you into structuring considerations, let me give you a better view of Soquem's assets and liabilities at the time.

- The most attractive asset was clearly the 50 percent undivided interest in the Doyon gold mine. Doyon had over ten more years of mining reserves. Annual output was 170,000 ounces of gold. At $500 (CDN) per ounce that is $85 million of revenues. However, Soquem had the back seat. Lac Minerals was the manager.

- Another 50 percent joint venture was with Teck Corporation in Niobec, arguably the world's third largest producer of niobium, a metal mostly used in alloys. Niobec had been operating since 1976. Although grades were not exciting by world standards, productivity was excellent and cash flow, although minimal, was steady. This time Soquem was the manager.

- A 100 percent interest in the Magdalen Island salt mine. With revenues in excess of $35 million, Seleine, as it was called, had not yet reached maturity. It was still losing money. In addition, rock salt as a commodity is anything but scarce and competition is fierce.

- Portfolio investments that came with board representation, principally in three public gold mining companies: Sullivan Mines, Aiguebelle Resources and Louvem Mines. The latter two were in ailing financial health and the former was a sleeper.

- A large, probably the largest, portfolio of mining properties—over 60—principally in the Abitibi area, one of the busiest mining camps in Canada; and,

- $100 million of debt.

STRUCTURING THE TRANSACTION

Some Parameters

In structuring this transaction a few obvious conclusions hit us. There was no way we could privatize Soquem as it was. I have yet to see a money-losing Crown corporation sell shares to the public. Second, salt and gold don't mix in the public eye. Third, aside from the salt mine, Soquem did not seem to have much control over its assets. Most of them were managed by somebody else. Images of a holding company with its discount in the marketplace came to haunt us.

It was therefore decided to segregate the assets and privatize only the gold assets in addition to Niobec. Furthermore, the process had to yield enough cash to enable Soquem to substantially reduce if not eliminate its own debt while at the same time providing her with a minimum interest of 25 percent and a maximum of 45 percent interest in the assets to be privatized.

One may question why the objective was set to reduce Soquem's ownership below 50 percent. In my view, governments' objectives over time do not mesh with those of individual investors. With ownership above 50 percent, the temptation is far too big for a government to meddle in the affairs of a company no matter what the initial commitments were at the time of privatization. The message here was clear—we are getting out. To reinforce this message of disengagement, another wrinkle was used. It was decided that there would be a mechanism whereby Soquem would automatically reduce its ownership sometime in the future. The instrument was the warrant.

As you know, a warrant is a financial instrument, an option if you will, that allows its holder to buy a share of a company at a predetermined price for a specified period of time. Here, in addition to a common share there was a warrant. And whereas a warrant is more often than not exercisable into treasury or new shares of a company, in our case, in addition to warrants of that nature we also had warrants exercisable into shares still held by the government, thus ensuring that the government's position would be further reduced. But I am getting ahead of myself.

Coming back to structuring considerations. For legal, accounting and tax reasons, the selected assets were to be transferred to a shell company, Cambior, and shares of Cambior were to be sold to the public. Comparing Cambior's assets to that of other Canadian and international gold mining companies and analysing its ability to generate profits and cash flow, one could say that it was a healthy baby. Pro forma trailing twelve months revenues and profits were $51 million and $11.9 million respectively. For good measure, $10 million of debt was transferred to it from Soquem.

Everything looked good on paper. The original report recommending privatization was presented to Soquem's management on October 7, 1985. By December the structure had been put in place, the numbers crunched. An issue of $150 million was suggested. The new government took power

December 2. For the next three months, time was spent—wasted—in putting the finishing touches to the project. What was to be launched in early February was postponed until mid-March, then mid-May.

Who Decides?

In retrospect, the controversy was simple. It happens in all cases of privatizations, I suspect, particularly in cases of partial privatizations. It happens in situations where management and employees of a Crown corporation see some assets disappear from under their control. What is going to happen to them? Don't they have a say in the new venture? They have been deprived of the benefits of public ownership while working for a Crown corporation, do they not have a chance to participate? Herein lie the roots of the problems that pervaded this privatization.

While Soquem's preoccupations were often real and well-founded —such as having a say in selecting new management, a board of directors, determining the pricing and above all selecting the assets—the confrontational attitude taken by existing management killed all likelihood that its views would be heard. The other side of the story is equally appalling. Here is a newly-elected government that has not seen power in ten years. It is presented with a privatization plan as an ultimatum. Give us money; privatize or go bust. Ultimately the government took over. In doing so, clashes developed. Numerous, ferocious. Leaks were made to newspapers. Public affiliates of Soquem sued or threatened to sue—one for seeing its shares included in the assets being transferred, the other for not being included. The union, as expected, made noises about layoffs. Political intrigue blossomed.

In retrospect, and retrospect is 20/20 vision, the solution lay in the dialogue that ought to have taken place between the government and the Crown corporation's management. An understanding of Soquem's residual role after Cambior's privatization would have been useful. A job description for those who stayed behind would have been an enormous incentive.

In the end the government won. It selected the board of directors, it put the final touches on the selection of assets, it selected the management, and it assisted in pricing negotiations. In my view, although this may not sound very sympathetic to some of you, I believe that in any privatization process it is up to the government—the sole shareholder, let's not forget—to decide on the agenda, influence the pricing, select the board of directors and senior management. Existing management, employees, unions, suppliers and clients should participate in the process, but they should not forget the government's prerogative as the sole shareholder.

A LOOK AT THE MARKETPLACE

A Key Variable: The Price of Gold

While these shenanigans were taking place, there were some real concerns about the marketplace. In the fall of 1985 and the spring of 1986, gold prices were not that robust. They had touched a low of $288 (US) an ounce just six months before and were only hovering around $340 (US) at the time serious pricing talks were taking place.

Various financial structures were tested, such as a straight common share offering, common shares and warrants, gold purchase warrants, and convertible preferred shares when it was still fiscally interesting to issue them. By mid-March the decision was taken to launch a unit offering consisting of common shares and warrants as I described a little earlier.

Who to Sell to?

Another question we faced was to whom to sell the issue. Not much time was spent on the subject, but the decisions that were taken were right. Inevitably, when one privatizes one has to be sensitive to the political agenda and the political climate. The constituency of a government is its voters, of which, as you know, only about one in ten has money in the stock market and only one in 1,000 can afford to lose, say $10,000, without affecting his quality of life. With that thinking in mind, the reminder of the prevailing dull gold market and the prospect of a large $150 million issue—which would eventually be the sixth largest common share offering yet done in Canada, the third or fourth largest for an initial public offering and the largest IPO ever done in Quebec—we took a close look at the alternatives.

With the presence of the Quebec Stock Savings Plan, the temptation was big to flood the local market and provide every Tom, Dick and James and Jacques with some shares in "their" company. In order to achieve that goal, we asked ourselves: should investment dealers do it alone or should banks and credit unions with their tremendous branch network be enlisted? This option was easily disposed of. Gold stocks are not for everyone. Gold prices go up and down and so do the stocks. I for one, as a general principle, and I know there will be exceptions, encourage extreme care and caution when privatizing resource-related companies. The financial, and thus political, downside is much too serious.

Interestingly, at the time this was happening the press about South Africa—by far the largest gold producer in the world—was heating up. Many investors, especially European, were starting to withdraw from South Africa and look for alternatives. Canada was one. Canada ranks third or fourth in the world in terms of gold output. There are well-known substantial Canadian gold mining companies such as Campbell Red Lake, Dome Mines, Lac Minerals and others. The decision was taken to seriously market this issue in Europe, a first in Canadian privatizations.

Creating Awareness

We have all seen or heard ads in England and France touting the characteristics of a company that is to be privatized. Little "how to invest" booklets are mailed to the general public. Payment is made easy. Privatization is everybody's business. Not so in Canada. In Canada we have not had the luxury to be able to enlist the public's support in our efforts for one main reason, the regulator—or regulators I should say, ten of them. I am speaking, of course, of the provincial securities commissions.

During the months of March, April and May, efforts were made in the form of corporate-type ads to create a profile for Cambior. After all, if Soquem wasn't known, how well do you think the name Cambior rang a bell with investors? Unbeknownst to us at the time, these ads were offside in terms of some of the provincial securities acts. Arguments, hearings, cooling off periods, all delayed the file by at least three to four weeks. This delay could have seriously affected the success of the operation. I shudder at the thought of this one year later.

Herein lies one of the great lessons of public privatizations. They cannot but work. They have to work. The political fallout from a failed issue is too large not only for the government of the day but for the province or the country as a whole. I would suggest it is high time our legislators got together to open the securities field and permit broad dissemination of financial and corporate data about Canadian companies including cases of privatizations with the help of the media.

Pricing

There are two aspects of the pricing of this issue I would like to cover with you briefly: one concerns the mechanics, the other the process. Let me start with the mechanics. In determining the pricing, I mentioned earlier that we did what any financial adviser would do—compared our proposed pricing with that of comparable investment alternatives, by that I mean comparing the pricing with that of other gold-mining stocks.

But there were other factors, some positive, some negative. For one, we were dealing with an internationally recognized commodity, gold. Clearly, we would have no problems arousing interest outside the country. By Canadian standards, Cambior with its anticipated annual production and its market capitalization was to rank easily in the top ten producers in the country, a clear alternative to most other senior Canadian stocks that many considered too expensive at the time. Finally, the issue was going to benefit from the eligibility to the Quebec Stock Savings Plan, not a small advantage when practically all other Quebec-based company issues were also eligible to that plan.

Consider now some of the negatives. Cambior was operational in only one province. Any counsellor will tell you to seek geographical diversification in your investments. This was not our case. Also, as I alluded to before, although Cambior was well-endowed in terms of assets, it hardly controlled the money-making ones, thus, the holding company syndrome with its associated discount to true break-up value. Also, a big hindrance was management or rather the absence of it. Nobody knew the capabilities of the new management team that had hastily been assembled two months prior to the issue. I would say it was our biggest hurdle. Finally, the delays and the occasional bad press and lawsuits did not help our case.

Given all those circumstances, it is fair to say that the issue was reasonably priced based on the data that was available to us at the time. But, more importantly, the price was perceived by the marketplace to be at a discount to where it could have been, based on strict numbers. In the end, perceived value made the issue successful.

The second aspect of the pricing of this issue you may find interesting is the process that was followed. As I mentioned before, there were three parties to this transaction, four if you count the underwriters. The three parties were the government as shareholder, Soquem's management and board, and Cambior's management and its new board. Partial privatization as opposed to en-bloc privatization adds one party to the negotiating table.

Although everybody's interest is in realizing a successful issue, the greed factor quickly enters and all three parties take different positions. Soquem's management takes the high road. It is, after all, the legal seller. It wants nothing but the highest price. On the other hand, new management's performance and compensation will be linked, after the issue, in large part to the performance of the stock. It wants the lowest price. Interestingly, but not surprisingly, the party that has the most to lose and to gain in the process is the government. It will take the middle road. On the one hand it wants to get fair value so as not to be accused of dilapidating the family silver. On the other hand and above all, it demands a successful transaction.

As it turns out, the level of comfort that the government required so early in the transaction (final terms were agreed upon on May 12, a full two and one-half months before the final prospectus) probably played against its interest in obtaining the best price. But, in my view, the political risk it was taking as well as the credibility risk for the province if the transaction did not work was far greater than the risk of leaving something on the table. Let us not forget that there was also a built-in mechanism to protect the government, in a way, from a sudden rise in price that may have been perceived as mispricing. It lay in the fact that the government kept a residual interest in Cambior of close to 32 percent, thereby ensuring it would participate in any rise in the price of the stock in the aftermarket.

The Issue

I realize that in the last few minutes I have been hinting at a very success-ful issue. Let me briefly comment on the issue itself. What was originally announced as a $100 million to $125 million issue ended up being a roar-ing success. The preliminary prospectus was filed May 15. The first week was slow. Local Quebec demand was gaining momentum, but slowly. Canadian road shows started on May 26. European road shows were held starting June 9. Within two weeks the books showed interest of $400 mil-lion, of which $200 million came from Europe.

What made this success possible? In my view, five aspects. First, the word "privatization." In the summer of 1986, especially in Europe, that word was still synonymous with quick profits. Secondly, as mentioned before, value. Value is the great equalizer. Whatever the political message, whatever the hype, one does not build a large transaction on anything but value. Thirdly, the stock market was on a roll. We were then and still are now in a buoyant market. Money was available. We had a winner! Fourth, the price of gold started rising. We simply got lucky. Fifth, local demand was enormous. Privatization can only work if local demand is present in force. In turn, this demand can only exist if there is a legitimate domestic capital market.

That, in a nutshell, is the story of the issue that was priced on July 24, 1986, a year ago today. The stock was listed on August 13, 1986. The first trade was done at $11 having been issued at $10.

Life after Privatization

As August 13th approached, anxiety started building. At what price were the shares going to open? As I just mentioned, they opened at $11. This, in itself, was already a miracle. From the day of pricing, officially July 24th,

1986, to August 13th, the price of gold went from $349 (US) to $385 (US). After a period of "shakeout" of fringe investors expecting to double their money in two weeks, real buying took place, fast and furious. In the following weeks, Cambior was often on top of the list of the most actively traded Canadian resource stocks.

In the ensuing months, the opposition's feeble attempts to discredit the transaction failed. New management was making its mark. Good news came from anticipated but up to then unconfirmed reports that the Doyon mine was going to deliver even better results. The price of gold kept rising. Canadian gold stocks rose even faster, Cambior with them. The peak was reached on April 14, 1987, when the unit consisting of one common share and one-half warrant that was issued at $10 was trading at $47.81. Mind you, gold had risen 27 percent between July 24 and that date and the Canadian gold sub-index rose 155 percent during the same period. As of last Friday, July 17, the unit was trading at $37.13.

The issue of privatization has now died down. Cambior is now part of the Canadian mining and stock market scenery. It has a substantial exploration budget. It is participating fully in the expansion of the Doyon mine. It is engaged in takeover activities. The company is making its own bed. How long will it last? Probably until the present government or a new one decides to dispose of its remaining block.

WHAT LESSONS DID WE LEARN?

Without wanting to sound pompous, I would like to suggest to you some lessons we can take from the Soquem/Cambior experience.

- A public issue was only one route available to the government. A private sale, a tender process, a piecemeal sale of certain assets—all were alternate methods. There is no magic in a public issue. The profit is high. The risks are higher.
- In Canada we often tend to look elsewhere, particularly to England or to the United States, for precedents. Although I am neither a historian nor a sociologist, I would suggest that no party in Canada, provincial or federal has in its roots, aside from periodical electoral platforms, any tradition that calls for equal access to wealth and equal opportunity to access that wealth. From this I suggest that it would be unwise for any government in Canada to expect to generate a following in the nature of a crusade to support its privatization efforts as we have seen elsewhere.
- Partial privatization is an awkward process. Management that is to be left behind should be well treated, cajoled almost. Think for a moment

what senior management or personnel of B.C. Hydro or Quebec Hydro would say if they were directed to sell part of their operations to the private sector. I will bet you they would not play dead.

- The need for political will. While I seem to have distanced myself from the British experience in my talk, we all have heard Mrs. Thatcher's commitment to privatize. Let us forget for a moment why she made that commitment and remember that she did it. Closer to us, here in B.C. the BCRIC experience that was so well researched by the Fraser Institute was also a demonstration of political will. In the Soquem/Cambior saga, government pressure and commitment was maintained. You need it to successfully privatize.
- Value is the key. The major world stock markets have witnessed boom times in the past five years. This will not, this cannot, continue forever. Be flexible in pricing. I would not like to be the underwriter or the minister in charge of the first large public privatization that enters a down market.
- Presence of a local capital market. To expect to generate local demand one has to be able to count on the existence of a viable domestic capital market.

Before concluding I would simply like to add what has been done in Quebec in matters of privatization besides Cambior in the last two years. A sugar refinery was sold to the private sector; Quebecair, the money-losing airline, was sold to Nordair-Metro after very public negotiations; a small fishing and fish-processing company was sold to local interests; the control block in Donohue, a publicly traded pulp and paper company was sold after a successful tender process, and there were other smaller situations. In all, a very successful privatization campaign. What it could do without major restructuring efforts, the government has done. What is left? Chronically money-losing propositions in iron and steel and in asbestos, for instance, and monopolies. I hope to be back in a few years to talk to you about their privatization, or perhaps they won't be privatized after all.

REFERENCES

"Privatization of Quebec Government Crown Corporations: Progress Report." Associate Minister for Finance and Privatization. March 1987.

"Report of the Committee on the Privatization of Crown Corporations. From the quiet revolution ... to the twenty-first century." Submitted to Mr. Pierre Fortier Minister Responsible for Privatization. June 1986.

"Privatization of Crown Corporations: Orientation and Prospects." Minister Responsible for Privatization. February 1986.

Preliminary prospectus dated May 15, 1986, and Final Prospectus dated July 24, 1986, of Cambior inc.

Privatization: Theory and Practice, T.M. Ohaski and T.P. Roth, The Fraser Institute, 1980.

"Crown Corporations in Canada. The Calculus of Instrument Choice," edited by J. Robert Prichard. University of Toronto, 1983.

"Privatization if necessary but not necessarily privatization," Institute for Research on Public Policy, T.E. Kierans, September 1984.

"La Privatisation de Soquem." Report submitted to the management of Soquem by McLeod Young Weir Limited outlining the process of privatization of Soquem, October 1985. Document tabled at the National Assembly in September 1986.

Soquem. Annual Report as at March 31, 1987.

Cambior Inc. Annual Report as at December 31, 1986.

WENDELL COX

(Introduction by Michael A. Walker)

We have been very fortunate in attracting Wendell Cox to Vancouver to discuss a particular instance of service privatization. Mr. Cox is a leading North American expert and a leading advocate for and a successful promoter of privatization of money-losing transit systems right across North America. He was graduated from California State University and Pepperdine University and has amassed a truly unbelievable record of experience in the politics and economics of contracting out, including advising transit operators on the appropriate strategy to minimize labour reaction to change.

A background in finance and strategic planning at the Crocker National Bank and an eight-year stint on the Los Angeles County Transportation Commission prepared Wendell for his career as an urban transportation consultant. In the latter capacity, he has advised and/or devised strategic plans for governments in California, Louisiana, Missouri, Colorado, Michigan, Georgia, Indiana, Oklahoma and Florida. He is a member of the board of the Joint Center for Urban Mobility Research and has been chairman of the American Public Transit Association Committee. Recently, I might tell you, he has been in British Columbia to advise the B.C. government on its transportation policy and the measures it might take to privatize its operations.

CHAPTER 12

PRIVATIZATION IN THE PUBLIC SERVICES:
Competitive Contracting and the Public
Ethic in Urban Public Transport

Wendell Cox

THE PRIVATE INTERESTS OF PUBLIC MONOPOLIES

Public monopolies were established by governments to provide essential services with the expectation that these organizations would serve the public interest first. It was assumed that motivated by the profit motive, public monopolies would be driven by the public interest, rather than by private interests. A public ethic would emerge wherein the good of the people or society would be the consuming preoccupation. The public ethic holds that activities undertaken in the name of the public should provide the maximum reasonable benefit to the public. Conversely, the public ethic is not operative if the activity undertaken in the name of the public results in a net loss to the public. In practice, the public has lost because public monopolies have been characterized by high and escalating costs, low quality of services, and arrogant treatment of customers. The failure of public monopolies is stark. It is widespread, and it is geographically dispersed. From the Soviet Union and China to Africa, Europe, the United Kingdom, Australia, and the Americas, governments are modifying or replacing public monopolies with competitive mechanisms to improve service to the public.

Why have public monopolies been so unsuccessful? Because, without the natural incentives of the competitive market, public authorities are inclined to replicate the excesses of private monopolies, and more (at least private monopolies are subject to government regulation—a rarity for public monopolies). Public monopolies are just as likely to pursue their own good as are private monopolies, to the detriment of customers and the public. This is consistent with the public choice theory developed by Nobel Laureate James M. Buchanan which holds that public officials are driven more by their own private interests than by the public interest. Public managers are not somehow a moral step above private managers; like private managers they are rewarded as the establishment grows, not as the establishment declines.

The problem with monopoly, public or private, has never been that monopolists are evil, it is that monopolists are human. Human beings in responsible positions rarely resist using the power available to them. This is why the theoretically pure form of government suggested in Plato's *Republic* has never become a reality. Competitive incentives are either absent or defective in the monopoly environment. Public monopolies were doomed from the start to become expensive failures.

The public monopolies did not develop a public ethic; instead a new private ethic emerged, the private interest of the public monopolies. Public monopolies evolved to primarily serve their own internal interest to the detriment of the customer groups they were established to serve. In response to this failure, privatization has arisen to replace or modify the public monopolies.

PRIVATIZATION: VEHICLE OF THE PUBLIC ETHIC

Privatization is the use of competitive market options to provide government services. Privatization is characterized by a public purpose, not by a private purpose. The thrust of privatization is to obtain quality services for the public at the lowest possible cost. It has two primary forms.

Sale or Transfer of Commercial Services

Some services that are provided by government are commercial (profitable, or could become so under competitive management). In such cases, privatization involves the sale or transfer of an enterprise to the private sector, and the enterprise competes for customers in the market. This provides financial gain for the government through the sale proceeds, subsequent taxes, and the elimination of subsidies. Consumers gain through the cost control and service quality that are the natural result of a competitive market.

Competitive Contracting of Non-Commercial Services

Other government services are non-commercial (unprofitable); if they are to be offered, they must be subsidized by public funds. There might be considerable disagreement about whether or not a particular service is within the sphere of appropriate government activity, but privatization is not concerned with that debate, it is rather concerned with the most economical production of services that have been determined to be public. Non-commercial services can be most economically provided through the competitive market.

> The issue is not whether more billions should be spent, but how to spend each pound to the best effect. Individuals do that, day after day. So do companies. They succeed, more or less, because they face choices as consumers and competition as producers. The minimum duty of a state should be to replicate such choice and competition in its own affairs, so that the billions it raises in taxes achieve the high-sounding aims it sets for itself. (*Economist* 1987)

If government has decided to provide a non-commercial service, then a form of privatization, competitive contracting (competitive tendering), can achieve that best effect in public expenditure. Through competitive contracting, government can obtain the competitive incentives of the market, by entering the competitive market as the purchaser of services for the users and taxpayers. The fact that operating revenues fall short of the programme expenses is not a barrier because services are still subsidized, but at a lower rate (chart 1). Competitive bidding is used to obtain public services from the most economical provider, public or private, subject to standards established by public authorities. Competitive contracting is under the full control of public authorities, and results in lower immediate and long-term costs, improved cost control and improved service quality.

This paper examines competitive contracting of public services by reviewing the experience of public transport in the United States.

THE PURPOSE OF PUBLIC SERVICES

The debate over privatization of non-commercial services (referred to as "public services" throughout this paper) is fundamentally a matter of values. These values go to the very heart of political philosophy: What is the purpose of public services and who are they established to serve?

A public service would not be established unless government had determined that it was essential for the service to be provided and that it

Chart #1

COMPETITIVE CONTRACTING CONCEPT
Cost Comparison for Unit of Service

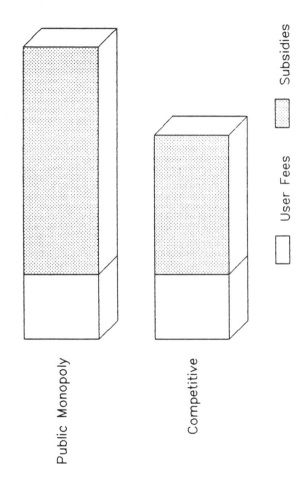

Public Monopoly

Competitive

User Fees

Subsidies

could not be reliably provided commercially. Public services are established to directly serve the general public or a subset of the general public (users). Thus, the purpose of an education system is to educate students; the purpose of a public roads programme is to build and maintain roadways for drivers, and the purpose of a public transport system is to provide mobility to passengers. (This may sound so elementary as to be absurd, but examination of public transport in the United States will demonstrate that, in practice, purposes other than service to users can assume a predominant position.) Public services are established to directly benefit the users, assuming a particular public funding level. The users are served by receiving more service, not less, and by better service, not worse.

Further, public services are established for the general welfare of society and are financed, partially or wholly by the taxpayers. All public services require support through tax revenues collected from these customers. Assuming a particular level of public expenditure, taxpayers are best served by lower, not higher taxes.

Government purchases public services for the specific good of the users and for the general good of society. Thus, it is proposed that *the purpose of a public service is to maximize the level of a particular standard of service to the users for the lowest possible expenditure of taxes.* This purpose is rooted in a public ethic, the basic test of which is the extent to which the activities of a public enterprise benefit the users and/or the taxpayers, and at a minimum that there should be no net loss to the users or the taxpayers.

PUBLIC TRANSPORT IN THE UNITED STATES

Urban public transport has undergone major changes in the United States over the last four decades. (Intercity bus or coach travel remains commercial in the United States and is not treated in this paper.)

Public Transport as a Non-Commercial Enterprise

In the United States, public transport is not a commercial enterprise. There are no systems, and few, if any individual routes that can be operated profitably. This is in contrast to Great Britain, where people use automobiles less frequently for urban trips. There, more than 70 percent of the deregulated public transport routes outside London are now being operated commercially (Balcombe, Hopkin, Perrett and Clough 1987). In the United States, passenger revenues account for less than 37 percent of costs. Annual passenger journeys declined by more than 52 percent from 1950 to 1980, and by 1980 there were only 28 annual per capita passenger journeys (calculated from American Public Transit Association 1985). This compares to more than 80 per capita trips in the United Kingdom (calculated from Department of Transport 1985).

An important difference between the two nations is the degree of urban population dispersion. The scattering of residential and commercial development has been very significant in the United States. For example, in 1980 population density in U.S. urbanized areas was 1,033 persons per square kilometre. This is more than a 50 percent decline from 1950 (2,089), and there is every reason to expect that this trend will continue. A recent study concluded that suburb-to-suburb commuting has become the dominant pattern, accounting for double the number of commuters as suburb-to-central city commuting (*Philadelphia Inquirer* 1987). The U.S. residential and commercial dispersion has been supported by the development of comprehensive highway systems and the proliferation of automobiles. Public transport is more often than not unavailable or extremely inconvenient to use in the newer suburban and exurban commercial areas. Employment growth continues to be greatest on and beyond the urban fringe, with central business districts being of declining relative significance. This trend may even accelerate as a result of a recent U.S. Supreme Court decision (First English Evangelical Lutheran Church versus County of Los Angeles, 1987) that will make control of dispersed development even more difficult for public authorities. In the not too distant future, the population density of U.S. urban areas could drop below that of some entire countries (such as 85 percent rural Bangladesh, which has 672 people per square kilometre).

One impact of this dispersion is that public transport has largely lost its discretionary market segment (customers who have automobiles but choose instead to travel by public transport). The discretionary market segment is small, and it is largely limited to peak commuting periods. Strong discretionary markets still exist in only a small number of core cities (New York, Chicago, San Francisco, Boston, and Philadelphia). Outside of these core cities, the discretionary market is limited to work trips to the downtown areas, where relative employment is declining. From 1970 to 1980, the work trip market share of public transport in larger urban centres declined by 30 percent in the United States. What remains is the "captive" market segment—those people who ride public transport because they have no other alternative. This market segment is characterized by persons with low income or with physical handicaps, and who have limited access to automobiles. Some reports have indicated that the average public transport rider lives on an income below the poverty line. It is therefore reasonable to characterize public transport in the United States as becoming a poverty programme.

Nevertheless, public authorities have considered it desirable to encourage increased use of public transport by automobile commuters. Thus, public transport in the United States has a dual purpose: to increase public transport usage and to preserve the mobility of the present users. National, state and local governments have determined that public transport, a non-commercial enterprise, is a public service.

Performance of Public Transport Monopolies

In the United States, because of the precipitous decline in patronage during the 1950s and 1960s, private transport monopolies became unprofitable. To retain public transport service, governments created new public transport monopolies that bought or assumed control of the transport systems. This transition was largely completed by 1970.

Cost Escalation

As the degree of public ownership increased, operating costs per vehicle kilometre escalated at higher rates.

Period	Public Ownership	Inflation Adj. Cost Increase	Annual Real Increase
1940-55	20.2%	16.7%	1.04%
1955-70	45.0%	29.9%	1.76%
1970-83	83.0%	51.8%	3.26%

From 1970 to 1983, operating costs per kilometre increased an inflation adjusted (real) 52 percent. This cost escalation outstripped virtually every element of the Consumer Price (inflation) Index, including both medical care services and fuel (chart 2). *If public transit costs had risen within the inflation rate, the same service and fare levels could have been provided in 1983 for $5,700 million instead of the $8,700 million*—a savings of $3,000 million.

Public subsidies were increased, and new subsidy programmes were established to ensure the continuation of vital transportation services to the needy, and to provide an alternative to the automobile for potential new customers after the gasoline distribution crises of 1973 and 1979. Yet the public obtained only $0.32 of benefit for every dollar of subsidy. Approximately $0.20 was used to reduce public transport fares in real terms, while $0.12 was used to increase service levels. Alternatively, $0.68

Chart #2

PUBLIC TRANSPORT COST INCREASES

Compared to Inflation and Medical Costs

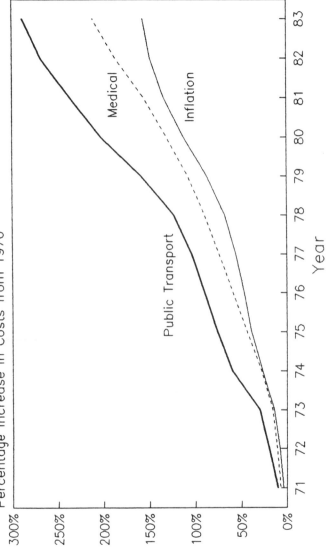

Percentage Increase in Costs from 1970

Medical

Inflation

Public Transport

Year

went to pay for cost escalation above the inflation rate (chart 3). If the public subsidies spent on cost escalation above inflation had been spent to expand services, 5,200 million kilometres of service could have been operated, instead of the 3,400 million kilometres that were operated.

This cost escalation has diluted the ability of public authorities to develop longer term transportation improvements. For example, in Los Angeles public transport cost escalation above inflation over the last decade has exceeded $1,000 million. That is enough to build the three urban rail lines under consideration, for which no firm financing is likely to soon be available.

Scanning the public transport literature over the last decade, however, one might be surprised to learn that costs have continued to escalate. A number of methods have been applied to public transport cost control, with great promise. In the late 1970s, improved management and performance monitoring systems were going to arm managers with the information necessary to bring costs under control. The impact of these programmes was imperceivable at the bottom line. Then came the negotiation of "part-time" labour provisions in labour contracts. Research has indicated that most of the savings achieved were cancelled by the higher wages and benefits for full-time workers that were exchanged for the part-time provisions (Institute of Transportation Studies, 1981).

There is increasing consensus that cost control is not possible under public transport monopolies. Even the proponents of public transport monopolies have abandoned their cost defences and have instead found justification for continued cost increases. One large eastern seaboard public transport monopoly anticipates that within five years real costs will increase another 50 percent. While cost control is the exception with public transport monopolies, cost control is inherent to the competitive private bus industry (see below).

Private Interests of Transport Monopolies

But the problems of public transport monopolies have gone far beyond costs. Public transport monopolies have pursued interests that are at odds with the public welfare.

A west coast public transport monopoly fought hard to deny a private bus company the authority to operate profitable commuter services during and after the 1973-74 gasoline availability crisis. The public transport monopoly alleged that the private operator diverted passenger revenue from the public transport monopoly. However, the public operator provided no competing service and had no plans to do so. The public

Chart #3

USES OF PUBLIC TRANSPORT SUBSIDIES: 1983
Calculated from 1970 Base

Fare Reductions
19.7%

New Service
12.4%

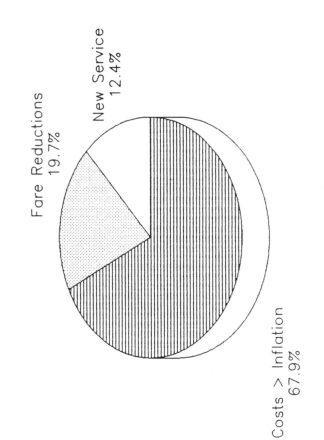

Costs > Inflation
67.9%

operator argued that customers should ride its service that required two transfers, a trip at least 30 kilometres out of the way, and more than two additional hours each way. There was no public purpose here, there was instead the private purpose of the public transport monopoly—the public transport monopoly sought to limit services available, thereby restricting choices available to the public.

A midwestern public transport monopoly, fearing that it might lose a service contract, offered to provide the service without charge to the customer. This increased cost to the public authority would have been in the face of planned service reductions that might otherwise have been avoided and unmet mobility needs in other parts of its service area that have been widely publicized. There was no public purpose operating here, there was rather the private interest of the public transport monopoly, which chose to expend the scarce public resources entrusted to it to consolidate power rather than to maximize service to the public.

In at least two cases, public transport monopolies have threatened suburban communities with sanctions if they undertook competitively contracted local services. These have included one threat to reroute a planned urban rail system away from such a suburb and another threat to cancel the services that the public transport monopoly would still have provided in the suburb. The public monopolies were driven by private purposes, not by the public ethic. They sought to use monopoly power to maintain and extend their own influence rather than to serve the public.

One public transport monopoly attempted what might be characterized as a strategy of predatory pricing to retain a suburban service that was to be competitively contracted. A suburban community was to award a contract for the service to a private bus operator at a substantial savings compared to the previous costs of the public monopoly. In response, the public monopoly submitted an unsolicited proposal (the monopoly had not bid in the competitive procurement) that was well below its previous year's price. This was despite the fact that the costs of the public monopoly were rising. Had this proposal been accepted, the result would have been to divert millions of dollars of public subsidy money from the public transport monopoly's core community (the only community in which the public transport monopoly had a legal mandate to provide service). The private interest of the public monopoly would have been served, to the detriment of both the users (a generally less affluent group compared to the suburban users) and the taxpayers.

Management

Public transport management has been understandably less effective in the non-competitive environment. For example, some large public transport monopolies have driver absenteeism rates that are shocking. Two large west coast public transport monopolies have average annual absenteeism rates of more than 30 days (not including vacations and holidays), more than four times the standard in private industry. When challenged by the press, one such monopoly set a goal to reduce absenteeism by 20 percent over three years—in other words from 30 to 24 days—still three times the national standard. A firm in a competitive environment would be fortunate to survive if its absenteeism rate approached one half the rate of large public transport monopolies.

Revenue vehicle fleets have been allowed to deteriorate so much that public transport monopolies have not been able to operate their daily service schedules. In Detroit, over a three-year period (from 1982 to 1985) the number of buses operated on a daily basis dropped from 690 to 270 because of maintenance management problems. In 1982, the fleet had deteriorated in Houston to such an extent that the public transport monopoly had to borrow buses from other public transport monopolies. Similar situations have occurred over the last decade in Philadelphia, San Francisco, Miami and Cleveland, and they will continue to occur if the non-competitive environment is retained.

Management, Labour and Public Monopoly

The performance difficulties cited are not intended to imply that the fault lies with management or with labour. Of course, there are skillful managers in public transport, and less skillful managers. But management can only make a limited difference in the non-competitive environment. Similarly, labour unions cannot be blamed for obtaining all that is achievable in collective agreements. Enterprises and people tend to seek what they perceive as their own good. People tend to prefer better life styles, not worse. Enterprises tend to prefer more power, not less. The problem is that in a non-competitive environment, the customary restraints of the competitive market are absent or of little influence. Consequently, public transport monopolies exhibit cost escalation and other behaviour that is at odds with the public interest. The interests of the users and taxpayers are plundered in the unbalanced non-competitive environment.

The Future

If the non-competitive environment is not replaced by a competitive environment, public transport users and taxpayers are likely to pay a heavy toll. Based upon public transport cost trends, it can be expected that unit costs will rise another 37 percent in real terms by the year 2000. This would require another $2,200 million in 2000 and $18,000 million in additional expenditures over the period, just to retain present levels of service. Alternatively, if the higher costs are absorbed by the public transport monopolies—without real increases in public subsidies—fares might have to rise a real 161 percent, service might be reduced by 16 percent, and patronage could be expected to decline by another 40 percent. This could result in the elimination of approximately 14,000 bus driver jobs (American Bus Association, 1987).

Public Transportation Monopolies and the Public Ethic

The performance of the public transport monopolies should be tested against the purpose of a public service which is *to maximize the level of a particular standard of service to the users for the lowest possible expenditure of taxes.*

Have the users and taxpayers gained or lost from the substantial public subsidies? Only 32 percent of the new public funding expended on public transport has been used to increase service or lower real fares. The users have lost 68 percent of what was to have been their benefit. They have foregone potentially lower fares and significant service increases that might otherwise have been provided. Likewise, the taxpayers have received a return of only $0.32 for every public dollar expended. The remainder, 68 percent, has contributed nothing whatever to the public welfare. The impacts on the customers of public transport have been:

Higher real costs for the users, which translate into:

- lower service levels at a given funding and service quality level, and/or
- higher fares at a given funding and service quality level,
- transit system improvements, which might otherwise have been provided, have been foregone.

For the taxpayers:

- tax rate increases that have largely supported the cost escalation of existing services rather than increasing service levels or reducing fares.

It is clear that the public has suffered a net loss—for every dollar of public gain, three dollars have been consumed by the public transport monopolies. Absurdly, public transport monopolies have come in practice to serve themselves first and only secondarily to serve the public. What is particularly distressing about this conclusion is that public transport's largest market segment is characterized by poverty level incomes.

Stated another way:

> much money is squandered and welfare services are run for the benefit of those who work in them rather than those who desperately need them (*The Sunday Times* 1987).

What was to have been a transfer of income from society in general (the taxpayers) to the users of public transport has become instead a transfer of income from the taxpayers and users to the public transport monopolies themselves. Public transport has not been driven by the public ethic because its structure does not permit it.

COMPETITIVE CONTRACTING AND PUBLIC TRANSPORT

As the performance of the public transport monopolies became more of a concern to public officials, private bus companies were employed to provide public transport services under contract. One compelling reason for this use was the favourable cost performance of such enterprises.

Performance of the Private Bus Industry

The opportunities that were made available by the increased public funding for public transport need not have been lost. In significant contrast to the cost escalation of the public transport monopolies, private bus companies have controlled their costs. These companies include intercity, charter, airport and tour operators. From 1970 to 1983 real costs per kilometre declined 3 percent as compared to the 52 percent real increase in public transport (chart 4). Relative to public transport costs during this period, private bus company costs declined 36 percent. Cost performance has improved since then. In 1982 the U.S. government enacted a deregulation bill that greatly increased competition in major segments of the private bus industry. This has resulted in even further downward cost pressures, with real costs per kilometre declining a further 6 percent from 1983 to 1985 (calculated from *Metro Magazine* 1987). This cost performance has been achieved while achieving an enviable safety record (chart 5).

Public officials are often interested in why private (competitive) costs are so much below public costs. The basic reason, of course, is that *competition results in better cost control* (better price control for the

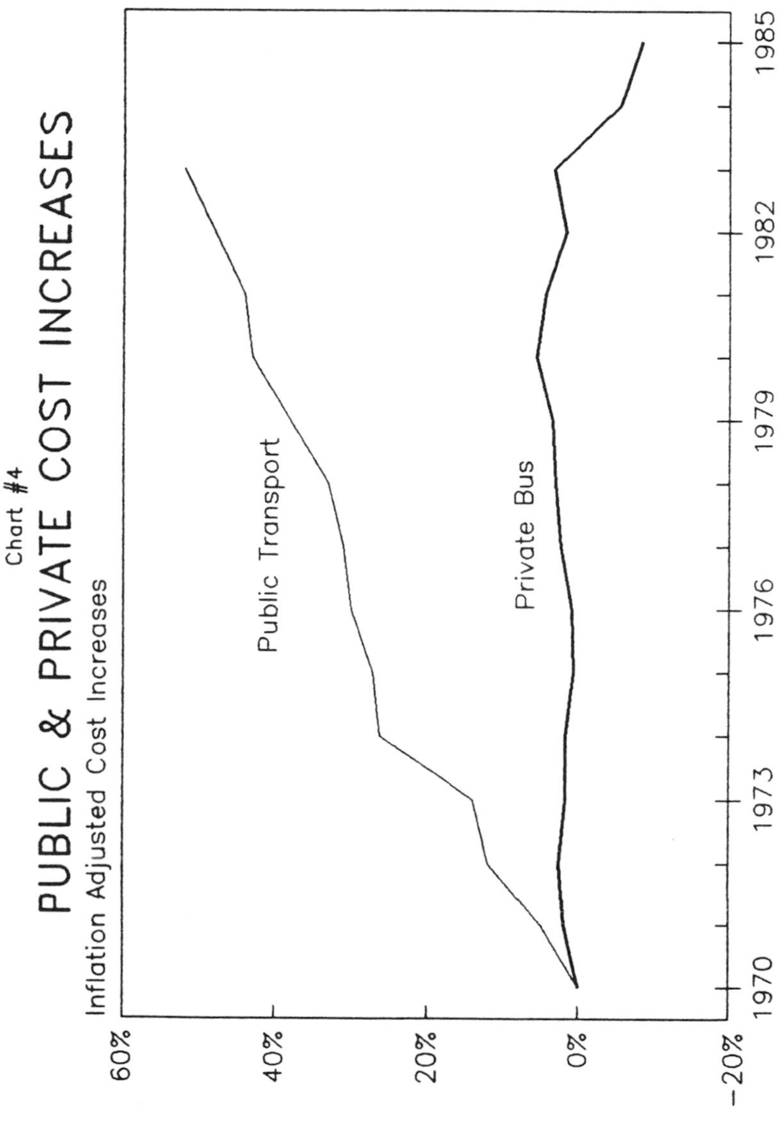
Chart #4
PUBLIC & PRIVATE COST INCREASES
Inflation Adjusted Cost Increases
Public Transport
Private Bus
60%
40%
20%
0%
-20%
1970
1973
1976
1979
1982
1985

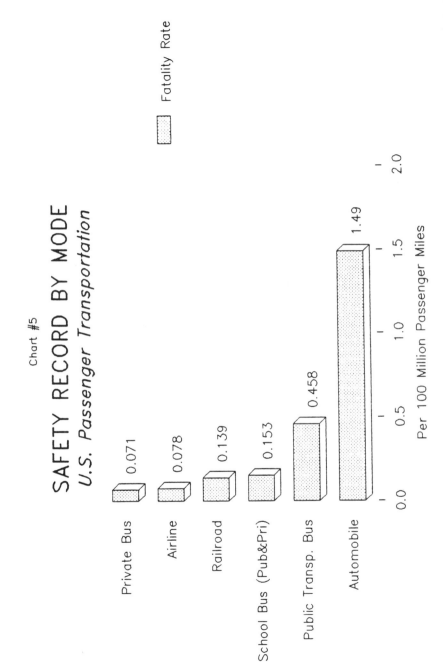

Chart #5

SAFETY RECORD BY MODE
U.S. Passenger Transportation

consumer). This is illustrated by the experience of other competitive markets. For example, specific airline markets in the United States may be served by one carrier or by more than one carrier. In monopolistic markets (one carrier), air fares are, almost without exception, higher than comparable competitive markets. One survey indicated that those differences range from 48 percent to 58 percent (*Frequent Flyer* 1987).

By contrast, it is possible to identify elements that operate differently in a non-competitive environment such as public transport:

• Wages and benefit packages tend to be more costly in a non-competitive environment, especially where there is no regulation as in public transport. The average hourly cost of wages and benefits for drivers exceeded $22 in 1985, compared to the private bus industry average of $9, and the national employee average of $10.55 (American Bus Association 1987). The labour unions, quite understandably, seek to obtain the best settlements for their members. The managers and public officials have little effective incentive, and even less political appetite to take the kind of strong negotiating position that would keep cost increases within inflationary bounds. This is illustrated not only by public transport in the United States, but also by the experience of public monopolies in the United Kingdom. The increase in management labour costs tends to track with the increase in driver labour costs. (In some states the highest paid public official is the chief executive officer of a public transport monopoly.)

• Management has less incentive to manage against expense control objectives in the monopoly environment. In a non-competitive market, managers manage toward revenue rather than expense goals. The answer to most substantive questions is more revenue, either from the users or the taxpayers. The management performance required by the public ethic is unachievable without competitive incentives.

COMPETITIVE CONTRACTING IN PUBLIC TRANSPORT

As a result of the cost control failure of the public transport monopolies, some public authorities have competitively contracted public transport services to private companies. More than half of the paratransit (dial-a-ride or demand responsive) service is competitively contracted, and competitive contracting of more conventional services is increasing.

How Competitive Contracting Works

Under competitive contracting, the lowest cost responsible and responsive producer provides public transport service, subject to quality standards established by the public authorities. Thus, competitive contracting does not necessarily mean private operation, it could mean public operation where public costs are lower than private costs. In such a case, a public authority can be awarded a contract under the same terms and conditions that would have bound a successful private bidder (as has occurred at London Regional Transport). The issue is not who provides the service, the issue is that the public should receive the most economical service that meets the quality standards established by the public authorities.

Competitive contracting allows full policy control of the service by public authorities. The public authority determines which routes are operated, where they are operated, how frequently they are operated, what fares are charged, and transfer arrangements. Most public transport authorities require that the vehicles be painted according to the public authority's specifications (liveries), so that all of its services, private and public, have an identical appearance to the customers.

The public authority seeks bids or proposals to operate a particular service for a particular period of time. Private companies respond, and the contract is awarded to the lowest responsive and responsible bidder or proposer. The private company has incentives to perform effectively: the contract may be cancelled for unsatisfactory performance; many contracts provide for penalties for unsatisfactory performance; and, the private company will be interested in being favourably considered when the contract is rebid at its expiration. The jobs of present public transport employees can be protected by restricting the competitive contracting conversion to the natural employee attrition (wastage) rate.

Results

Four basic impacts have been noted:

Lower costs

Competitive costs are lower than public costs by an average of 30 percent. Cost savings have ranged from 10 to 60 percent (Teal, Giuliano and Morlok 1986; American Bus Association 1987). For example,

- In Los Angeles, three large contracts have recently been awarded, with savings of from 37 to 50 percent.
- In Houston, private park-and-ride service is operated for 33 percent less than public costs.
- In Seattle, private express service is operated for 37 percent less than the previous public costs.
- In Chicago, privately provided service for the disabled is operated at cost savings of more than 50 percent.

Improved cost control

- Competitive costs rise less steeply than non-competitive costs. This has been demonstrated in a number of California contracts and in Houston. Competitive costs have generally risen at or below the inflation rate, as has been the experience in the private bus industry generally.

Improved public cost performance

Finally, a competitive environment improves public cost performance. This has been documented in a number of cases in the United States.

- Lower cost increases have occurred in San Diego and Norfolk.
- The competitive environment has considerably improved labour settlements in San Diego, Los Angeles, San Antonio, Phoenix, and other cities as it has become clear that there are alternatives to public monopoly service provision.
- The mere threat of competitive contracting can be a powerful incentive to improved public monopoly cost performance. One public transport monopoly threatened to discontinue service for three months during 1985 unless additional public revenues were obtained. At the same time, local public officials became interested in competitive contracting and became convinced that the transport system could be operated competitively for significantly less. In threatening this environment, the public monopoly found ways to continue operations through the year without additional revenues, and has continued to operate despite a deteriorating public funding situation. Two years later fares had not been raised, and service had not been reduced.

Improved service quality

- More and more, there are reports of improved service quality under competitive contracting. This impact has been noted in Los Angeles and Seattle. Similar experience has been noted at London Regional Transport.

San Diego and Competitive Contracting

These public benefits have been clearly demonstrated in San Diego. In 1979 a very costly labour settlement brought driver wages to over $10 per hour, the highest in the United States at the time. This controversial settlement induced communities in the San Diego area to begin competitively contracting for public transit service. From 1979 to 1984, the percentage of service competitively contracted rose from near zero to more than 15 percent without causing the layoff (redundancy) of a single public transport employee. San Diego has also realized other benefits as a result of competitive contracting:

Competitive costs were lower

On the average, the costs of service competitively contracted were approximately 50 percent below those of the public transport monopoly.

Cost control was improved

Not only did competitive costs rise within the inflation rate, but the public transport authority greatly improved its cost performance. Before competitive contracting, costs at the public monopoly, San Diego Transit, had increased at a rate similar to that of other California public transport monopolies. However, the competitive market induced cost control at San Diego Transit. From 1979 to 1984, real public transport costs in California rose 24 percent while real costs at San Diego Transit increased less than 2 percent. And system-wide, including both public and competitive operations, real costs declined 3 percent (chart 6). By 1984, the comparative improvement in cost performance had saved the San Diego area more than $40 million.

The net financial gain from competitive contracting was of assistance to San Diego in building capital intensive rail systems, in contrast to Los Angeles (see above). The San Diego experience demonstrates the positive impacts of competitive contracting. No similar long-term and comprehensive successes can be claimed by any of the other cost control options available to transport managers (see "Opposition to Competitive Contracting," below). The competitive environment has made it possible for public transport to operate in a manner consistent with the public ethic.

Opposition to Competitive Contracting

Opposition to competitive contracting comes from two primary sources, public transport labour unions and some public transport managers.

Labour Unions

Public transport labour unions are opposed to competitive contracting because they fear loss of power. This opposition is understandable but short-sighted, because to deny the flexibility to make public transport more financially secure through competitive contracting will surely threaten the job security of present employees in the future. Labour has used the following arguments against competitive contracting.

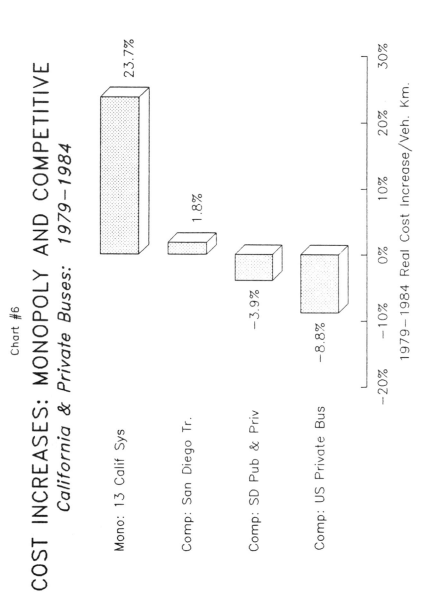

Chart #6

COST INCREASES: MONOPOLY AND COMPETITIVE
California & Private Buses: 1979-1984

Mono: 13 Calif Sys — 23.7%

Comp: San Diego Tr. — 1.8%

Comp: SD Pub & Priv — -3.9%

Comp: US Private Bus — -8.8%

1979-1984 Real Cost Increase/Veh. Km.

-20% -10% 0% 10% 20% 30%

Union Busting

Competitive contracting is alleged to be "union busting." It is not, because nearly 60 percent of the private bus industry in the United States is unionized, and there are no barriers to unionization in the remainder of the private bus industry.

Layoffs

Competitive contracting is alleged to threaten the wholesale replacement of public transport workers. This is not so, because the rate of competitive contracting is effectively limited to that permitted by the natural employee attrition rate. To proceed otherwise could require invocation of federal section 13(c) labour protections that guarantee up to *six years' pay* for employees dismissed because of competitive contracting (a level of protection that is limited to public transport and the railroad industry—not even the heavily unionized automobile industry provides protections that begin to approach this). It should be noted that section 13(c) protections do not apply where the public transport monopoly is reacting to a reduction or limitation on funding. By allowing competitive contracting, the labour unions could, in effect, eliminate the possibility of layoffs of their members resulting from budget difficulties.

Exploitation

Competitive contracting achieves its savings by exploiting workers. The logic runs as follows: It is exploitive to pay bus drivers wages and salaries below that paid to present public transport drivers. At odds with the "exploitation theory" are the following:

- Public transport wage rates have been permitted to rise artificially high by the non-competitive environment.
- School bus drivers, who move more passengers annually than public transport drivers, are paid competitive rates well below the public transport monopoly rates. Are these drivers, who are responsible for transporting our children, any less important than their counterparts in public transport?
- Private bus companies and public school authorities have no particular difficulty in obtaining skilled drivers, even though they employ more than ten times the number of drivers that are employed by public transport monopolies and pay competitive rates that are substantially below monopoly rates.
- By paying more than the competitive rate, the users receive lower service levels, and taxpayer funds are less efficiently used.

• Unemployment remains a problem in the United States. People are denied employment by policies requiring artificially high wages, which unnecessarily limit job creation. Not only are the unemployed denied jobs, but they remain on public relief rolls—or worse. This support for higher levels of unemployment is for the protection of bus drivers who are not yet even employed.

The exploitation theory is not a valid argument. It leads to a logical conclusion that the great majority of U.S. workers—those who are paid competitive wages—are by definition exploited. In fact, those who are exploited by the present monopolistic arrangements are potential workers who are denied jobs by artificial limitations on job creation, and users who receive lower levels of service than would otherwise be available to them. It is private interests, not public interests, that are served by paying more for public transport than is necessary.

Prevailing Wage Requirements

Any competitive contracting should be subject to "prevailing wage and conditions" clauses, or in an environment of compulsory unionization. Of course, the intent of such provisions is to prevent the application of competitive wage and benefit packages to public transport. Such protections serve no public purpose, rather they serve the private purpose of extending costly protections to public transport workers who are yet to be hired. Why should potential public transport workers be granted protections not available to current public employees already employed, such as those in education, school busing, and mental health or even in the private sector?

However, labour has primarily relied on its still very considerable influence in political processes at the national, state and local levels to limit opportunities for more effective public service delivery through competitive contracting. With public funding for public transport declining in real terms, and with the national budget deficit and state and local funding difficulties, failure to permit attrition rate contracting could result in the loss of union jobs. As the public transport financial picture becomes more clouded, and as costs continue to escalate (as they must in the non-competitive environment), large scale layoffs of union members could occur—something that cannot happen under an attrition rate approach.

Managers

Some public transport managers have expressed opposition to competitive contracting, and there is little if any support among transport managers for requiring its use. The public transport monopolies have lobbied hard at the national and state levels to avoid any competitive contracting requirements such as have been placed upon London Regional Transport by the Parliament. This opposition is understandable. Managers, like other people, generally prefer more latitude to less and more power to less. Further, as the number of direct employees declines through the use of contractors, transport managers justifiably perceive that their advancement, both in position and in remuneration, may be limited. Few transport managers will publicly express outright opposition, instead it is typically heard that "competitive contracting is only one of the options that public transport managers have to control costs." While that may be true, it is also true that only competitive contracting has produced any serious bottom line cost savings. Stated another way, among this array of cost containing options, only competitive contracting has made a perceivable difference.

The Future

If U.S. public transport authorities were to adopt an attrition-based competitive contracting programme, the escalation of operating costs could be contained. Inflation adjusted costs would rise only 1 percent between now and the year 2000. Fares would rise only 7 percent and service levels would decline only 1 percent if those increased costs were absorbed by the public transport systems without additional public funding. Finally, no bus driver jobs would be lost (American Bus Association 1987). This is a very conservative estimate that does not take into account the direct public authority savings that have routinely accompanied a more competitive environment and which would surely further improve cost performance.

The Trend toward Competitive Contracting

There is an undeniable trend toward competitive contracting in U.S. public transport. Virtually all new public transport systems have been competitively contracted. Even some of the more reluctant public transport monopolies have begun to incorporate competitive contracting. As of 1985, 9 percent of U.S. public transport services were provided under competitive contract, and these services consumed 5 percent of the public transport operating costs. Further, there is no indication of any return to public monopoly service provision. There have been no competitive contracting failures. Services that have been competitively contracted have not been returned to private monopoly operation.

Competitive Contracting and the Public Ethic

The experience of competitive contracting should also be tested against the purpose of a public service: to maximize the level of a particular standard of service to the users for the lowest possible expenditure of taxes.

The results of competitive contracting have been lower real costs for the users, which translate into:

- Higher service levels at a given funding and service quality level, and/or
- Lower fares at a given funding and service quality level
- Public transport improvements that can be financed with the savings.

For the taxpayers:

- Because present service and fare levels can be preserved with present public resources, tax rate increases are unnecessary (or, alternatively, new taxes can be used to pay for new services, lower fares, or capital projects).

Competitive contracting passes the test of the public ethic, because it represents a net gain for both the users and the taxpayers. At least as much public benefit is obtained as is paid for—for each public dollar expended a minimum of one dollar in public benefit is delivered. It is clear that if public transport is a public service designed to serve the users and taxpayers, there is no proven alternative consistent with that purpose other than a conscious programme of competitive contracting.

Policy Choices

In analysing public transport monopolies, the appropriate public policy questions are the following:

- Should more be paid for a public service than is necessary?
- Should fare levels for riders be minimized, assuming a particular public funding and service level?
- Should new taxes be used to increase service and/or to reduce fares?
- Should new public transport employees be paid the competitive rate?

If public transport is a public service, then the answer to all of the above questions must be yes. If the answer to any of these questions is no, then it might be argued that public transport is not a public service, and efforts to minimize its public financial support could be justified.

It all comes down to a simple question. Does public transport receive public revenues to serve its customers, the users and taxpayers, or to serve itself? It is suggested that if public transport is a public service, then its purpose must be to serve the users and the taxpayers. For public transport to become a genuine public service, it must be restructured to serve the users and taxpayers. That restructuring involves the incorporation of competitive incentives. The case for competitive contracting is compelling. Competitive contracting is fully consistent with a genuine commitment to public transport as a public service, and with primary concern for serving the users and potential users of public transport.

COMPETITIVE CONTRACTING APPLICATIONS

Competitive contracting can obtain similar benefits in Canada.

Public Transport in Canada

The Situation

The public transport market situation in Canada is more like that of the United States than that of the United Kingdom. While Canadian passenger fares contribute a higher percentage of operating costs than in the United States, at 53 percent (Canadian Urban Transit Association 1986), public transport is still far from profitable in Canada. Public transport is non-commercial, and it has been deemed to be a public service by provincial and local public authorities.

There are, however, important differences. The development of Canadian cities has been more favourable to public transport than in the United States. For the most part, high capacity limited access highways have not penetrated Canadian cities, and commercial development has remained more concentrated and centralized. This is despite the fact that automobile availability is high in Canada. These factors have preserved a larger discretionary market share for Canadian public transport monopolies, and transport patronage has increased in recent years. From 1950 to 1980, public transport ridership declined only 6 percent, compared to 52 percent in the United States. Annual per capita public transport journeys are 54 in Canada, compared to 28 in the United States (Canadian Urban Transit Association 1986).

Cost Performance Compared to the United States

Before describing this cost performance, it is important to understand a crucial difference in public funding in Canada. In the United States, unlike Canada, there is a large national transport programme that through its regulatory process dictates subsidy conditions, and severely limits local control. And, public funding has been more easily available to U.S. transport systems, while Canadian systems have been under pressure to justify capital expenditures and capital improvements.

For example, in the United States bus replacement capital funding is readily available, while operating assistance is more limited. This has resulted in less than effective maintenance, because maintenance is an operating expense (this has absurdly induced one U.S. snow-belt public transport monopoly to not use anti-freeze, an operating expenditure, because capital funding for engine replacement is more readily available). Public transport authorities in the United States routinely replace buses that are 12 years of age. These same buses are operated by private companies in the United States for more than 20 years. Similarly, in the more rigorous Canadian funding environment, British Columbia Transit (B.C. Transit) has an average bus age of 17 years. B.C. Transit operates vehicles comparable to those operated by U.S. public transport authorities. The crucial difference is that B.C. Transit must petition Victoria for capital funds on a case-by-case basis, rather than routinely receiving a formula grant for capital purposes from Ottawa, as would be the case in the United States.

Undoubtedly, the fact that Canadian transport authorities have been required to more carefully account for their expenditures has assisted those authorities in achieving cost performance that is superior to that of their U.S. counterparts. A critical factor contributing to this more favourable performance is that public transport policy is made not in Ottawa, but rather in Victoria, Edmonton, Regina, Toronto, et cetera. Nonetheless, Canadians have paid a price for public monopoly operation of public transport.

Cost Performance

Public transport costs per vehicle kilometre increased 27 percent, after adjustment for inflation, from 1970 to 1985. It cost $350 million more, in real terms, to operate the Canadian public transport systems in 1985 than it did in 1970. This is enough to pay all fares and operating expenses of B.C. Transit for more than three years.

Competitive Contracting in Canadian Public Transport

Competitive contracting is already being used in Canadian urban transport in a limited manner, both for conventional public transport services and for demand responsive (dial-a-ride) services. Most of the transport systems in British Columbia, outside of Vancouver and Victoria, are competitively contracted. B.C. Transit, which manages these systems, established these arrangements well before any significant competitive contracting of public transport was under way either in the United States or in the United Kingdom. The competitive environment has assisted B.C. Transit in containing operating cost increases and improving service quality. Some smaller transport systems are also competitively contracted in Ontario.

The Future

If public transport costs continue to escalate as they did from 1970 to 1985, it can be expected that a 19 percent real cost increase will occur from 1987 to the year 2000. On an annual basis, nearly $500 million more will be required to operate present service levels after adjustment for inflation. The gross cost above inflation for the period is projected to approach $5,000 million (figures based upon a linear regression analysis).

Applicability of Competitive Contracting to Public Transport

While Canadian transport cost escalation has been less severe than in the United States, and while some competitive contracting is already under way in Canada, there is much more that can be obtained for the users and the taxpayers through a more ambitious programme. The private bus industry in Canada is relatively strong. (For example, the largest school bus company in the United States operates 14,000 buses, equal to one-third of the U.S. daily public transport total and 3,000 more public transport buses than are operated in Canada. This large company is Canadian owned.) Competitive contracting can make a positive contribution in Canada, as it has already in the United States and at London Regional Transport.

Competitive Contracting of Public Services

It is suggested that competitive contracting is appropriate for consideration in virtually all public services because the mere consideration of competitive contracting induces improved performance on the part of public authorities. Phoenix, the London Borough of Wandsworth, and other general governments have particularly noted this effect. In Wandsworth, competitive contracts are being awarded in subsequent periods at lower real rates than in the first contract period (Beresford 1987). Competitive contracting has even been a success in the United States Postal Service, which few would consider an efficient enterprise. Since 1947 the postal system has competitively contracted the surface shipment of mail, and costs have been rising within the inflation rate, despite considerable cost inducing federal regulations.

Approximately one-third of the school transportation in the United States is operated by school bus contractors. In Canada, varying percentages of school bus services are already competitively operated in each province and the two territories. These successes have induced legislative bodies to consider requiring competitive contracting by local authorities to improve service to the users and taxpayers:

• In the United Kingdom, the Local Government Act would require the competitive contracting of certain municipal services.

- In Colorado, an act would require the competitive contracting of all state services.
- In California, the Public Transit Competitiveness Act would require competitive contracting of some public transport services.

Ready, willing and able private suppliers already exist in some markets, such as public transport, school transportation, and refuse collection. And the lack of ready, willing and able suppliers is not a significant long-term barrier. The creation of profit opportunities through competitive contracting will attract capital, just as capital attracted to British privatization issues has far exceeded that which the experts had considered possible. For example, a number of firms have entered public transport competitive contracting (American Bus Association 1987). In the long run the critical issue is not the availability of the supplier market, rather it is the existence of profit opportunities. Where entrepreneurs can make a profit, while providing quality service and saving public money, a supplier market will develop.

COMPETITIVE CONTRACTING: ACHIEVING THE PUBLIC ETHIC

Competitive contracting represents a useful policy option for the provision of public services. Through this form of privatization, public authorities can serve the users by providing quality service while serving the taxpayers by providing that service as economically as possible.

Beneficiaries

Unless public monopolies are subjected to a competitive environment, decay will set in, and a less secure future awaits the users, the taxpayers and ultimately, the employees of the monopoly:

> No government in a democracy can forever turn its back on the market. Unless nationalization produces mechanisms for ensuring that goods and services are produced of a kind that customers want at a price that customers will pay, there is no long-term future for the output that is being produced. If, for example, poor productivity and poor control of costs cause prices to rise beyond the level that the market will stand, either subsidies have to be sought or customers look elsewhere in cases where they have freedom of choice. A spiral of unprofitability sets in; it may be tolerated for a while; but then abrupt structural changes are necessary. (Moore 1983)

Who benefits from competitive contracting, and who does not? In the long run all will benefit from attrition-based competitive contracting programmes:

- *The users* will receive more service and will pay less for it.
- *The taxpayers* will get more value for their tax contributions and will experience lower taxes in the long run.
- *Public employees* will have more secure employment job security with layoffs unlikely in the improved financial environment of competitive contracting.

In the United States, competitive contracting has been supported not only by conservatives and Republicans, but also by liberals and Democrats. The supporters of competitive contracting have included those interested in limiting the costs of government and those interested in maximizing public services to the customers.

On the other hand, the opponents of competitive contracting have little or no interest in limiting the public costs, and betray their interest in maximizing public services to users. Their disingeniousness is exposed by support for requirements that siphon off public moneys for the public monopolies themselves, and deny service to the very users that the public services were established to serve. Concern about unemployment is inconsistent with anti-competitive requirements that limit job creation, and thereby sustain unemployment. Similarly, concern for the poor is inconsistent with anti-competitive requirements that limit public services to the poor.

The Public Ethic

Liberals and conservatives can debate ad nauseam about whether a particular service should be a public service. But once the decision is made, it is in the public interest to provide that service in the most cost effective manner possible. This might be through direct production, or through production by others, through competitive contracting:

> The essential function of government is deciding. Government may later, itself, do what it has decided should be done. But equally it may not. Its basic intention is simply to see that what should be done is in fact done. (Citizens League of the Twin Cities 1983)

The public monopolies have not performed in the best interests of either the public service users or the taxpayers. The users have not been given the highest levels of quality public service that could have been purchased with the public funding available. The taxpayers have seen their contributions unnecessarily committed to paying higher prices for public goods than are necessary. It will only be through the injection of competitive incentives that the interests of the users and taxpayers—the public interest—will be served.

Competitive contracting is in the public interest. Through competitive contracting, a public service is provided by the most economical producer, subject to quality standards set by public authorities. Competitive contracting is a reliable strategy for achieving the public ethic in the public services.

REFERENCES

American Bus Association, *Optimizing Public Transit Service through Competitive Contracting*. (Washington: 1987)

American Public Transit Association, *Transit Fact Book, 1985*. (Washington: 1985)

Balcombe, R.J., J.M. Hopkin, K.E. Perrett, W.S. Clough, *Bus Deregulation in Great Britain: A Review of the Opening Stages*, Transport and Road Research Laboratory, Department of Transport. (Crowethorne, Berkshire: 1987)

Beresford, Paul. Presentation to the London Privatization Conference. (1987)

Canadian Urban Transit Association, *Urban Transit Facts in Canada, 1986*. (Toronto: 1986)

Citizens League of the Twin Cities, *Enlarging Our Capacity to Adapt*. (Minneapolis: 1983)

Department of Transport, *Transport Statistics Great Britain, 1974-1984*, Her Majesty's Stationery Office. (London: 1985)

The Economist, "Britain's Underclass." (23 May 1987)

Frequent Flyer (Magazine), "A Squeeze on the Wallet." (July 1987)

Institute of Transportation Studies (University of California), *Part Time Labor, Work Rules, and Transit Costs*, Office of the Secretary of Transportation. (Washington: 1981)

Metro Magazine, 1986-87 Fact Book, Bobbit Publishing Company. (Redondo Beach, California: 1986)

Moore, Rt. Hon. John, M.P., "Why Privatize," Speech (1983)

Philadelphia Inquirer, "Study: Suburb to Suburb Commuting Now the Norm," (Philadelphia: 27 June 1987)

Teal, Roger F., Genevieve Giuliano and Edward K. Morlok, *Public Transit Service Contracting*, Report prepared for the United States Department of Transportation, Urban Mass Transportation Administration. (1986)

The Sunday Times, "A Stark and Simple Choice." (London, 14 June 1987)

DISCUSSION

Edited by Michael A. Walker

Question: In Canada there is a tendency to regard transit as an uneconomic service. But as you talked about the kinds of savings available from contracting out, I thought that perhaps it's not an inherently uneconomic service but rather a service that's been rendered uneconomic by its means of production. Is that a possibility, or is it really an uneconomic service?

Answer: It's a possibility, and I think it is a much greater possibility after having spent some time in London recently talking to Department of Transport people. I really didn't expect deregulation to work in Great Britain, and it seems to be working quite nicely. However, I think one thing you have to consider in Canada is what you want your cities to look like. In a sense, you have more concentrated cities in Canada than in the U.S. You have more concentrated business districts than in the United States; you don't have freeways going into your central cities for the most part. Because of some decisions you've made with respect to land use, land control and urban form, it may be that while you might be able to make it more commercial, you might not want to for reasons having nothing whatever to do with that kind of policy.

Question: You mentioned that a competitive contractor may be a public or a private body. Do you really believe that public and private bodies will compete on an equitable basis? How do you ensure that a public competitor is in fact dealing on an equal basis?

Answer: It's a matter of political will. We have some cases, Phoenix, Arizona, for example, where the city administration has basically enforced that kind of policy on its own departments for solid waste collection and it is working well. In other cases we have planning agencies over the public transportation agencies which are doing that. It is a very serious problem. But in a situation where you already have an existing transit authority, I think it is important to try to set up a situation where they can at least compete. Don't give them a special situation, but I think it's very important not to get hung up on seeing privatization as an end in itself. It is a means of policy, not an end in itself.

Question: Isn't it true that public transit was once private transit? That it was fare regulation and interventions of that kind that killed it?

Answer: Yes, any number of things. First of all, I'm no great devotee of the former private transit because it was essentially a monopoly situation. But at the same time, there was incredible interference on fares and routes and all sorts of things from the regulatory side. U.S. transit people like to point to that as being private failure, and largely we've been able to deflect that one. I've taken the position that it's hardly worth arguing about what should or should not have been twenty years ago.

Question: There seems to be a public perception that safety standards in the private sector are not equivalent to those in the public sector. You hear a bit of that in talk about the airlines these days—they're cutting costs by not keeping safety standards up. In the area where I live I think it is a perception among the public that private companies run old buses, and they don't maintain them as well as they should. How do you overcome that? How do we prove to the public that with private competitive bidding, as you describe it, the safety standards that the public system is perceived to have will be maintained?

Answer: What you have to do is make sure you have the political will to require that your public administrators who remain in charge are enforcing safety rules and inspecting and that kind of thing. I know that perception exists, but the statistics say otherwise. There have been any number of cases I know of in the United States where quick inspections of public transit agencies have yielded results that are every bit as bad as the worst private sector thing you've ever heard of.

Question: What is an attainable revenue fare-to-cost ratio—50, 60, 70 or 80 percent—even by contracting out?

Answer: It depends. Clearly, there are some services that could become profitable in a competitive contracting situation. I do not believe that there is a single route in the U.S. at the moment that makes money under public operation. But it is conceivable that you could see some routes making money.

Question: Do you believe that publicly owned and privately run transit can be effective?

Answer: Presuming that by "privately owned" what we mean is competitively operated, I think it can be very effective. Quite frankly, if we in the United States have any interest whatever in preserving public transit, it's the only way we can go. I say that because there is incredible resistance from bureaucracy and unions not to let this competitive contracting thing go very far. If we continue on the road of being committed to the public monopoly approach, we are going to pay in the long run with our transit systems.

Question: What has been the history of requiring handicapped services, kneeling buses, et cetera? How much has it cost?

Answer: It ranges from zero to billions, depending on who you talk to. It is either successful or unsuccessful, depending on the will of the transit agency that you're talking about. It has gone back and forth. At one point virtually all transit vehicles were expected to be equipped with handicapped lifts or that kind of thing. Now, the regulations have changed so you can provide alternative services, and various agencies are doing different things.

Question: Gordon Tullock was in town last week. He mentioned some work he had seen which showed that it would have been cheaper in most areas of the United States to provide each handicapped person with his own van with a lift rather than to augment the public transit system. Whether that's true or not, I don't know.

Answer: One basic problem you have, as we heard from Minister Rogers this morning and others before, is a political thing. Who is willing to stand up on television and tell a group of handicapped people in motorized wheelchairs who have gone onto the freeway that they can't get on the bus? It becomes an incredible political thing for our elected officials to deal with, unfortunately.

Question: Rather than a municipality running a bus system to satisfy a minority group who are disadvantaged for one reason or another, you mentioned the alternative of the dial-a-ride system. Could you explain how to organize a dial-a-ride system to provide the equivalent service, and what would it cost in terms of investment on the one hand and operating costs on the other?

Answer: I'd be willing to provide you with a proposal to do some work for you on that. I really can't answer the question except to tell you that there's a point, based upon patronage levels, where a dial-a-ride service becomes uneconomical because you end up having to run so many vehicles to operate the system. Generally, cost differences on a vehicle-hour basis on the private sector dial-a-ride tends to operate in the neighbourhood of $20 to $25, including capital, where equivalent bus service tends to run $35 or so.

Question: But you might organize a dial-a-ride system with some form of voucher or access on a controlled basis. You dial a taxi-cab, and the taxi-cab company bills the municipality.

Answer: That's being done in any number of communities in the United States, and I should have mentioned it. Pittsburgh, Cleveland, and others have a voucher system for the elderly and the handicapped and use either taxis or the taxis have special vehicles for them. It generally works very well. There probably would be some applications for that kind of thing in Canada; I don't know if there are any existing systems here.

Question: Has competitive contracting increased the usage of public transit in the United States?

Answer: No, frankly there isn't much you can do to increase public transit usage in the United States besides high capital programmes that nobody can justify on any other basis than the fact that federal money is there to build them. I am convinced that if the Arabs ever cut us off again, we'll be on motorcycles before we're back on public transit. One has to recognize that our land use patterns are such that public transit doesn't even go where the people work. It's not like Vancouver or Edmonton or Calgary or Toronto, where perhaps by far your biggest commercial centre is downtown. In our country the worst traffic congestion is now routinely in the suburbs, and many of our largest business centres are arising in the suburbs. By 1995 northeastern New Jersey, the suburbs of New York, will have more office space than Manhattan despite what it looks like from the air.

Question: A recent study by the Federation of Canadian Municipalities indicated that the estimated cost of infrastructure replacement in municipalities in Canada is $100 billion, and the federal government is being approached to cover the cost as it is an onerous amount for the local property taxpayer. I want to link that up with something you said about federal funds; that is, that federal funds had corrupted the local transit systems in the United States. How have they done that? Should Canadian municipalities have a fear that if they get involved in a programme with the federal government to upgrade infrastructure, it is likely to have the same effect?

Answer: Presuming your federal government works in some way similar to ours—I don't know how yours works—I would say yes, there is a very great risk. For example, a particular section of the Urban Mass Transportation Act, section 13(c), basically says that on any federal grant the union has to sign off. That means that if you build an operating facility that's going to be around for fifty years, the union has to sign off. That agreement they sign off on may say something like, this bargaining unit has to provide all the work for this company for time immemorial. The federal intrusion on local decision making has been absolutely incredible. Beyond that, we have seen federal requirements take the cost of purchasing buses to a level that you simply can't believe. We've seen the same kind of thing happen in urban programmes as well. I would certainly urge you to try to avoid those kinds of programmes. Deal with Victoria or with Edmonton or with Regina, but don't deal with Ottawa. Let them do their own thing and try to stay away from them. I'm not suggesting you secede or anything.

Beyond that, let me give you a couple of other examples. In the city of New Orleans a democratic mayor was elected last year. Because of the oil difficulties, the city of New Orleans was virtually bankrupt as perhaps some of your municipalities that might be similarly inclined in Alberta might be. The first thing he did—a liberal, democratic mayor with labour support—was say, "I'm going to save money by contracting out solid waste collection," and he laid off all his employees. The transit agency in that community is in every bit as bad a situation. They can't even talk about the possibility of laying off employees because of federal involvement.

Finally, just an advertisement for my successor here today. In terms of infrastructure needs, they ought to be talking to Davis Schwartz and other people like him and perhaps some of the underwriters. We heard discussions in London about some major infrastructure projects with private involvement. I hope municipalities would look very seriously at private alternatives for developing those things. I don't know much about it, but there is sure a lot there.

DAVIS SCHWARTZ

(Introduction by Michael A. Walker)

Davis Schwartz is directly involved in the privatization of services in a very practical and pragmatic way. Mr. Schwartz was educated at the University of Minnesota, received a Masters of Business Administration at the Graduate School of Business at Stanford University, and did further graduate studies in urban and regional planning at George Washington University. He is the national director for state and local government services for Deloitte Haskins & Sells in the United States. He has had very extensive experience in the subject area which was dealt with by our previous speaker. He was his firm's partner in charge of mass transit practice for the western United States. More recently he has been working in a very practical way with state governments on the awkward question of privatizing the provision of other services within the state apparatus, in particular maintenance services of various kinds. We're very fortunate to have Davis Schwartz with us today to describe some of his experiences with the state of Washington which has recently undertaken some very innovative and interesting privatizing operations.

CHAPTER 13

PRIVATIZATION OF STATE AND LOCAL GOVERNMENT SERVICES IN THE UNITED STATES

Davis R. Schwartz

INTRODUCTION

I'd like to begin my discussion with a question. Which of the following goals and objectives is the concept of privatization intended to accomplish?

- Improve efficiency and effectiveness.
- Reduce short-term budget deficits.
- Reduce the scope of government.
- Finance public works projects.
- Expedite the development of capital projects.
- All of the above.
- None of the above.

Obviously, if you've taken a lot of tests you realize it's always the final answer. So, the answer to the question here is "none of the above."

The true answer, in my opinion, is that it depends on what you mean by privatization. I hope to add a little additional insight on that from south of the border this afternoon.

Three Definitions of Privatization

When talking about privatization, and from what I've heard serving state and local government around the United States, we encounter three different kinds of definitions.

The first is the competitive contracting of services generally provided by state and local governments that Wendell Cox so eloquently spoke about.

The second definition is the one on which most of this conference is focused and which describes the U.K. experience in particular: the sale of government assets acquired through public programmes, previous nationalization, or in some cases, by default.

I'll touch on the third definition only briefly this afternoon, but I think it is really the opportunity of the future: the public/private development of capital facilities that are traditionally constructed by governmental enterprises or public works programmes.

THE PCEM PROJECT IN WASHINGTON

Let me follow up some comments Wendell made about competitive contracting and describe the project that has been under way in the state of Washington for the past year and a half. Having just been approved by the governor within the last month, it will be going on as a pilot programme for the next two and a half years. We call this PCEM (project cost evaluation method) for roadway construction and maintenance. Let me briefly highlight some of the reasons this study is going on before getting into the primary issues and recommendations and some of the things that are going forward.

Essentially, this study arose out of a continuous perennial battle each year concerning how roadway construction and maintenance were going to get done in Washington. The players involved in that perennial battle included the Association of General Contractors, the Association of Washington Cities, the County Road Administration Board, the Washington Asphalt Pavers Association, the Washington State Association of Counties, and the Washington State Department of Transportation.

About two and a half years ago, the legislature started to tire of constantly getting jaw-boned and beaten up by both sides each year, so they authorized a project under the control of the Legislative Transportation Committee, a joint committee of both the House and the Senate, to determine the most cost-effective way of handling roadway construction and maintenance for both state and local government within the Washington jurisdiction. Although the primary concern was for cost effectiveness, it was very quickly broadened to encompass two other concerns: the efficient work-force utilization of people already employed by state and local government and quality control over the maintenance and minor construction areas.

Scope of PCEM

To give you a little bit of perspective about the nature of the beast that we were trying to get more cost effectiveness out of, in 1984—the base year before this study began—the state of Washington was spending about $1 billion a year in roadway construction and maintenance. About 71 percent of the dollars are spent for construction; another 29 percent are spent for maintenance. By and large, construction is contracted out, as you might expect, and maintenance is routinely done in-house.

The scope of our project for the Legislative Transportation Committee, centred on four things.

* Compare the accounting procedures and costing techniques used by governmental agencies and private contractors to determine how they were the same and how they were different.
* Recommend any changes in what are called "bars" in the state of Washington, that is, the budget accounting and reporting standards that apply to local government.
* Identify and develop a methodology in which we could compare government and private contractor costs on a project-by-project basis for true cost effectiveness, whether it be done in-house or outside, forgetting for the moment whether it was construction and maintenance and what the bid thresholds were.
* Identify desirable changes in state and local laws, ordinances, and regulation that would facilitate the ongoing use of this kind of cost-effectiveness evaluation.

Approach to the Study

We surveyed all 61 cities and 39 counties, the largest of the cities and all of the counties, and received a 71 percent response rate. We held forums with county engineers and with private contractors. We did some selective interviews to try to get a representative feel for the issues and the nature of doing business around the state from both the public and the private side. They certainly were not random samples but a good way of getting a feel for a methodology that would apply throughout Washington.

What we were trying to get at and what we found through this initial round of data collection—through interviews and site visits throughout the state—was a range of issues that we essentially broke down into two sets. Let me identify them and give you a very quick answer to what we concluded so as not to spend a lot of time supporting the analysis but rather on what came out of it.

Clearly, one of the primary issues was the nature of the cost accounting systems. We were concerned about two things. First, the comprehensiveness of the cost accounting systems; that is, does it capture all the costs for the project? For example, in cases where a project is going to be bid out, does it include the administrative costs of putting together the package that has to be reviewed by legal counsel and the purchaser? Does it also involve inspection and the compliance monitoring that has to go on in a contracted-out project?

We were also determining what kind of consistency we were getting. Are we getting comparison of apples and oranges or apples and apples when people make claims that the public sector or the private sector can do it more efficiently?

A second major issue we addressed was the nature of overhead cost allocation. Although Wendell didn't talk about it, one of the things that the issue of competitive contracting very quickly centres on, if you decide to get involved in that business, is how does the public sector side deal with its overhead? We were interested in both the central services of payroll departments and data processing that may be provided to a district such as the public works department or a state DOT as well as the indirect costs of administering that kind of department.

A third issue was accounting for materials.

What the Research Found

I'll give you some short insights into what we found. We found that the main difference is really in material overheads that are picked up elsewhere in terms of cost allocations. But there were not significant cost differentials between roadway construction and maintenance in terms of major differences in procurement, storage and distribution. Similarly, we did not find the accounting for equipment to be significant when looking at it in the case of public works for either the State of Washington or the local jurisdictions.

We looked at self-insurance costs. We looked at the issue of the local tax impact of contracting out work. One of the claims always made by the private sector is that it is generating taxes, and the taxes come back to the public sector. When we did that analysis at the local level, we found the differential was about 1 to 2 percent when it really came down to it, so we dismissed that for the rest of the study.

Similarly, we also got rid of some other red herrings. One typically goes under the guise of "the level playing field," that is, that either the government or the private sector has cost advantages or disadvantages which we ought to try to equalize to put them on a comparative basis. The fact of the matter is that businesses and governments are not equal. Governments may have a lower wage rate, but they need to employ public works employees year round. A contractor may have more flexibility in hiring on a project basis. We decided not to get mired down in methodology designed to equalize everything, when that is in fact not the way the world works.

We dealt with some other issues in terms of inspection and quality control, the impact of bid limits and day labour requirements, labour agreements and practices, inter-agency contracting, and essential services provided by governmental agencies. These were all clearly relegated to a secondary status.

RECOMMENDATIONS

We recommended eight basic points to the state of Washington and that is now going forward in a pilot project. The legislature, based on the mandate for doing the study, was prepared to make this a state-wide mandate for state and local government. We said we had better be more sure of the effectiveness and the administrative costs of the methodology itself before making such a mandate. So, as I indicated earlier, we recommended a two-year pilot programme to test this methodology.

The first point was to adopt the concept of full project costing—with some qualifications which I will explain more carefully within the PCEM. By full project costing we meant: get all of the project and get all of the costs. We identified the need to modify certain project cost accounting techniques that I'll skip over here in the interest of time. We made it very clear that you have to allocate overhead costs to project estimates to figure out whether to do the construction or maintenance work inside or outside. I'll come back to some distinctions we want to make between fixed and variable overhead.

We identified some other changes in terms of better definition, better documentation of inspection and quality control procedures, bid limits, day labour limits, and so forth. We identified areas where we would have to waive some state laws or local ordinances or get some kind of special dispensation or court rulings in order to carry out a successful pilot project for two and half years.

Lastly, we got our steering committee to adopt some proposed definitions in four major categories. These may seem fundamental, but they are clearly at the heart of a workable methodology. The first one is, what is a project? The second is, what is construction? The third is, what is maintenance? And the fourth is, what are essential services? It may seem simplistic that those should be well-defined and well understood, but I dare say, whether you go to Washington or any of the other 49 states, you'll find that there is no ready agreement of what they mean or how they are applied.

PCEM Elements

There are four key elements in terms of structuring this methodology. The first is to **allocate overhead costs to projects**, so agency and contractor costs can be compared on a full-cost basis, making sure that we do have an apples and apples comparison to the extent that all the costs are relevant in a given situation. I'll explain that more carefully in a moment.

We were very careful, however, to **recognize the distinction between fixed and variable overhead**. There are elements of indirect costs or central services costs that will in fact vary over time depending on how much work you do inside versus contracting it out. If you do more contracting out, you may use more purchasing. As a result, your indirect or central services costs may go up. By the same token, your payroll costs may go down. Clearly, the key issue is the time frame you are measuring to determine whether the overhead is fixed or variable.

What we wanted to do in the methodology was allow some breathing room, some flexibility. In cases where there were under-utilized resources, we would in fact not necessarily look at all total costs because some of them may not be relevant in a given situation. What we wanted to avoid was a very interesting paradox. If you are contracting out or competitive contracting on a project basis, you could conceivably contract out each and every project on a micro basis within a given year or biennium. But you would have the fixed costs associated with running a public works department or a state DOT, and on a macro basis, you would end up with the worst of all possible situations. So you need to be very careful about this overhead and not simply say that we have to compare all overhead in order to get apples to apples.

The third element in PCEM was **documenting decision-making procedures and the economic rationale** used to identify the work that was going to go to contractors or be performed in-house. What we are essentially trying to do here is create what came to be known in the 1950s at General Electric as the Hawthorne effect. That is, if someone in an experiment knows that others are looking at them and observing and monitoring them, there tend to be improvements even when there's no difference between what the two groups are doing. The fact that they are being monitored, and know there is a more careful scrutiny of the criteria as well as the process for applying the criteria, can have a very beneficial effect.

The **fourth element in PCEM is a feedback group.** We decided to recommend putting together some documentation on actual project costs done both in-house and outside by contractors, after the fact—not a large onerous amount of paperwork but a summary of costs—so there would be some intellectual honesty. There would be some going back to see how reliable the estimates were inside and outside. We could then use that kind of information to tweak the methodology, either during or following the pilot project, before seeing something like this methodology mandated throughout the state.

Building the Methodology

Without going into a lot of detail, it was a fivefold process. First, preparing contractor estimates solicited from contractors or prepared in-house based on the historical experience of the department by contacting similar agencies that had been involved in similar projects. Since many of these are identified on the basis of unit costs, that tends to be fairly easy to do.

Secondly, preparing agency estimates that would reflect the labour, materials, equipment and the overhead costs that would be relevant in a given project.

Third, comparing the agency and contractor costs. We also came up with a process to streamline this using an ABC technique to identify projects that were going to be contracted out for reasons other than cost effectiveness. If the costs were not in a 15 to 20 percent range of each other, largely driven by other factors such as the need for special equipment or specialized expertise, we didn't spend a lot of time doing a comparison of the numbers. By the same token, if the costs were 20 percent under in favour of the in-house group, that fell into the C category, and we expedited the process for applying the methodology there.

In other words, in the end you find that you're comparing the grey areas. We wanted to concentrate the analysis where costs were going to be within 20 or 25 percent of one another at the margin. That is where we thought the state and local governments in Washington had the most to gain by looking at things on a cost-effectiveness basis rather than on the basis of tradition.

Fourth, there is a bailout aspect to the methodology, something we call operational factors. These factors tend to fall into three major categories: urgency, resource availability, and the availability of bidders. After all, in areas in eastern Washington where there may not be a whole host of contractors to bid on the work, it's kind of a no-brainer to figure out that we're not going to spend a lot of time doing an analysis to see how much money we'd save on the contracting side. That might be, as Wendell said, a monopoly situation because there is only one contractor. We are looking at the cost effectiveness that comes from the competition, in this case competition from the inside versus the outside.

The last part of the process was to prepare an annual report of the projects. We came up with a one-page summary in two parts. Part A identified all projects automatically contracted out to the private sector for reasons such as specialized equipment and so forth; projects automatically done in-house for other types of reasons; and projects that because of the operational factors, such as an urgency situation like a bridge collapsing, were exempt from PCEM due to the nature of the situation. In Part B we recorded the dollar amounts of the projects actually contracted out, what the bids were, and what the actual results were. We recorded similar estimates for in-house work versus outside work.

Implementation Recommendations

How did we recommend implementation of the plan? Initially we suggested a one-year programme. We ended up with a two-year programme. In addition to applying the methodology on a project-by-project basis, we also wanted it to be used in the annual planning and budgeting process. And, we wanted to give the Hawthorne effect time to operate, so people would do a more careful job of packaging their projects during the planning process and in preparation for submitting their annual budgets. We wanted to give that a fair chance to operate.

The pilot programme for state and local government includes six cities, three counties, and all six DOT districts in the state Department of Transportation. To get a fair amount of participation during the pilot programme, we have representatives from management and labour as well as from the Legislative Transportation Committee and trade associations and the cities and counties. So no one has the opportunity to say they didn't have any input or didn't know how the pilot programme was applied, which would have lessened the opportunity to have the results reviewed at the end of two and half years. We have to go back to the legislature and say, "here are the results, and we think you should do this, this, or this."

When the governor signed the legislation authorizing this project earlier this month, it allowed these particular jurisdictions, particularly the cities and the counties, to waive bid limits and the day labour rates that are applied in construction or maintenance projects. That applied only to the people involved in this project; otherwise, the whole effort would have been thwarted.

As I mentioned, we divided projects into three categories. We are using PCEM primarily for project decision making in the B category, the grey area where we think there is the margin for improvement. As continuing consultants on the project, we will be involved in monitoring both the decision-making process and the results in particular situations during that two and a half year period. Then we will prepare the results of that pilot evaluation for the Legislative Transportation Committee.

SUMMARY

In summarizing this Washington experience, there were four major reasons for the pilot programme. One is that we ourselves wanted to ensure the most effective application of PCEM possible. We did not want to come up with an administrative nightmare—another thing talked about but not necessarily applied in earnest. We also wanted to make sure a sufficient support system would be available in some of the smaller cities or rural counties. Simple things that some of us might take for granted may very well not be available. A simple cost allocation and reporting system or well-documented cost accounting policies and procedures might not be available in some of those cases. Another reason for the two-year period is that we'll actually spend some time helping some of those governments in those particular areas.

We wanted to minimize the administrative costs of PCEM and tweak it so it would have the least administrative burden possible consistent with getting some acceptable results. And, as a number of the speakers have talked about, we wanted to facilitate labour's involvement and support of PCEM for competitive contracting purposes. That was very clearly the case. We have three different labour unions involved in the steering committee for the project.

PRIVATIZATION AND THE FUTURE

Other Privatization Candidates

Let me just point to a couple of other privatization candidates, some of which have been talked about here. Municipal utilities have gone from traditional garbage collection to privatization, particularly in California where we've just passed enabling legislation to facilitate privatization in waste water treatment, solid waste management and hazardous waste management, one of the things that seems to be looming on the horizon. I'm sure there will be all sorts of questions about safety requirements and standards and compliance with those requirements. Transportation systems have been talked about here. Another area I think we'll see is institutional care, whether it be in the form of nursing homes or public facilities. The Lyndon Baines Johnson School of Public Policy at the University of Texas in Austin published some privatization studies on all aspects of state-run institutional care in Texas.

Finally, correctional facilities, simply because there is an absolutely dire need for them in an increasingly conservative population in the United States. The governor of the state of Texas is under a $24 million a month court decree. If he doesn't improve the overcrowding in Texas state prisons, he has to let them out or pay the fine. We have the same thing in Santa Clara County. Judges are regularly putting the supervisors in jail or holding them in contempt of court for not dealing with those kinds of situations. I suspect that if necessity continues to be the mother of invention, you will find privatization in correctional facilities coming to fruition very quickly.

Focus on the Process

I'd like to emphasize how concerned the privatization should be to focus on the process. Several other speakers touched on it before me, but I don't think we can emphasize it enough. As in planning, the process is more important than the document. What is most important about privatization is doing it correctly. It is a means; it is not an end to itself. It should not be caught up in the rhetoric. It should be applied correctly and effectively.

The kinds of privatization studies we tend to get involved in are not the kind that say "you should do this." Firms like ours, whether it be the public accounting and consulting business or any kind of consulting business, ought not to substitute our judgement for that of elected officials and appointed management. In fact, we ought to be advising our clients on how to do it effectively—what the issues are and what to be aware of. For example, in San Diego County we set up an entire process including how to identify candidates, how to screen them to quickly get down to a short list, how to evaluate them, how to put out the contracts, how to administer them, and how to evaluate whether the process itself is working.

Similarly, we've gone into places like Dade County School District. They came to us and said, "show us how to farm out school bus maintenance." We said, "how do you know you should farm out school bus maintenance?" In fact, we found such an absence of information that the decision to go ahead could be based on nothing more than a gut feeling that this was a good thing to do and was politically expedient. Some of the things we're doing down there now make it appear as if that would have been a very bad idea in that particular situation.

In a recent study we completed for the State of California, Office of the Legislative Analyst, the fiscal adviser to the legislature asked us to identify the advantages and disadvantages—not apply our own particular value judgement of whether it's a good idea, but just give people a list of the issues and the things they ought to think about in deciding whether they want to go forward with contracting.

Capital Projects for Turnkey Development

I want to touch briefly on one of the things we see looming on the horizon in the United States. I don't think this has been talked about a lot at this particular conference, and maybe it's appropriate. It is probably one of the most promising areas for private sector participation in government services. It involves packaging capital projects for turnkey development and implementation by the private sector. This will allow us to expedite the schedule for capital projects, like dealing with the overcrowding situation in jails if there is that kind of court order, and shift some of the risk for budget overruns to the private sector. We have no shortage of horror stories as to huge budget overruns, percentage-wise and in actual dollar terms, on some of the light rail transit projects going on around the country. It would also reduce the total procurement costs for public projects, once again having this concern for the administrative costs of projects. I just can't emphasize enough that when you're doing competitive contracting, you need to recognize that one of the costs is the cost of administering the competition. That needs to be factored into the total cost.

The other thing that's exciting about this particular area is that, unlike selling off governmental assets or doing it outside versus doing it inside, this is a situation which doesn't have any zero sum implications. A number of these capital projects simply might not otherwise be done without private sector involvement or some kind of private/public sector partnership. I think you will see many, many consortiums getting into the business to the extent that they are allowed to bid on these projects on a turnkey basis; that is, to take the risks but also to stand to gain the rewards if in fact there are performance incentives and other things for bringing a project in ahead of schedule and under budget.

DISCUSSION

Edited by Michael A. Walker

Question: A recent national study by the Federation of Canadian Municipalities found that all municipalities face a major problem in infrastructure replacement. The estimated cost is in the order of $100 billion, and the federal government is being approached to cover the costs as it is an onerous amount for local property taxpayers. Is there anything that can be done at the municipal level to develop private sector involvement in the replacement costs of existing sewers, water lines, roads, parks, et cetera?

Answer: I think there are a number of things municipalities can do to deal with the infrastructure problem. It's an area that I've been involved in for about three years. As a matter of fact, I sit on the executive committee of a group called California Business for Infrastructure, about twenty companies that are pushing legislation in the state of California to attempt to deal with some of the infrastructure financing and management problems.

There are three things, at a minimum, that local governments can do. One that my own home city, San Francisco, has been doing for several years is extortion. They've done it in three categories. For example, when a major construction company builds a commercial office building in San Francisco they will now be extorted to contribute to a pot in three areas: one will typically be for housing, one for mass transit, and one for day care. So, there is a way for them to get involved, although I'm not sure it's totally voluntary.

A second area is in pushing for support of local tax increases. A phenomenon that we saw starting in Silicon Valley was the option for additional taxes—and it was largely pushed by the private sector, a group of the manufacturers in Silicon Valley—in this case a one-half cent optional sales tax applied throughout the county to support infrastructure requirements. It would support everything from filling potholes to any other things that wouldn't typically be covered in a highway or transportation plan.

A third area—and one of the things we're doing in California right now—is trying to get legislation passed to set up infrastructure loan guarantee programmes, so there would essentially be more opportunities for bond pools and revolving funds that could be used to support private development of infrastructure.

The last area would be the typical kinds of things we're seeing that come under several categories called value capture or joint development, wherein you use something like a light rail transit system to fashion development. For example, in areas outside Minneapolis or Fairfax County, Virginia, around Tysons Corner, you get the private sector to give up part of the appreciation and the real estate value brought on by something like a light rail transit system to help support the debt service on its capital costs.

Question: The U.K. experience seems to indicate that even if there is no local contractor, or only one, the potential existence of a competitor is enough to lower costs. What is your reaction to that?

Answer: I don't buy that one. Basically, I agree with Wendell that competition is the key here. I would go a step further and say that it is real competition, not perceived competition. The folks in the private sector out in eastern or rural Washington, for example, who know that they're the only bidder within fifty miles for some contracted out snow removal, can figure it out real quick.

CHAPTER 14

PANEL DISCUSSION

Edited by Michael A. Walker

Oliver Letwin: I wasn't struck at all by the complacency of the Canadian experience. On the contrary, I was struck by the extent to which things—which I didn't know about—had happened. The things we were told at lunch were extremely impressive and very realistic. The feel that gave one for what it's like to be inside a privatization was extremely close to the impressions I've had in a number of them. The doubts, the hesitations, the worries, the seeming impossibilities and, as one genuinely hopes, the final triumphs, all seemed utterly true to life. The description we had of contracting out, which has gone on in the United States and could be transplanted here, was also extremely impressive.

Let me, however, take issue with the gentleman (Mr. Thomas Kierans) on my left, inevitably, who had some extremely interesting and important things to say with which I deeply disagree. To focus the issue, it's easiest if I just talk about Petro-Canada. Let me immediately declare a non-interest; I am not employed as an adviser on Petro-Canada—never have been, may very well never be, particularly after these remarks. I'll tell you what I would have said if I'd been hired. I think you were telling us what you would have said if you'd been hired, so we're on all fours.

To give the gist of what you said, if I'm not misleading the audience, you said that the Petro-Canada share is a volatile item very different from a utility. It shouldn't be sold very widely to ordinary people who haven't previously invested in shares. And, in any event, you can raise $1.5 billion from investors within Canada and major institutions overseas and that's how you should generally pursue it.

I would have given exactly the opposite advice. I think it's possible to get rid of the whole of Petro-Canada more or less in one go. It may very well be that it would require some form of installment. But given its potential, particularly on the downstream side which is generally underestimated, I'm quite convinced it would sell. Very often, people don't realize how much downstream activity—less volatile, more profitable —Petro-Canada is involved in through many subsidiaries which actually operate petrol pumps and so forth.

The fact is that the two sides of your argument made one another consistent. It's true that if you restrict an offer like that to the ordinary, traditional investors, you will not succeed in selling a very large proportion of that company in one go or indeed perhaps ever.

Let me take you to a case of a far more volatile company with far less downstream, and that was far less well known, which went out to a large number of new small investors, namely Brit Oil. It was not a great success to begin with. We learned from that. What we learned was that we hadn't gone out for the small investor enough. In subsequent tranches it got a lot better.

In BP, a very large, highly volatile oil stock where the remaining section to be sold off is going to cost about 8 billion pounds or $16 billion (CDN), we at Rothschild intend to get six or seven million people to buy those shares. It will be subscribed across the world, and we expect to get rid of $16 billion (CDN) worth in one shot. I'll bet you here and now that it will be massively over-subscribed precisely because we shall be going out to huge numbers of small investors. Those investors will know very well that they're taking on a volatile stock. They buy gasoline and can see the prices rise and fall, and what happens to oil prices, generally, has very high exposure in the newspapers.

I think what I was saying yesterday applies. It's a good thing, not a bad thing, for people in a small way—not mortgaging their houses or selling off everything they've got, but in hundred dollar units or thousand dollar units at most—to buy a stock and watch it rise and fall and begin to understand what it's actually like being part of an economy as an actor rather than as a passive recipient. It's only when you get to that stage that you can conceivably float an issue of that size, because that's the only way you create the scarcity which makes the institutions come in.

It isn't the case that there were two policies in Britain—one for small investors and the other for selling these large items to large numbers of institutions—on the contrary, they're part of the same policy. It's by creating an atmosphere of scarcity when the institutions begin to realize that there are massive numbers of small investors looking for the stock, that the institutions come in and overbid. They know they'll get scaled down. That, in turn, creates an atmosphere of expectation in the rest of the world and the rest of the world piles in. It's all part of one scheme.

I would offer the government here that piece of rather more heroic and neck-putting-out advice. Give it to Rothschild's, and we'll try to sell the lot —fast, to everybody.

Thomas Kierans: We live at a different point in the market. First of all, I'm at a little bit of a disadvantage here, which I will clearly acknowledge, as I am the government's adviser. From the point of view of the Canadian privatization process at this point in time, I think we want to make sure we get it launched properly. We're not coming in at the end of the British process; we're at the beginning of our process. That's an important distinction I should make.

A second distinction to make is that from the government's point of view, beginning the privatization of Petro-Canada is a good thing to do. However, that would not be do-able from the political point of view if the government turned a substantial portion of the equity, as opposed to the voting control of the company, over to people who are not Canadians. It wouldn't be feasible. We're settling for a significant component of half a loaf here.

Another thing is that we don't have mechanisms to restrict how much Canadians would be allowed to own. Consequently a large number of Canadians could wind up on the losing side of it and the government will therefore absorb a heavy burden. The prospect of that would be that the government would be disinclined to do it at all in the first place.

The third aspect would be that if the government were going to do it that way, they would begin to look at a special share, to which I alluded this morning, in which you had a preferential dividend arrangement for ordinary people. The problems with that, again, are those to which I alluded this morning. The government doesn't get any significant return from its enduring position in the company. Secondly, the moment you say you're going to preserve a 4 or 4.5 percent dividend—when integrated oil stocks yield 1.5—in a way you're pretending that it isn't an oil stock.

So, my own judgement of how to handle this, particularly at this stage of the Canadian privatization process, is to understand the government's position. On the one hand, the government will make sure all Canadians buy it through the post office, because it will be an advertising thing. Secondly the government will therefore feel a sense of responsibility for it. And thirdly, that's going to muck up the whole process. The point is to get the process started at this point in time, not to preclude it.

Question: Where does the notion of political feasibility come from? We've heard about billions and billions of dollars of privatization in Canada and elsewhere. Where does the notion come from that it is not politically feasible to do something?

Thomas Kierans: That is purely in the minds of politicians. That doesn't exist in the minds of this audience or this panel. In the final analysis, politicians will call the shots; we will only advise.

Michael Walker: Right. But what sort of advice are they getting at the moment? Is the federal government getting advice that you can't do it?

Michael Burns: Can I speak to that for a moment? Six months ago, I would have given the same political advice as Tom Kierans did. In British Columbia, I would have told you that Bill Bennett was carrying BCRIC around on his back, that they blamed him for it, that the public was intolerant of that—they thought it was a bad thing to do—and that it should never be done again. We were very much surprised by the research we did in the last six months. We found that British Columbians as a whole thought privatizing BCRIC was a good idea. They did not blame the government for the disaster that ensued, and maybe they wouldn't blame them for oil prices. They felt that the responsibility for the problems of BCRIC was squarely on the shoulders of management—very insightful, I think, on the part of the public. When asked if it should be done again, even those who bought and lost on the product said yes. I think we may be selling the public short on some of these items.

Oliver Letwin: I absolutely believe that. Moreover, there's an interesting point here about the role of financial advisers. Perhaps this is an odd thing for me to say as I am, I suppose, mainly a politician by vocation but a financial adviser by hobby. But I don't think a financial adviser's role is to tell the government what the financial adviser thinks is politically feasible or isn't. I think it's the role of the financial adviser to tell the government what is technically possible. I'll bet my shirt and my suit and anything else that it is technically possible to sell Petro-Canada—massively, within Canada, limiting foreign ownership to 15 or 20 percent, like most of the privatizations around the world have done—and to have a massive success on your hands. When presented with that advice, whether the government judges that it is or is not worth taking what is always a large risk is up to politicians.

But as a matter of practice and technique, I think it would be entirely feasible. You could protect the company against depredations from abroad in every conceivable way through special shares and so forth. Technically, again, I don't think you need to enshrine a dividend or do any monkey business of that kind to get people in and get them to stay there. I don't think there would be any likelihood of the markets suddenly turning around on you and biting the hand that fed them. On the contrary, I think you'd see development of the capital market, particularly in Toronto, on a scale completely unprecedented in Canadian history. Indeed, it might be unprecedented in anybody's history because Petro-Canada is a much larger company vis-a-vis the stock market capitalization—the Toronto Exchange being roughly a third of the Canadian market—than most other stocks that have been done at that stage in a privatization programme anywhere in the world.

I think it's essential, if the government is serious about these things —I'm now speaking as a politician—that it should actually take that risk. If it sells Petro-Canada largely to the traditional institutional investors, the upshot will not be that the privatization programme has gotten off to a brilliant start and is widely acclaimed but, on the contrary, everyone will say, what's new? Nothing has happened. Some fat cats have got hold of the thing and are going to make money out of it.

If you asked me to guess what's going to happen to oil in the next six months or a year, I would say that it will either go up a long way or go down a long way. It is unlikely that it will stay still. It's just as likely to go up as down. If it goes up, those fat cats are going to get rich beyond the dreams of imagination. If they get rich, there is going to be one hell of a political price to pay in Canada, because it will not have been the small man in his millions who is getting rich, which is fine—who can oppose that?—it will have been the people who are already very rich getting a great deal richer.

As a politician, I think the risks run the other way on the whole. But as a financial adviser, I'd merely advise them that it is technically feasible. It seems to me that a government has a right to expect that kind of advice from financial advisers rather than political advice. I think it's terribly important for the financial adviser to understand that difference. It's all too easy to have a political opinion and convey that as if it were a piece of financial advice. I'm not suggesting you're doing that, but it can happen easily. I think a lot of the French houses got into that kind of trouble.

Thomas Kierans: As a point of clarification, it has been suggested that the government's bankers are giving political advice. The fact of the matter is that the Canadian government and its public servants are very sophisticated. They're not interested in our political advice at all; we didn't tender it. What I tried to give this conference is a balanced view, so you could look at the thing from point one to point two.

The second point is that in terms of launching a privatization, the government is interested in encouraging Canadians to participate in Petro-Canada as opposed to actually selling the whole thing out—that's not part of the mandate; this is a notion that should be understood. Number three, as I said this morning, the whole thing is political. That has never been at issue.

Graham Walker: One more argument that you didn't use is that we have ten securities administrators in Canada. To do this massive offering across the country, it would be a horrendous task to convince ten administrative bodies—starting with Ontario—that unsophisticated people should have the right to sell a stock. Should Petro-Canada buy that stock through their credit cards or at service stations or at the post office?

Question: Wendell Cox made a sound case for competitive contracting of transit. Is privatization of transit operations by sale to private operators or to public employees by share issue a practical alternative?

Wendell Cox: While one might be able to make a technical argument that you could follow the British example and do the kind of thing they've done with the National Bus Company, my view would be that there is probably not the public policy support for that in Canada at this time. In many ways, Canadian urbanized areas have operated on the assumption of a regional public role in the provision of public transportation services. If you should ever get to the U.K. model, I think it's going to take an intermediate step of competitive contracting.

Question: Why do you think Canadian investors are incapable of assessing the risks of purchase shares in industries such as those of Air Canada and Petro-Canada? This seemed to be your premise in your attitude toward the distribution of shares in those two companies.

Thomas Kierans: I don't think that's a fair characterization of what I said, and I don't think Canadian investors are incapable of making those assessments. But people ought to understand that when the government of Canada or the Premier of the province of Alberta go out on either a Canada Savings Bond campaign or some such thing like that, Canadians tend to feel safe, in terms of their investing habits. If you're dealing with investors as opposed to citizens, I don't have any problem.

The moment you begin to launch an advertising campaign, you're dealing with citizens as opposed to investors. Then there's a problem that begins to bother me. As some of us discussed at lunch, if the government were to stand up and come clean and say, "listen, oil prices are volatile, stocks go up and down and you had better be damned careful about whether you buy this thing or not, but we'll make it available through the post office," that's one thing. But we all know that is not what they're going to do.

If they did that, it's a perfectly valid conclusion that somebody who gets hurt, gets hurt. But the moment you assume that they're not going to do that, or they assume they're not going to do it, then they will decide they must bend over backwards to protect the small shareholder.

Oliver Letwin: The central point is a very interesting one. If you're right about what the government would in fact do, then I agree with you. But I think the government would be very wrong to act in that way, and it isn't the way the British government acted. I don't mean to hold up Britain as a paragon, God knows we've made enough mistakes. But if you look at British Airways, for example, which—exactly as you were saying about Air Canada—is a highly cyclical business in a very uncertain state, as the present takeover plans for British Caledonia show, the mini-prospectus which was produced has statements like "the airline business is very risky" written all over it. It's a two-page job, for very large numbers of people, millions of them, and written all over it—apart from everything else on the grounds of prospectus liability and nobody wanting any civil suits—are statements like, "this company may go bust." I can't quote it, but that was the gist. If you read it carefully, you would never have bought shares in British Airways. Yet, one and a half million people bought British Airways and, I think, know quite clearly that it's risky, not least because a few years ago British Airways was comprehensively bust and known to be. It could happen again.

I think governments need to own up to the public about that. Part of the important role of a financial adviser in preparing a prospectus is to make sure the government is protected by doing that. If you were writing a prospectus for them, I'm sure that's just what you'd do, and I'm sure they'd take your advice.

Thomas Kierans: It's naive to assume the prospectus is capable of protecting people. It's well known by practitioners in both the United States and Canada that by the time you get through a 130-page document you haven't learned anything. There's no point in contrasting British Airways with Air Canada, because to my knowledge it's not the government of Canada's intention to privatize Air Canada through an offering through the post office to all sorts of people who wouldn't read the prospectus.

Let's talk about British Telecom, which is a better example. I was there when the first advertisements came across. I'll tell you how the advertisements went, and just talk a little bit about subliminal advertising. First of all, you had the Queen opening the House of Commons. She was reading the Speech from the Throne. Then you had a cutaway to the part where her ministers were going to privatize British Telecom. From there you went back to a very soothing voice-over about all of the desirable things about privatizing British Telecom. It went on and on. The subliminal message was very simple—the Queen was telling you to buy the stock.

With British Telecom basically an unregulated monopoly with a licence to steal when all was said and done, at that stage of the market it was probably a worthwhile gamble. I have to tell you that I don't agree with pulling that stuff with Petro-Canada in Canada for the reason Graham Walker just mentioned, and because when you engage in that kind of advertising with ordinary citizens as opposed to investors you begin to acquire some baggage.

Question: One of the major problems with contracting out municipal services is second and third round bidding and making sure that those rounds of bidding are competitive. It's frequently the case that some learning or information is gained by providing the service such that when the incumbent gets around to the second bidding they have a competitive advantage. Is there a way to structure the contracts and the tendering process to deal with that problem and create a level playing field for subsequent rounds of bidding, or are those the types of services that perhaps shouldn't be privatized at all?

Wendell Cox: I think the critical thing to recognize here is that we're not trying to treat the private contractors fairly, with all due respect. We're trying to get the public the best deal. If a contractor, in doing the job for five years, manages to gain a professional advantage and his competitors can't do a better job of bidding for the service when the contract comes up for rebid, then more power to him in my view. The idea is to get competitive rates for the public. I think we always have to keep in mind the purpose, which is public service not private gain.

Davis Schwartz: I would second Wendell's comment. From a technical point of view, you can make information available to the second round bidders in terms of costs and actual experience and so forth. But just as in the Washington study where we said that trying to create a level playing field is not a goal in and of itself, I would agree with Wendell—more power to them.

Keith Alexander: My question is a practical one about ideology, if that doesn't sound altogether too contradictory. We heard a fair amount during the last two days about the absence of ideological concerns in the pursuit of privatization. Three of the U.K. speakers made that point. I think it certainly emerged from the luncheon speech by Mr. Stein yesterday, and I felt I heard some of that coming through in Tom Kierans' remarks as well. What concerns me is that the kind of work and discussion we've had in the last two days is simply too good to go to waste, and my fear is that it's going to unless we provide decision makers, i.e., the politicians, with the kind of ideological armour they're going to require to offset the opposition to privatization, which is distinctly ideological in this country.

I don't want to get too convoluted about this, but I want to make the point that Tom brought up this morning. His concern was to get what he called macro and micro sectoral public policy sets right. That was the adviser's job in a technical sense. Tom also noted, and I think quite correctly, that the government has dismantled the NEP, for example, which is a more important economic force than energy privatization, for example.

What he didn't mention was, of course, that the government had all kinds of macro/micro sectoral public policy sets when it set up the NEP in the first place, and it got all kinds of technical advice on how to do that. Unless we are prepared to directly provide advice that arms the politicians with some kind of ideological offset to the attacks that are being made, then all of this simply falls in the same category with what happened to the NEP—which many of us in the west think was a disaster. For exactly the same reason, I suggest, you may well lose the discussion in terms of privatizing such things as Petro-Canada, Air Canada and many of the other Crown corporations either federally or provincially.

My experience parallels Oliver's in a lot of ways, because I too am an ex-politician, and I want to say this from an ex-politician's point of view. I had some sympathy with the minister this morning who simply said that unless he is able to generate a greater sense of public support, it's very hard to do privatizations. While we have said some enormously scholarly, intellectual and clever things in the last couple of days about providing technical support, who cares, unless we can stiffen up the spines of the politicians who will make the decisions.

My concern is that while the policy mix is unquestionably valid, it may also simply be some sort of intellectual smokescreen behind which politicians can retreat if the going gets heavy when they confront the ideological left which isn't without its resources for obfuscating the issues and making the lives of politicians very difficult. They come up with such things as selling the silverware or the family jewels and that kind of thing. It's not easy to cope with that unless we arm the politicians with sufficient offset for that kind of discussion.

I agree with the remark you made almost parenthetically a moment ago that privatization is—in the minds of some of us, mainly conservatives—in fact good in and of itself. I hear too many people at this discussion backing off from that idea because they're providing quality technical advice on how to do it. How to do it doesn't matter unless someone gets it done.

It used to be that governments needed a clear reason for ownership of assets and services. That has completely flopped over, and it's now incumbent upon politicians to find a clear reason to divest. From the British experience and certainly from our own idea of social ownership, I think we have seen that it is inefficient, costly and wasteful. We endorse private ownership and incentives because it is efficient.

Can we realistically expect much progress in reducing the size and the scope of government? Specifically, can we expect progress in such things as privatization without helping politicians face the ideological opposition on its own ground?—not some ground it's not playing on and not willing to play on. The minister said he has to knock on doors in East Vancouver. As any politician will tell you, you don't have time to develop a policy stance. People don't care about that. They want to know "why are you selling the family jewels?" What is the answer? Can we realistically structure the answers we do have, and at which I think Tom is a master, as though they are technical but are pointing clearly in some direction or other?

Thomas Kierans: Before those of us who are pro-privatization start beleaguering ourselves to the ground, I think the answer is that we can expect a lot of privatization in Canada. What we have to understand is that the experience in Canada is quite different from that in Britain.

Let me just deviate for a second and talk about the philosophical differences and why Canadians look at the commercial Crowns differently than the British would have looked at nationalized industries. In Britain, when they nationalized industries they were doing so from a socialistic, ideological point of view that these things would behave at once equally efficiently on the one hand and yet somehow socially or compassionately. The whole profit motive would be expunged from them, and somehow nirvana would flow through. Of course, it was quite easy—not easy, but it was less hard—to turn on that notion when it became quite clear that they weren't performing, and that they were the subject of very large blockages in a free market system and that the losses were enormous. So something had to be done.

The Canadian experience is not that. We didn't nationalize these things by and large. We created them collectively, positively, as part of a nation-building effort. By and large, until the very early '80s Canadians had much better experience with their commercial Crowns than the British had with their nationalized industries. So we are working in a different social and psychological environment. Therefore, it follows that unless some prime minister feels that he has to break these things immediately as an end in itself, he is going to approach it somewhat differently from a different perception.

Having said that, and I think it was Michael Burns who said it this morning, these things have now become a panacea for good management. It is becoming progressively accepted in the public mind that the ability to privatize is a function of efficient government. This is getting across. But it will get across in Canada, for the reasons I've given, slightly more slowly and evolve in a slightly different way.

Michael Burns: I just want to thank Tom for the excellent commercial message. That's our business, and we think it is do-able. Ideologues can't assail government without bullets. If we apply some good political research to some of that, I think we can take those bullets away from the ideologues. But the problem is, as Tom describes it, not one where we've got people in the streets disaffected with the performance of Crowns. When we took a couple on, we found that they're pretty much in love with them. The opposition will find all the bullets there are to shoot at you, and it's damned hard work. But some of us have been trying to do some of that work.

Oliver Letwin: That seems to me absolutely right. I'm sure that the more ammunition the ministers have the better. But, perhaps against the grain at this meeting, I take the view that in the end no amount of theoretical ammunition is going to win this battle. I absolutely understand the point that you're coming from a different position in Canada and that people regard nationalized industries here quite differently from the way in which they regard them in England and in France and many other countries. Not least, perhaps, because Canadians are rather better at running things in general than the English people tend to be, so these things run rather better just because they're Canadian rather than because they're nationalized.

I hope I'm not too rude or it isn't going to sacrifice too much potential business on my part, but I thought there was a very interesting contrast between Minister Rogers, who arrived and made a speech which said one terribly important thing which I'll come to in a moment, and the ministers from the federal government, who didn't arrive and didn't make a speech and have probably gone underground. My guess is that they're terribly worried and they think that if they keep quiet long enough it will all be all right and blow away and somehow there will be some easy time when you can creep in and do a privatization without anybody quite noticing until it's over. Then, when it's over, pray God that the rain will stop. I don't think that's true.

The important thing that Minister Rogers said—he is absolutely right, and it gave me considerable faith that things are going to come to pass in British Columbia—is that there's going to be a very nasty period for him between the time when he announces it and the time it happens. Any ammunition that you or other people can give him is good stuff, but it isn't going to be enough. It's going to be a nasty period, and he and the premier are going to have to ride that out if they're serious about it. Mrs. Thatcher had to ride it out. Everybody who has tried it has to ride it out.

That's one of the reasons you have to go quickly. If you let these things drag on for three years before anything happens, the will will disappear because there is too long a period of attack and too little upside. If there is a relatively rapid movement, a politician who has real strength of character and some real oratorical ability can probably just about get away with it. Then, when it has been done successfully, you really have the ideological ammunition. It's the best kind of ammunition; namely, there are people on the ground who have seen that it works and believe in it and want to be in the next one. Once that happens, when you go knocking on doors the position is completely different. You're not being asked, "why are you selling the family silver?" You're actually being asked, "when is the next one coming?" That's the only hope, but you need strength at the beginning.

Thomas Kierans: Just a clarifying point. The British didn't go quickly. Their process acquired momentum only in Mrs. Thatcher's second term. I take issue with this distinct paternalistic attitude that "we've proven that what's good for us is good for you, you ought to accept it despite our different conditions." It's nationalized industries versus corporate Crowns.

Oliver Letwin: Let me come back on that second thing. I'm not suggesting that. The mistake we made was to go much too slowly, and it almost destroyed the whole process.

Let me take you to 1981 and Keith Joseph, the Minister for Trade and Industry. He was told to go away and privatize the telephone industry, and he desperately wanted to. He ended up by deregulating headsets. That's how far he got. By the end of that exercise, everyone in Whitehall was absolutely one hundred percent convinced you could not privatize the telephone system. As time went on, they became a thousand or ten thousand percent convinced. It was only actually because we had a looming budget deficit and a chancellor who desperately needed money and a prime minister who was madder than she'd ever been in her life because she hadn't got a policy, that we got it done. If we had done it quickly, we would actually by now be through electricity, coal, steel, and probably on to some of the other things. So, it's not at all that I'm being paternalistic. We made a lot of mistakes, and I think you can learn more from our mistakes than from our successes.

Herbert Grubel: What came through to me in these two days is how difficult it is. In the last few years, politicians have sold their votes to special interest groups. How do they do it? A Crown corporation builds a facility in some outlying district in order to get the votes in that district. That is what Mr. Stein said yesterday. He has to examine whether a proposed privatization is consistent with a political objective. That's what we mean by political objective. What we're asking politicians to do with this technical advice is throw away one of the main instruments by which they compete with each other for votes. It is totally unrealistic to think they're in a world in which there are no outside pressures. They are not.

We need a crisis like in England—a world power going down to second rate status—or we need pressures like those in California, a tax revolt. Or we need a man like we had this morning who says, "I am doing it for ideological reasons." We need leadership, and that's what is apparently missing, certainly from what I heard from Mr. Stein and Mr. Kierans. In Ottawa things are going so well, politicians are saying we have such a promising future—why should we tie our hands behind our backs?

Wendell Cox: Clearly, timing and the situation is absolutely crucial. Around the United States we have seen these kinds of situations. In our case it has tended to be competitive contracting, but in some of our jurisdictions that's every bit as difficult as selling a commercial Crown. We found that the best thing to help us move toward those kinds of innovative approaches was a crisis, as you indicated in the California situation and others.

Perhaps some of your provinces and municipalities aren't ready to begin doing some of the things that have been talked about in the last couple of days. But I think a day will come, for instance in my own field here in Vancouver, when there's going to be a big fare increase in BC Transit. Somebody is going to get up and say, "why don't we begin doing some of that competitive contracting so we can keep fares down or so we don't have to cancel services?" The same thing will happen, perhaps with ferries or some other Crown corporation down the road.

At least, perhaps through what's happened in these two days and the work that the government will be making public in the next month or so, all of you will be aware of the alternatives and will be prepared to take them when the time comes.

Thomas Kierans: I think the Canadian problem is a much less devious and much more pervasive issue. It has to do with the distribution of wealth in a federal nation. It has to do with an issue of leadership. I will deal with these two issues. I stress that I deal with them in a neutral sense, I'm not partial to one point or another. Ontario is the sweetbread of the country, the heartland of the country. It's very rich. In Ontario you find the greatest degree of complacency, obviously, and it is in Ontario that you will find the greatest degree of suspicion about privatizing Petro-Canada. The country is rich; it's worked out well. Our commercial Crowns have supported the country well. The attitude is, "why rock the boat?" This is a major thing for a politician to deal with.

If it was a unitary state it would be bad enough, but in a federal state it is compounded by the fact that that attitude can get reflected in the views of a provincial government, which will then reinforce them and give them a degree of legitimacy that they simply wouldn't otherwise have. So, that's a real problem, and that's not a Buchananesque-type of situation.

The second problem has to do with the question of leadership. I think it is trite to suggest that the government hasn't provided leadership. I have given examples in certain areas where I think they have provided real leadership at considerable political risk and political exposure. Having said that, to question leadership on this issue risks fracturing the stability of the society itself. Union support for the system, which might not be a very high priority in British Columbia because of your own particular situation, certainly in the Ontario case is not something that any politician is going to take on easily. One would spend some time wooing the labour constituency away from its more militant leaders before you took it on.

Here again, our national experience with labour union leaders is somewhat different from that in the United Kingdom. We have not got the arteries clogged so much in the system that radical approaches are going to naturally be espoused by politicians. So, I think to raise the Buchananesque notion is trite. I think there are other larger issues that have to be overcome.

I hasten to explain to Oliver that this is not the advice I give the federal government.

Question: There was some implication that it was okay for governments to hold a major percentage of Crown corporations being sold. This is against the whole rationale for privatization. How can you even remotely suggest that this be tolerated?

Graham Walker: I don't know the answer to that. What I said earlier was that 50 percent is the magical number. When government is selling off a Crown corporation, it isn't always possible to sell the whole thing at one time. It happened in AEC and in Sask Oil. When it was perceived that the government didn't own 50 or 51 percent of it, it immediately became more attractive to institutions. It was already attractive to individuals, because they bought it. They didn't care about the government; they're quite comfortable with government ownership, perhaps more than they are with the company being strictly private. But in order to create a market for the stock, you have to interest the institutions.

Thomas Kierans: I agree with the thrust of the question. We had a better regional experience with mixed enterprise in the west of Canada than we have had nationally. The Alberta Energy situation, politically, was clearly one such example. But, there is very real concern in my mind about that kind of model. Essentially, it is the worst of both worlds. As long as politicians have a substantial component, you're going to get non-commercial interests coming in. In addition to that, you have politics coming in. We had a very bad experience with CDC. You can buy the stock at $17 now, but it wasn't so long ago that it was $5. The difference was the holding of shares by the federal government. So, I agree with the thrust.

Dealing with it pragmatically, it's a completely different issue. If the government determines that it doesn't want the equity—this has nothing to do with the golden share—of Petro-Canada being sold to non-Canadians in the majority, then you have to recognize that it's going to be a workout situation. You then seek to handcuff them to make sure that future governments will not get you into a CDC type of environment. To do that, you tend to use the AEC model. Certainly, if you're going to privatize, you should privatize and be done with it. I don't think there's any question about that, but it is the pragmatics that exist within a nationalistic country which is shaped largely by its influence with the United States.

Question: Have any studies been done to evaluate actual government tax reductions as a result of privatization plans?

Graham Walker: I don't think there's any way of knowing whether they reduced taxes or not, but the Potash Corporation of Saskatchewan recently issued their financial statement in the legislature and showed a loss of $103 million. If they didn't own that corporation, they would be $103 million better off and perhaps earn some interest or earnings on the billion dollars they invested in it that they're going to have to write off. I don't think there's any way of telling, but that's an example where you'd be better off.

Davis Schwartz: I would seriously doubt that you would have any realistic data on privatization that you could point to with any kind of confidence as a causal relationship rather than some kind of accidental relationship at this time. I would doubt it even further because when you are in a period of change, whether implementing a new computer system or a new policy, there is typically a transition cost. In fact, you might expect some burden in the very short term rather than an immediate reduction. So, I would seriously doubt that there is any data. If there is data that says there was an immediate reduction, I would doubt that it would be accurate or reliable.

Wendell Cox: For there to be any reduction in taxes there first has to be a reduction in expenditures. As Davis indicated, while there are not any studies that have indicated taxes have been reduced in any case, I think there are two very good examples from the U.K. where expenditures have been reduced and where it may be reasonable in the long run to expect some taxes to be reduced. Government subsidies to London Regional Transport are substantially lower than they were before LRT started competitive contracting. Private operators are providing service less expensively, and London Bus, the public subsidiary of LRT, is also providing service less expensively than it would have otherwise.

Secondly, and far more spectacularly I think, outside London where they have deregulated public transport they are looking at what they expect to be approximately an $8 billion (CDN) reduction of public transit subsidies as a result of making approximately 77 percent of the service commercial. So, with respect to competitive contracting and deregulation, where government has actually withdrawn from a particular service if it's commercially viable, you might well see some tax reductions in the U.K. attributable to it in the long run.

Oliver Letwin: I think there is some evidence. The London borough which has done the most contracting out in the U.K. is Wandsworth. It sits next to another borough called Lambeth, which is run by people who would be out beyond the sea to the left. The contrast is one on which many of us played happily. Once Wandsworth started contracting out, its property taxes were almost exactly half of those of Lambeth. So there were people on one side of the street with taxes exactly half that of people on the other side of the street because the border goes down the middle of the street. I don't say that contracting out is the only thing that has brought this about, but certainly Wandsworth is reducing its taxes way below the average of other boroughs.

At the macroscopic level—this is not a study and it's not an academic observation that I can prove—sitting in cabinet committee watching ministers trying to wrestle with the public spending programme and balancing the budget, you get a very strong impression that for very good political reasons the chancellor, or the finance minister, is extremely preoccupied about the extent to which any tax cut is going to eat into his manoeuvring on budgets and, in the end, deficits. The ready presence of a large accumulation of seats over the next few years through privatization puts him in an entirely different mood when he comes to the table. It makes him aggressive both in terms of tax cuts and, paradoxically, on spending, because he gets the idea that there's a chance of knocking another couple of pennies off the absurdly high tax rates in the U.K. That makes him think that if he can only get one and a half pennies worth there by privatization the other half a penny will come on spending. So, my impression is that psychologically there is a profound impact on taxation, though it would be very difficult to prove that except by reading cabinet minutes and trying to reconstruct what one person was saying to another and what tone of voice they used.

Question: If all the provinces and the federal government were to suddenly take entities to the marketplace for privatization, would there be sufficient capital in the money markets to support such a large undertaking, if done at one time?

Thomas Kierans: The answer is yes. There is no lack of supply of savings, it is the utilization of savings. It's not a problem.

Michael Walker: On that very hopeful note of potential, it's my duty to bring the conference to a close. On your behalf, I'd like to thank the panelists for their insightful and spirited dialogue and to wish us all many happy returns from future privatizations.